Academic Leadership

Academic Leadership

A Practical Guide to Chairing the Department

Deryl R. Leaming
Middle Tennessee State University

Foreword by Robert M. Diamond

Anker Publishing Company, Inc.
BOLTON, MASSACHUSETTS

Academic Leadership

A Practical Guide to Chairing the Department

Anker Publishing Company, Inc.
176 Ballville Road
P. O. Box 249
Bolton, MA 01740-0249

Composition and design: Boynton Hue Studio

ISBN 1-882982-22-3

About the Author

Deryl R. Leaming is Professor of Journalism and Dean of the College of Mass Communication at Middle Tennessee State University. He earned his Ph.D. in Mass Communication from Syracuse University, his M.A. from the University of Nebraska, and his B.A. from Fort Hays State University. He is also a graduate of a special program at the Menninger School of Psychiatry. Dr. Leaming served nearly 20 years as a department chairperson at four different universities. He is an active member of the Society of Professional Journalists, having also served on the society's national board and as a regional director. He and his colleagues at Marshall University won the coveted First Amendment Award from the society in 1993 for their courageous support of the university's student newspaper and the principles embodied in the First Amendment. He has also published a wide variety of journal articles.

To LML

About the Author

[illegible]

Contents

Foreword

Faculty may be viewed as the heart and soul of the institution, but the department chair is the glue, serving as the link between faculty and administration, between the discipline and the institution, and occasionally between parents and faculty. As chair, your primary responsibility is to ensure the quality of your department, including its courses, curriculum, teaching, and research. You play a major role in the recruitment and selection of faculty, in the induction of new faculty into the culture of your unit and institution, in the development of a fair and appropriate reward system for your faculty and staff. You are also looked to as the department's advocate in negotiations for budget and space. You are responsible for the day-to-day workings of a complex organization, one that includes individuals with varying roles, priorities, and perceptions.

As chair, you are a change agent, entrepreneur, leader, manager, fundraiser, mediator, strategic planner, the "human face" of the administration, and consensus builder. When problems arise, you are also the first person that administrators, faculty, students, and parents turn to for help. You will most likely be overworked, under-resourced, underpaid, and too often unappreciated. However, if you want to have an impact on your institution, on the faculty, and on the lives of students, you could not be in a better spot. As challenging and difficult as the role of department chair is, it can also be exciting, rewarding, and a great deal of fun.

A PERIOD OF CHANGE

Higher education is entering into a period in which the role of chairs is expanding as never before. A recent survey of department chairs reported on by Helen Giles-Gee and M. J. McMahon (1997) revealed that 79% of respondents had experienced an increase in their responsibilities. Chairs attributed the increase to more responsibilities in 1) administrative responsibilities, 2) personnel tasks such as evaluating and hiring faculty, 3) legal issues such as sexual harassment, 4) accountability reports to address state and federal mandates, and 5) budgetary requirements to contain costs (Giles-Gee & McMahon, 1997, p. 18).

Throughout the country, institutional leaders are beginning to realize that for any college or university to be successful, the energies of its faculty and its total resources must match the rhetoric of its mission and priorities. This realization has led to increased requests for each unit of an institution to state its goals clearly and to develop ways to measure its success against these priorities. Boards, trustees, governors, legislatures, parents, business leaders, and students are becoming increasingly vocal in demanding that colleges and universities become accountable and that there be a match between what we say and what we do. For example, in a landmark report "Making Quality Count in Undergraduate Education," Roy Romer, Governor of Colorado and Chairman of the Education Commission of the States, wrote:

> I continue to be amazed at the resistance I encounter to examining whether we can measure and report on effective learning at individual institutions and provide good information to inform consumers about their choices. I also continue to be amazed at the inability of policy makers and public leaders to create meaningful and useful accountability systems for higher education. Finally, I am amazed at how many people are content to rest on the laurels of the past and insist that our higher education institutions need not change because they are the best in the world.
>
> . . . For all its rich history, there are too many signs that higher education is not taking seriously its responsibility to maintain a strong commitment to undergraduate learning; to be accountable for products that are relevant, effective, and of demonstrable quality; and to provide society with the full benefits from investments in research and public service. Thus, the challenge to higher education is to be sufficiently responsive and adaptable in light of these new demands and to propel our nation to the forefront of a new era. Unless political leaders, educators, and the public accept this challenge, higher education soon may be a worn-out system that has seen its best days (Romer, 1995).

The department controls the quality of the academic program and determines what the priorities of individual faculty will be. Recognizing that for an institution to continue to grow, there needs to be an active involvement of the entire community and that the process must include departments that have different priorities, goals, functions, and strengths, administrators are turning more and more to the academic department as the appropriate site for initiating change and to the department chair as the individual who has the responsibility for implementing the necessary specific changes. As a result, many department chairs find themselves being asked to provide information that was in the past never requested. While you may find yourself being given more degrees of freedom than your predecessors, you may also find that you, your department, and your faculty are becoming far more accountable.

What makes the role of chair in this changing world even more challenging is that as faculty, one is rarely prepared for it. While some institutions, Arizona State University being one of the first, are developing comprehensive support systems for their chairs, these programs are the exception rather than the rule. When one assumes the role of chair, the first steps usually include asking for help from experienced colleagues, building on the successful approaches learned from experienced chairs. We often find ourselves relying on our natural instincts and, in times of high stress, quite a bit of prayer.

In *Academic Leadership: A Practical Guide to Chairing the Department,* Deryl Leaming draws on his own experience to provide an easy-to-use, comprehensive reference on how to handle many of the more complex situations faced by department chairs. You will also find practical advice on budgeting, faculty morale, recruiting, politics, and other more basic areas—often overlooked—that are essential to being effective in this role. The examples and advice are down-to-earth and realistic, and the suggestions are excellent. The book provides a context in which to work and will be a most useful reference as you deal with the many complexities of your role. If there is another book out there that presents so much useful information so succinctly, I have yet to find it.

Good luck, keep your sense of humor, and remember, good chairs are among any institution's most valuable assets.

Robert M. Diamond
Institute for Change in Higher Education
Syracuse University

REFERENCES

Giles-Gee, H., & McMahon, M. J. (1997, Summer). System-wide and institutional development programs for chairpersons. *The Department Chair: A Newsletter for Academic Administrators,* 8 (1).

Romer, R. (1995). *Making quality count in undergraduate education.* Denver, CO: Education Commission of the States.

Preface

Department chairpersons play a vital role in the university administration. They, more than other administrators, work closely with all who make up the university family—students, faculty, and staff members. Their duties and responsibilities are broad and vast. They must see the "big picture" while at the same time give meticulous attention to minute detail. If they provide strong leadership in their roles as department chairpersons, the university is made stronger.

The department chairperson is responsible for the administration and promotion of all affairs pertaining to the academic well-being and morale of the department. This responsibility involves such activities as faculty counseling and guidance, student advising and counseling, curriculum planning, scheduling, maintenance of academic relevancy, and all budgetary considerations. The maximum participation in the administrative decision-making process is encouraged at the chairperson's level. Every effort should be made to foster departmental autonomy and to assure that decisions are formulated closest to the students and faculty affected.

Despite the enormous responsibility assigned to chairpersons, universities do little to orient or train new chairpersons: They are thrust into the job, often without knowing what is expected of them. Most faculty members have no idea how many responsibilities chairpersons have, the number of important decisions they must make, or how they spend their time. Most of the training is left up to the secretary. Pity the poor newly appointed chairperson who must take over a department and hire a new secretary at the same time! Chairpersons learn from doing, and most are kept so busy in the first few years after their appointment that they have no time to do anything but serve as caretakers.

PURPOSE OF THIS BOOK

This is a practical book. It is based on the 20 years of experience I had as chairperson at four different universities, one private and the rest public. In 20 years, chairpersons face most of the problems they will ever have to deal with. They will make some mistakes along the way; I certainly did. But I learned from them and hope to pass on what I learned.

This book is written to assist chairpersons in carrying out their many duties and responsibilities. Its purpose is to provide a supply of good ideas and information that will be useful to all chairpersons, especially those who are new in the job. The chapters are brief and their content spans the range of a chairperson's roles and responsibilities. You'll find chapters on providing leadership, the seven habits of successful chairpersons, dealing with sexual harassment, dealing with difficult faculty, understanding the Americans with Disabilities Act, developing outcome assessment programs, time-saving tips, and surviving the technology revolution—among many others. Each is as practical as possible, and each presents many options for effectively managing the responsibility. The chapters will give you an idea of what's expected of you as a chairperson and they'll provide examples of ways that specific tasks can be handled.

Because departments vary in size and mission, it would be impossible to address solutions to every problem department chairpersons face. The suggestions and ideas presented in this book may have direct application for some departments and minimal application for others. Nonetheless, if they cause chairpersons to analyze their own departments and develop their own approaches to solving problems or improving their departments, the book will have served its purpose.

A word of advice: If you are a recently elected chairperson and from time to time find you're not sure how best to address a specific problem or opportunity, ask for help from others—chairpersons, deans, or senior university officials. The best way to master your new administrative responsibilities is to understand their requirements and implications.

And keep in mind that your primary job continues to be that of a scholar/educator. Universities exist not simply to dole out data, give tests, award diplomas, and keep precise records. Their larger purpose is to promote the discovery, preservation, and transmission of knowledge; to help students grow intellectually; and to enhance their cultural and ethical values. Becoming a good administrator is a worthwhile goal; using the skills of efficient administration to enhance teaching is a far greater accomplishment.

ACKNOWLEDGMENTS

I had the good fortune to work for and learn from honest, talented deans. Most were straight shooters—I didn't have to play games with them. I also had the good fortune to work for strong department chairpersons before I took on that position. I remain indebted to the two that I worked for—both were competent, honest, hard-working, and caring chairpersons. Much of what I have tried to do as a university administrator is modeled after their behavior. I am pleased to thank Art Langvardt and Ralph Lashbrook; I will always be grateful that I had the opportunity of working in a department you chaired and attribute much of my success as a chairperson to you.

I am deeply indebted to a number of people for their assistance with this book. I owe the most to my long-time friend and soulmate, Wallace E. "Ed" Knight. Without his help, I doubt that this book would ever have been finished. He gave me lots of advice, suggestions, and encouragement. He also helped me to laugh on occasion.

I thank Alan B. Gould, Director of the Drinko Program at Marshall University. Alan was my dean and later my vice president for academic affairs, and it was he who suggested that I write this book. I appreciated his help and encouragement.

Many colleagues have influenced and helped me. George Arnold and Ralph Turner, my special Marshall University friends, did much to support my efforts as department chairperson and director of the W. Page Pitt School of Journalism. Some of the people who were chairpersons at Marshall University when I was taught me much about doing my job. The ones I still remember as influencing me are Ken Ambrose, Elaine Baker, Margaret Phipps Brown, Don Chezik, Kathryn Chezik, Sam Clagg, Charles Lloyd, Charles Moffat, Harold Murphy, Dan O'Hanlan, Simon Perry, and William Sullivan.

I am indebted and grateful to individuals who read my manuscript and offered suggestions for improvement: Douglas Anderson, Director and Cronkite Endowment Board of Trustees Professor, Walter Cronkite School of Journalism and Telecommunication, Arizona State University; Jim Brooks, Chairperson of the Department of Speech and Theatre, Middle Tennessee State University; James Brooks, Chairperson of the Department of Music, Middle Tennessee State University; R. Ferrell Ervin, Chairperson of the Department of Mass Communications, Southeast Missouri State University; Jan Quarles, Associate Dean of the College of Mass Communication, Middle Tennessee State University; Harold Shaver, Director of the W. Page Pitt School of Journalism and Mass Communication, Marshall University; and Molly Whaley, Chairperson of the Department of Health, Physical Education, Recreation and Safety, Middle Tennessee State University.

I also thank my graduate assistant, Jeff Spurlock, and two secretaries, Deborah Hall and Sandra Neely. Without their help this project would have been more difficult.

Because they made my work enjoyable, Anker Publishing Company staffers deserve special recognition. Their regular encouragement and desire to produce a book of high quality meant much to me. Thanks Jennifer, Susan, and Jim.

I thank George Arnold, previously mentoned, for giving many hours to reading page proofs. Although others will not see the intelligence you've added to this book, I will always be mindful of it, George.

I thank Barbara Haskew, MTSU's provost and vice president for academic affairs, for her support of my efforts. She's a cone mover (see p. 116) and a dedicated, effective administrator.

I also thank Bob Diamond for contributing to this book and for adding considerably to what I have to say. Bob is held in high esteem in academic circles; I pray that his reputation will not be diminished because of his association with this book.

Finally, I thank my family for their patience and understanding.

While those who helped or inspired me are due thanks, none is responsible for any mistakes. Those are my blunders!

Deryl R. Leaming

1

Advice to the New Department Chairperson

There is a human tendency to try to please everyone, but for a chairperson that is simply impossible.

Almost no chairperson that I know was provided training for the position before undertaking the job. Moreover, not much in the way of training is provided after a chairperson assumes the job. Seagren et al. (1993, p. xvi) points out that "Training for department chairpersons can be characterized as casual to nonexistent, oriented only toward understanding administrative procedures, and situational rather than holistic or systematic." Chairpersons are left on their own to acquire the skills needed to succeed in the job. Their success is determined on how well they adapt to the role of leader, how much support they have from faculty and their dean, and myriad other factors over which they have little or no control.

As a new department chairperson, you are going to make mistakes. If the mistakes you make are small, some will not even be noticed and the ones that are will likely be forgotten in a short time. On the other hand, if you make a large mistake or two, you may not be able to survive as chairperson, and even if you do survive, you may have a hard time living down your blunder no matter how much good you do. Obviously, my advice is to keep your mistakes small.

How? Here are some guidelines I wish I had been given when I first became a chairman.

- **Consult others.**

Chairpersons have many duties and responsibilities. Many are time-consuming and complex. When you are faced with difficult decisions, consult others on campus who can be of help. Many of your fellow chairpersons across campus will have faced similar problems and will gladly offer advice.

Four years ago I accepted a new deanship, and I cannot tell you the number of times I telephoned my fellow deans to get their advice. Each was always helpful, and they certainly made my job easier.

- **Learn to say "no."**

There is a human tendency to try to please everyone, but for a chairperson that is simply impossible. Some of the most ineffective chairpersons I've ever known were those who never learned how to say no. They somehow had the notion that they could win respect by pleasing others.

Most faculty members know that some of their requests are going to be denied. They expect it. Likewise, they expect to be treated fairly. They want fairness far more than they want you to make promises you can't fulfill—which is what happens when you don't know how to say no.

Saying no can sometimes be painful, but knowing how and when to say no pays rich dividends. You may have to struggle to find the key to success, but not being able to say no will provide a quick, sure ticket to failure.

- **Be somebody who cares.**

While you must learn how to say no, you must also be caring. You must genuinely like people. You should feel a need to help others and to do what you can to make people more productive and happy. If this isn't you, chances are you will not be terribly happy or successful as a chairperson. Let's face it: Most of your time as chairperson is given to people's problems.

Unfortunately most chairpersons have not had training in counseling, and they feel helpless trying to work with troubled faculty members. You've known faculty members who were so distraught that they became self-destructive; some have attempted suicide and a few have even succeeded in taking their lives, while others have ruined their lives engaging in destructive behavior.

What can you do as chairperson to help faculty, short of going back to school to earn a degree in counseling or social work? You can read everything you can get your hands on about working with troubled faculty, you can consult with trained counselors, or you can bring in trained colleagues to help. You can also care: You can listen, empathize, and use your best instincts to recommend a course of action until you can persuade troubled faculty to seek professional help.

Some years ago in trying to find help for my son, who in time was diagnosed with attention deficit disorder (ADD), my wife and I went to all kinds of medical practitioners in search of help. Time after time we were told that there was nothing wrong with him, though we knew otherwise. Eventually we had the good fortune to meet a specialist in ADD and hyperactivity. I told him of our difficulties in getting help, concluding with, "The only thing I knew to do was to give him love." The physician looked at me with tears welling in his eyes. "Love is very powerful medicine," he said softly.

The lesson from that, it seems to me, is that if we have distressed faculty, they deserve to be helped, and while we may not have the expertise to provide professional help, we can give love. We can let faculty members know that we care.

- **Develop written policies and procedures (and follow them).**

The best way to assure that all faculty members are treated fairly is to have written policies and procedures governing such things as travel funds, released-time assignments, allocation of departmental funds for equipment, supplies, faculty development, etc.

You should be able to provide new faculty members with written policy statements that outline promotion and tenure procedures. New faculty members deserve to know what is expected of them, how and when they will be evaluated, and what they must do if they are to be promoted and granted tenure. Written guidelines on these questions will go a long way to ease tensions and misunderstandings in your department.

- **Keep good records.**

You will find it helpful to make some kind of written record of any important meeting you call. It should include the date and time of the meeting, who was present, what it was about, what decision was reached, whether any action is to be taken, and whether follow-up is expected. Faculty members, after all, are human. And you will be surprised at how often their memories of meetings and decisions will reflect what they wish had occurred, rather than what in fact did occur. As one especially capable chairperson told me recently, "Over the years I have discovered that this is one of the most important things one can do."

Likewise, it is helpful to keep good correspondence files and a record of all budget transactions. It is impossible for most of us to remember all the details of every meeting we attend and all we wrote in a letter or memorandum. You will discover how true this is the first time you have to go back a few years to refresh your memory about an important meeting.

- **Get to know your faculty.**

You should find some reason to see faculty members regularly in their offices. Just stopping to ask how their classes are going is reason enough. It is important for you to know their research and teaching interests. Encourage them to give you copies of articles or papers they write. And of course if they respond, you must read their papers. Sending a brief note commenting on their scholarly endeavors is an appreciated follow-up.

You will be a better chairperson if you get to know something about each faculty member's personal life. Knowing how faculty members spend their time away from the university will provide you with information that will help you understand why they behave professionally as they do.

You should want to know what faculty members are thinking, and have a sense of their moods, attitudes, and goals. What you learn about faculty members will help you provide leadership for your department.

- **Be upbeat, steady, and predictable.**

There will be days when it's difficult to put a smile on your face, but as a chairperson you will create morale problems if you are regularly glum and moody. Faculty should not have to ask the secretary, "Is he or she in a good mood today?"

- **Learn what is expected of you.**

Before you accept any administrative job, ask for a description of it, and then discuss the specific expectations of the person or people you will report to.

It will also help to determine your supervisor's style of leadership. Is it one that you find agreeable? For example, you may find it hard to work for someone who tends to micromanage, and you sense that your supervisor-to-be is prone to do that. Should you accept the job? Is it something you can clear up before accepting the position?

You should know precisely what the expectations are before you take a job so that you don't have to come back later and say, "Gee, I didn't know I was supposed to do that." You will have to assess your level of comfort with all the areas of responsibility. Determine also how much support you can expect in those areas in which you might be somewhat weak. Seagren, Creswell, and

Wheeler (1993) recommend that chairpersons gain a clear understanding of their role and tasks in accepting or continuing in the position of chairperson. "Update your roles and responsibilities if you are already in the position. Given the variety of institutional types, individual talents, and units' needs, negotiate priorities and agreements, using the suggested checklist of roles and responsibilities [found in Appendix A of Seagren et al.] to aid in clarification" (Seagren et al., p. 81).

- **Be sensitive to the needs of faculty, staff, and students.**

Having worked for insensitive supervisors, my constant prayer is that I will always be sensitive to the needs of others, especially those who report to me. Am I treating them as I would want to be treated?

Is it possible to have high standards and at the same time be understanding of others? I think so, especially when faculty and staff have the right incentives. Of course, we cannot always offer pay that meets all expectations, but we can make the department a challenging, enjoyable place to work.

I've found that I can get more work out of faculty and staff members by trusting them rather than breathing down their necks. I have high standards and high expectations, and I communicate that to faculty, staff, and students as fully as possible, but I don't try to be the departmental timekeeper. I have known chairpersons who were martinets, always determined to get their 40 hours a week out of everyone. While that was going on, it became my job to insist that many faculty members leave work because they were putting in too many hours—often more than 60 a week.

- **Plan.**

I can't say enough about the importance of careful planning. You need a set of goals and a vision, and you need an honest assessment of the department's strengths and weaknesses. Moreover, you must determine what resources are needed to accomplish your goals.

> The literature on departments and chairs contains little discussion of long-term visions for departments. Departmental leadership cannot afford to be shortsighted, however. Discussions about the current and future stages and needs of the department ensure the projection and development of needed leadership. To achieve the department's stability and continuity of leadership requires a serious commitment and understanding that planning is more than

> hiring good people and maintaining the usual routines (Seagren, Creswell, & Wheeler, 1993, p. 81).

In good times, the importance of planning will be less obvious. However, when resources are not plentiful and enrollments take a downturn, the lack of planning becomes painfully obvious. Careful planning not only helps you assess needed resources, it also helps you make good use of available resources.

- **Be careful when hiring, and be honest when evaluating.**

A colleague said to me not long ago that hiring was at best a "crapshoot." While he may be right at times, careful checks of a potential faculty member's background can increase the odds in your favor.

Check all listed references carefully; then always call some who are not listed. Let's face it: Potential faculty members are not going to list people as references who are likely to have negative things to report.

A few years ago, when I was the dean of liberal arts at another school, a chairperson brought me the name of a candidate to whom he wanted to offer a job. I had interviewed the person and felt uneasy about making the candidate an offer. Something didn't seem right. I got on the telephone and after one call discovered that the individual in question had many, many problems. After several more calls and a discussion with the chairperson, we decided not to make an offer. I am convinced to this day that we saved the department and the university much grief.

It is just as important to be honest and thorough when evaluating faculty members as it is to be careful when hiring. The only thing worse than making a bad hire is to renew the appointment of the bad hire.

I've worked with dozens of chairpersons over the years, and I've encountered many who tended to give above-average evaluations to weak faculty members. They did so for any number of reasons, but mostly because they had not worked hard enough to document a weak evaluation. Or sometimes they simply wanted no hassle; they wanted to be nice. Providing a less-than-honest evaluation is unfair both to the person involved and to your department and institution. Moreover, if you end up having to extend tenure to a weak faculty member, it is unfair to the other faculty members.

No matter how much work is involved and how difficult it is to explain to a faculty member that he or she has weaknesses, it is worth the time and anguish.

- **Encourage change and innovation and forgive failures.**

If your department is going to be dynamic, it must have faculty members who are willing to take risks and be innovative. You must encourage change. Likewise, you must be patient with those who try new things but fail. Don't be afraid of change. Departments that resist change are likely to face troubled times as we move into the Information Age.

Chairpersons must be catalysts for change. This is one of the characteristics of good leadership. In fact, if you are not planning for change, you are failing as a chairperson.

- **Pay attention to the budget.**

If allocating, accounting, and purchasing practices did not differ so much from one university to another, I could offer much help on budgeting. Because that is not the case, I can provide only a generalized budget discussion.

I caution you to pay close attention to all budget matters. Having a bright, efficient secretary who is good with budget matters is essential to your mental health and even to keeping your job.

I have difficulty keeping my personal checking account balanced, so I leave budget monitoring to my secretary. She is exceptional: She keeps me informed, and above all, she knows that I tend to be conservative in fiscal matters. I will not permit spending more than has been allocated.

- **Use your creative talents.**

If you want to set yourself apart from the run-of-the-mill department chairperson, be creative. You need to do more than answer the mail and see that classes are covered.

Start some new initiatives: Create a scholastic program to interest high school students in your region and state in your discipline; create an alumni organization; publish an alumni newsletter; raise funds to establish money for faculty development; establish an annual high school career day.

Departments should be like dynamic, living organisms that grow and change continuously. Be prepared to face resistance from faculty members who are comfortable the way things are. They will resist change. Indeed, to some the idea of change is obscene or repugnant; they fear it and will fight to protect their ways of doing things. Read Chapter Eighteen for more discussion about dealing with faculty members who resist change.

- **Work at effective communication.**

I complain constantly about being inundated with paper, yet I really get upset if I do not get information that I need. Effective communication can be achieved without flooding your department with paper. Try always to see that faculty members get the information they need: about ways to serve their students, and about matters such as salary increases, schedule changes, activities, etc. There are several effective ways of relaying information. Holding regularly scheduled faculty meetings is one. Memoranda and telephone messages have their place in the communication scheme. Whatever the medium, if faculty members get information they believe is useful, and if it gets to them on time, they appreciate it.

- **Keep your hand in teaching.**

Most of you can skip this section because you have no choice about teaching; it's required. However, for those who chair large departments and are not expected to teach, I urge you to find a way to teach at least one course.

Even as dean I continue to teach, and getting out of my office and into the classroom helps me to keep my sanity. An added benefit is that I am forced to keep up-to-date in my discipline. Moreover, I get to know students—beyond those who come to my office to complain—and I think teaching helps me understand the concerns that other faculty members have.

- **Make time to develop a professional development plan for yourself.**

It is all too easy to overlook your own development after you become department chairperson. In addition to keeping your hand in teaching, you should try to find time for research. Also, you should find ways to improve your skills as chairperson. Attending workshops for chairpersons will enable you to learn more about areas for which you are responsible. To learn more about workshops for chairpersons, you can contact some of the sources listed in the appendix. Others are also available.

- **Don't back yourself into the corner when making decisions.**

There are times when we back ourselves into corners without thinking. We do that when we make decisions that leave no room for us to back down without losing face. One of the things I learned in the Armed Forces Leadership Program was that we should always leave room for an out for ourselves and for others. It is tempting at times—usually when we are overcome with anger—to box others in, or to put them out on a limb with no way to escape. We should avoid that temptation. An absolute yes or no, if awarded too soon, can be a dangerous matter indeed.

- **Avoid favoritism.**

You can't afford to have faculty members believe that you give special treatment to some of their colleagues. There is no question that some faculty members are easier to work with than others. Even so, you cannot give favorable schedules or allocate funding on the basis of congeniality. "Resources of all kinds are limited and are invariably outpaced by demand. Do not concentrate most of the resources on a few: All members should receive their fair share. However, make public the criteria for the distribution of departmental funds and use those criteria consistently: Otherwise, you'll be (rightly) accused of favoritism or shiftiness" (Arslanian, 1990, p. 5). Faculty members may perceive favoritism where none is intended, so be very careful to avoid even its slightest suggestion.

- **Set a good example for faculty.**

If you are to be an effective leader, you must lead by example. You must have a good work ethic and demonstrate the other qualities that you would like to see in faculty members and in your supervisors. It's hard, for example, to reprimand faculty for not showing up for a department-sponsored event when you fail to show up at certain events faculty members are involved in. Keep in mind that others look to you as a role model. Many will try to pattern their behavior after yours.

- **Study the art of decision-making.**

As a leader, you must learn to be decisive. There are many decisions that you can make jointly with your faculty, which is as it should be. However, there will be others that you must make alone. Unless you are willing to make decisions—no matter how difficult—you are not likely to be successful as an administrator. Moreover, you must learn how to make good decisions.

- **Employ a good secretary.**

If I were to say that good secretaries are worth their weight in gold, it would be a cliché, but it would be true. A trusted secretary is indispensable. To the general who would say "War is hell," a chairperson would answer, "Have you ever tried running a department with a weak secretary?"

I have no idea who wrote the following, but it summarizes the power of the departmental secretary:

The dean—Leaps tall buildings in a single bound, is more powerful than a locomotive, is faster than a speeding bullet, walks on water, gives policy to God.

The department chairperson—Leaps short buildings in a single bound, is more powerful than a switch engine, is just as fast as a speeding bullet, walks on water if the sea is calm, talks with God.

The professor—Leaps short buildings in a single bound, is almost as powerful as a switch engine, is faster than a decelerating bullet, walks on water in an indoor swimming pool, talks with God if a special request is approved.

The associate professor—Barely clears a quonset hut, loses tug of war with locomotive, can fire a speeding bullet, swims well, is occasionally addressed by God.

The assistant professor—Makes high marks on the wall when trying to leap tall buildings, is run over by locomotives, can sometimes handle a gun without inflicting self-injury, dog paddles, talks to animals.

The instructor—Runs into buildings, recognizes locomotives two out of three times, is not issued ammunition, can stay afloat with a life jacket, talks to walls.

The student—Falls over doorsteps when trying to enter buildings, says "look at the choo-choo," wets himself with a water-pistol, plays in mud puddles, mumbles to himself.

The secretary—Lifts buildings and walks under them, kicks locomotives off the tracks, catches speeding bullets in her teeth and eats them, freezes water in a single glance. She is God.

REFERENCES

Arslanian, A. (1990). A few suggestions to new department chairs. In J. B. Bennett & D. J. Figuli (Eds.), *Enhancing departmental leadership*. Phoenix, AZ: ACE/Oryx.

Seagren, A. T., Creswell, J. W., & Wheeler, D. W. (1993). *The department chair: New roles, responsibilities, and challenges*. Washington, DC: The George Washington University.

2

Seven Habits of Successful Chairpersons

One of the biggest complaints I hear against administrators is that they don't give faculty members straight answers.

Successful chairpersons are always easy to identify. They and their departments are viewed on and off campus as somehow special. Indeed, an air of energy usually surrounds a department headed by such a person; it is evident in the behavior and attitude of the faculty and students. Pride seems to emanate from the department itself.

So what is it that these chairpersons have in common? Is it something others can acquire? I will try to answer the first question; you can answer the second.

1. Successful chairpersons have goals.

Their goals are no secret. They are well articulated, shared with the faculty, and pursued until accomplished.

I learned something recently about developing goals, and I don't know why it took me so long to discover it. When our provost and vice president for academic affairs asked each dean to submit goals for the year, she said to limit them to not more than four or five. "I don't think you can focus sufficiently on too many more than that," she explained. She's right, I think. Four or five important goals are sufficient for any year. Obviously each may have many parts, so it's not as if you are accomplishing only a few things annually.

No matter how many goals you settle on, it is important that you define and develop them fully. You then must commit the department to carrying them out, and you must see that sufficient time and resources are made available to satisfy the goals.

2. Successful chairpersons get to know their colleagues and fellow administrators.

They know the interests of faculty members, both professional and personal. They know something about their personal lives. They come to know the potential of each person in the department, and they give them room to grow and develop—even to make mistakes.

Have you ever noticed how much harder you are willing to work for someone who seems to understand you, who inquires from time to time about your family, who remembers your favorite baseball team, and who does not get angry and hold it against you forever if you make a mistake? As chairpersons we need to be sensitive to the needs of the faculty, and we cannot do that unless we get to know them.

3. Successful chairpersons are agents of change.

He or she understands that the status quo—even if comfortable—often may stunt progress or fail to meet the needs of students.

We must look as far into the future as our best lights permit. What's out there? And what does it mean to students who will be in the workforce 10, 15, or 20 years from now? What are the scientific, technological, social, and economic forces that are shaping society? Are we helping our students to understand these forces?

With the world changing so fast, we must be knowledgeable about directions and tendencies. We must be avid readers and observers of new professional developments, and we must be persuasive enough to engage the faculty in this pursuit.

4. Successful chairpersons understand and appreciate teaching, research, and public service.

While most chairpersons have heavy administrative burdens, they must try to find time to keep their hands in each of these areas. Faculty members respect chairpersons who are active in areas in which they are evaluated. They resent administrators finding fault when the administrators themselves have not proved themselves in teaching, research, or public service.

I remember how faculty members at another school resented a dean who often rejected applications for promotion because the applicant supposedly "had not done enough research." They resented his assessment because the dean himself had never done any research. The point here is that as a chairperson, you are expected to serve as a good role model when it comes to fulfilling basic responsibilities that you expect of others.

Successful chairpersons must provide leadership for the assessment of teaching, scholarship, and service. Chapter Sixteen deals directly with these matters.

5. Successful chairpersons are honest, forthright, decent people.

They make tough calls and are decisive even when the decision goes against those whom they would most like to please. Also, they make clear that they cannot respond favorably to all requests.

One of the biggest complaints I hear against administrators is that they don't give faculty members straight answers. They say what others want to hear rather than what must be said.

I've worked with many different kinds of administrators, many honest ones, and some who were less than honest. There were some I always had to play games with. I am fortunate now that the person I report to is not like that at all. She is honest. There's no game playing. As a consequence, I like my job all the more, and I will do all I can to meet her expectations.

6. Successful chairpersons are fair and evenhanded.

No matter how principled we are, it is difficult not to want to show favoritism toward those we get along with best.

For your own good and for the good of the department, you must learn that everyone profits from fairness and evenhandedness. Many of the faculty members in your department will be resentful and unsupportive if there are lapses.

7. Successful chairpersons are consensus builders and good communicators.

Their leadership style is to develop ideas and persuade others to support them. They are good, and they also are good at communicating their ideas.

I've watched and evaluated many different chairpersons. I have seen some try to lead without first trying to build consensus. I have seen them fail, even when they had good ideas. Faculty members need to be involved in the department and its changes. Failure to involve them generally means that new ideas are not going to be accepted. Successful chairpersons understand this and work carefully to keep faculty members informed and to get their support.

There undoubtedly are other character traits that successful chairpersons have in common. Those enumerated here seem to stand out above all others. I know that if you have these qualities, you are likely to succeed. Faculty members will give you their support, and you will find that your dean and provost will provide support as well.

Of course when you are successful, the job is more enjoyable. Others notice and praise your work, and, above all, your students are the big winners. They are studying in a stronger, more vital department, and they are being taught by people who are happier with their jobs.

At the beginning of this chapter, I raised two questions: 1) What do successful chairpersons have in common? 2) Can these traits be acquired? I indicated I would try to answer the first question and leave the second to you. However, I can't resist trying to answer the second as well. I strongly believe that these successful habits can be acquired. With hard work and practice, we can all learn to develop goals, get to know people who make up the department, and become agents of change. Likewise, we can develop an understanding and appreciation for teaching, research, and public service. Furthermore, we can be honest and fair, and we can work to be consensus builders. In short, it seems to me that all of us have a chance to be successful if we acquire these habits.

3

Duties and Responsibilities of Department Chairpersons

First and foremost, you serve as the spokesperson for the interests and the welfare of the entire department.

As a department chairperson you have a wide variety of duties and responsibilities. On any given day you may be teaching a class, preparing annual reports, putting together next semester's schedule, counseling a faculty member, conducting a faculty meeting, or developing a plan for getting outside funding. While the time that you must give to the management of your department depends in part on the size and the nature of the department, the responsibilities are nonetheless time-consuming.

The roles and expectations of chairpersons may vary from institution to institution and are not well defined at many colleges or universities. We can even see different interpretations of what a chairperson is and what he or she should do from department to department on the same campus. It is interesting to see how this could be. One explanation is that most universities have no written job description for department chairpersons. Thus, department chairpersons themselves define their role in accordance with:

1) their own comfort level
2) wishes of the faculty in the department
3) how their predecessors have defined the job
4) how some of the campus's more seasoned chairpersons interpret their roles
5) how their dean defines the position
6) a combination of the foregoing

Chairpersons have a long list of responsibilities, and in order to accomplish them, they assume different roles. Tucker (1992) lists 28 possible roles that chairpersons assume to some degree at one time or another. No matter how long the list of responsibilities is, it remains clear that the chairperson's role is "ambiguous, unclear in terms of authority, and difficult to classify as faculty or administrator" (Seagren, Creswell, & Wheeler, 1993, p. iii) according to studies of the role and responsibilities of chairpersons.

Gmelch and Miskin (1993) see four main roles as critical for department chairpersons: the faculty developer, manager, leader, and scholar. They describe them as:

Faculty developer. This involves recruiting, selecting, and evaluating faculty as well as providing the informal faculty leadership that enhances faculty morale and professional development.

Manager. These are activities such as preparing budgets; maintaining department records; assigning duties to faculty members; supervising staff personnel; and maintaining finances, facilities, and equipment.

Leader. This involves providing long-term direction and vision for the department, soliciting ideas for improvement of the department, planning and evaluating curriculum development, and planning and conducting faculty meetings. It also involves providing external leadership such as representing the department at professional meetings, working with alumni, etc.

Scholar. This involves the continuing need to teach and keep current in one's academic discipline.

If we conclude—and I think we must—that chairpersons in the past had demanding, critical jobs, then it seems fair to say that today's chairperson is burdened in ways not imagined by his or her predecessors. Today's department chairperson must deal with ever-increasing demands for public accountability at a time when resources are declining. Thus, the chairperson of today must be an astute manager. Seagren, Creswell, and Wheeler (1993) point out that the importance of the chairperson as manager is expected to increase with fewer resources. However, managing is not enough. Exceptional leadership skills are required if we are going to meet the challenges that come with changes we can expect in the decades ahead. Department chairpersons will have to provide the way for their faculty to discover new ways of teaching and learning, and for helping faculty members to adapt and learn new skills to meet the challenges of the future. If universities are to change as profoundly as many people seem to believe they must, then the role of a chairperson as a leader is even more critical than ever.

In this chapter we will examine the most important roles, responsibilities, and challenges of today's chairperson, elaborating on roles and responsibilities that are not covered in detail in later chapters.

First and foremost, you must serve as the spokesperson for the interests and the welfare of the entire department. Your role of chairperson, therefore, is one of communicator and facilitator. You must learn to recognize the strengths and weaknesses of the department and its faculty, and seek to improve strengths and correct weaknesses. You must assist and counsel faculty members with a sense of fairness, open-mindedness, and concern. As a spokesperson for the interests and the welfare of the entire department, you have a responsibility to see that your department gets its fair share of resources and that department faculty are not shortchanged when salary increases, promotions, sabbaticals, faculty development grants, and other faculty benefits are made available.

If you are aggressive in fulfilling this role, you may at times cause some other chairpersons to resent or be jealous of you. This is certainly true if you succeed in getting more than your fair share of university resources. Still, you need to be fairly aggressive in your role as spokesperson for the interests and the welfare of your department. It's your job, and if other chairpersons are equally aggressive, then all things will tend to balance out in a way that should not be seen as a lack of collegiality. Note that I said "fairly" aggressive, as I believe you must learn how to be persistent and aggressive without being unpleasant and unbearable. Learning how to be aggressive and still be liked and respected calls for a certain amount of finesse and the fine-tuning of your interpersonal skills.

ORCHESTRATING CHANGE AND PLANNING FOR THE FUTURE

Strong interpersonal skills are also called for in bringing about change. The time has passed when chairpersons could serve as caretakers without hurting their department; they must now be agents of change. Indeed, those who study change believe that in the past, departments—and even universities—were often rewarded for not taking risks and that the modern department or university that does not take risks will suffer. Some may even perish.

In your role as the leader of the department, you will be expected to keep the department current and to light the way for the future, a responsibility that will challenge all of your leadership skills. You will find faculty members who will resist even the slightest, most noninvasive change. All too often these are senior faculty members who wield a lot of power and influence, and those who support change often will not do so if it means confronting the department's power structure. Added to this is the perplexing problem of getting a fix on what the future holds. In today's fast-paced, ever-changing world, it is difficult enough to say confidently where we are at present, to say nothing of the difficulty of seeing into the future.

Here are some suggestions for assessing how the future may affect your department:

- Keep up-to-date with what's happening in your discipline by reading books and journal articles and attending conferences.
- Stay in touch with those outside the university who employ your graduates. Recently I have conducted several focus groups made up of industry leaders in our region to hear from them about what changes they see.
- Stay in touch with your alumni to learn as much as you can about what they learned—and didn't learn—in school that they regularly use on their job.

One important responsibility you have as a department chairperson is that of planning, and an important first step in that process is developing a mission statement and assessing core values. Not enough is written about the importance of a well-written and intelligently conceived mission statement. Gmelch and Miskin (1993) provide a solid "how-to" for developing a mission statement, while the words "mission statement" are nowhere to be found in a number of important books on chairing the academic department. Although so little is said about the importance of having a good mission statement, that should not minimize its need. A mission statement should, in my estimation, be written, and it should clearly explain a department's reason for being. In my mind's eye, I see a department chairperson who is without a mission statement waving "this way" to his or her faculty members and shouting, "Follow me," only to be asked: "Where are we going?" and "How are we going to get there?" A mission statement should answer those questions. It is a roadmap to the future: It helps to show where you intend to go by indicating your core values.

A good leader can lead without a well-written mission statement, but he or she can lead even better with a mission statement that provides a vision. During the troubled times of the *Saturday Evening Post*—the late 1950s and early 1960s—the editor Robert Fuoss explained that he saw editing the *Post* as something like leading troops into battle without knowing why we're at war. He proclaimed, "We had no reason for existence" (Leaming, 1968). Some departments appear to be groping for direction just as did the *Post* under Fuoss. You as a department chairperson can remedy this situation by working with faculty members to develop a mission statement and assessing the department's core values. Gmelch and Miskin (1993, p. 44) remind us that a "mission statement need not be couched in sophisticated rhetoric nor presented in perfect strategic format." Gmelch and Miskin (1993, p. 54) go on to add:

> The format and wording of your mission statement is not the important issue. Informal, but consistent, communications are sometimes just as effective. The critical issue is to develop your mission and identify the key outcomes with sufficient faculty input, involvement of relevant stakeholders, and your dean's approval. Be certain that your university, your college, your department, and your constituents value achievement in each of your identified key outcomes. Once developed, you must share it. Post it in the department, distribute it to clients, publish it in the newsletter, initiate a memo, or include it in your annual "state of the department" correspondence.

Coupled with your efforts to make needed change is long-range planning. It, too, is often neglected because of the day-to-day work that must be done to keep the department functioning. Long-range planning nevertheless is crucial. Here are some key questions to be answered:

Long-Range Planning Questions

1) What are enrollment projections for the next five years? Given resources of the department, should we expand or curtail our efforts to recruit? Should we limit enrollment?
2) What resources are needed to meet anticipated changes? Will resources be available to meet the changing needs of the department? If university funding is inadequate to meet these needs, can outside funding be obtained?

3) Are our current facilities adequate to meet changing needs?
4) What kind of faculty additions will we need in the next decade? Is the makeup of the current faculty appropriate to meet changing needs?
5) What will the educational needs of students be in the coming years? What curricular changes should be made?
6) What are the department's equipment needs for the coming years?
7) Are new instructional methods called for?
8) If the department has an accrediting agency, are new standards anticipated? If so, how can they be met?
9) Do planned changes fit in with the institution's mission?
10) Is the planned change of such magnitude that it requires approval by the academic planning committee and other university bodies before implementation?

Questions of this nature should be a part of any long-range planning. One does not have to be a futurist to respond to them, although precise answers may not be easily found. Indeed, it might be necessary to involve the institution's research center in order to acquire information to frame well-reasoned answers. Obviously, if you keep abreast of your discipline and stay current with the broader issues of higher education you will find it easier to answer these questions and to plan ahead. It might be prudent to appoint a departmental planning committee and charge its members with developing plans about where the department is going and how it is going to get there.

Much has been written about strategic academic planning. While the concept itself is fairly simple, to most chairpersons the idea is fuzzy. For the department, the concept is related to how the department achieves its mission and requires resources to carry out that mission as it responds to changes in the external environment. Unless you have some control over the allocation of resources, strategic planning is largely a waste of time. Also, the process should not be a lengthy, involved one with a lot of information gathering. The reason for this is simple: Strategic planning should be driven by ideas, not by data and paper. However, you have to take a long, hard look at your department's strengths and weaknesses and what they mean for its future success and match your ideas to realities.

Chairpersons and others who do strategic planning often make a mistake in writing a so-called strategic plan. The process should result in common understandings, shared expectations, and a shared sense of direction. Thus, if you write a plan, it should be about how to implement these common understandings of where the department is going. You should also keep in mind that a strategic planning document is never anything other than a plan that is incomplete and always in need of revision.

OBTAINING AND ALLOCATING FUNDS

You are responsible for obtaining funds and determining how the funds are allocated and spent. You must determine the cost of operating your department to carry out its mission. In this light, you also must be aware of changes in your department's mission and anticipate the costs associated with any changes. As indicated in Chapter Six, you must understand your university's budget process and know how your funding level is determined. You also need to understand how to plan a budget and develop priorities for spending.

A growing number of chairpersons are expected to engage in fundraising as more and more public universities are looking at the private sector to supplement their meager budgets. Chapter 15 provides information to help in getting started as a fundraiser.

You should consult with all of the faculty members of your department to determine funding needs. You must assume responsibility for providing equipment and supplies needed for instruction and academic activities. Moreover, you must bear responsibility for seeing that each faculty member has the wherewithal to fulfill his or her research and service responsibilities.

CARING FOR THE CURRICULUM

Managing the curriculum is another important responsibility. You should evaluate (see Chapter 22) the curriculum regularly to see how well all courses support the overall educational objectives. You need to keep up with changes within your discipline and those of your department if more than one is represented, maintain professional contacts, and keep abreast of literature—not just within your discipline, but also on the wider issues that affect higher education in general. As a corollary, you need to see that assessment programs (see Chapter 16) are in place to determine whether students are getting what they should out of the educational programs of the department. Likewise, you should provide leadership in assuring that all faculty members remain abreast of current advances and practices in their fields.

SUPPORTING RESEARCH AND DEVELOPMENT ACTIVITIES

Encouraging faculty members to become involved in research and faculty development also is one of your important responsibilities. This is especially challenging when faculty members appear to have no real interest in pursuing such activities. They always can provide good reasons (note I did not say excuses) for not doing research. Heavy teaching responsibilities can be a legitimate reason for limited research activity. Moreover, if the faculty members spend a lot of time advising students and working with them out of class, if they sponsor student organizations and serve on committees, and if they are active in the community, they may not have appreciable time for research. Some faculty members seem to get involved in research despite these obstacles, however. For this they deserve appreciation and should be encouraged to apply for faculty development grants offered by the university, research grants through the graduate school, or the option to work with the staff of the research and development center to seek other grants.

It is important for you as a chairperson to set a tone that emphasizes the importance of research and faculty development. Faculty meetings should include discussion of what might be done to encourage research and faculty development, and how the department might support these efforts through rearrangement of teaching, advising, and activity sponsorship assignments. Indeed, it might be possible to give faculty members released time on some kind of rotation basis. If this can be arranged, accountability must follow; those who are given released-time must show that they are using the time on worthwhile projects.

WORKING WITH STUDENTS

While much of what has been said up to this point has dwelt on faculty-related matters, I have had no intention of minimizing the importance of your relationships with and responsibilities to students. Certainly it is necessary to get to know students and to work closely with them. You need to know how students feel about their course work, faculty, department-sponsored activities, and the department in general. Students can be especially helpful on many matters of special concern. They can help plan and implement student recruitment efforts, for example, and help evaluate the effectiveness of student advising. Moreover, most are eager to be asked to help. If you do not take advantage of student participation in department affairs, you are missing a good opportunity.

One method of involving students is to create a student advisory committee. It can be assigned a number of important tasks: Members can assist with administering student evaluations of the department; individuals can serve on faculty search committees; and they can meet with candidates for faculty positions. Also, the committee can be useful in serving as a link between faculty members of the department and the general student body. Students who have complaints or concerns about departmental matters can be invited to bring them before the student advisory committee. Some students will share such matters with other students when they are reluctant to discuss them with the chairperson or faculty members.

There are many ways to put together a student advisory committee. One example is the way it has been done in a couple of journalism programs that I have directed. There the presidents and vice presidents of each of the three professional student groups—the Society of Professional Journalists, the Advertising Club, and the Public Relations Student Society of America—along with an elected graduate student, make up the Journalism Student Advisory Council.

MENTORING FACULTY AND SERVING AS A ROLE MODEL

The first-time college teacher should not be left alone to devise his or her approach to teaching. Some department chairpersons are guilty of doing little more than providing new faculty members with old course syllabi, telling them what courses they will teach, and pointing them in the direction of the classroom. You should do whatever you can to make new faculty members feel a welcome part of the department. You also might assign a veteran faculty member to serve as a mentor for the first-time college teacher. In this role, the veteran professor would meet regularly with the newcomer to discuss teaching methods, grading, handling absences, or any number of other problems or concerns. This dialogue should ease the frustration of the new faculty members.

You should serve as a role model for young faculty. In addition to having senior faculty serve as mentors, you should make it clear to new faculty members that they can come to you with questions or for advice. It is so easy to forget how uncertain many young faculty members are. There undoubtedly will be times when they need to talk to someone about a problem when their assigned mentor is unavailable. I was reminded of this not long ago when a first-year teacher came to me to ask whether he should assign an incomplete grade to a student who was requesting it. He said the student had quit coming to his class by midterm and had told him that she didn't have time for his class because she had been too busy with her other classes. The faculty member said he was inclined to give the student an incomplete but wanted my advice on the matter.

I explained that incomplete grades are for those who have legitimate reasons for not being able to complete course requirements, and that based on what he had told me I definitely would not give this student an incomplete. He said he understood but was having a hard time reconciling that with his Christian duty to help others. We had a long talk. I pointed out the unfairness to the other students that could result, as well as how giving students something they had not earned was not, in my judgment, the Christian thing to do.

New faculty members also deserve to be told as precisely as possible what is expected in order for them to win promotion and earn tenure. For example, what level of research is expected of faculty members, how much time are faculty members expected to give to office hours, etc. Finally, they also need to be told something of the history of the department, what its tradition and goals are, and how it fits into the structure of the college and university.

MAKING THE DEPARTMENT A PLEASANT WORKPLACE

Promoting the morale (see Chapter 12) of all of the department's faculty members is another of your responsibilities. You need to let faculty members know when they have done a job well. It does not take much time to write a short letter showing appreciation for a job well done. Likewise, a note or a card sent to a faculty member who is ill or dealing with personal adversity means a lot.

You should make a habit of meeting regularly with faculty members to see how they are doing, finding out what they need, or what concerns they have. Faculty members like to talk about their work, and it boosts morale for the chairperson to say occasionally, "Tell me how your classes are going."

Morale can be a problem if you fail to respond quickly and fairly to faculty conflicts. Honest differences of professional opinion always exist, and when differing viewpoints are expressed with civility they can be healthy. Debate causes faculty members to think and respond to ideas. Yet, when faculty members see these differences as personal attacks, conflict results. You often can deal effectively with such problems by getting the involved faculty members together to talk about the problems and to see if differences can be resolved. Participants must understand the importance of avoiding personalization of professional differences.

The department can be a pleasant place to work and study if you work to foster a feeling of participatory membership. Reference to "the history family," "the journalism family," or "the marketing family" can be an outward sign of an attitude that fosters togetherness—if it is really meant. Sponsoring department activities that bring faculty, staff, and students together also can be meaningful. For example, many departments regularly sponsor school picnics, Christmas parties, and an end-of-the-year awards banquet. Each activity does much to bring faculty, staff, and students together; students develop warm feelings toward the department and members of the faculty and staff; and most become supportive alumni. Symbolic team building is something chairpersons generally don't do enough of because, as one outstanding chairperson said to me recently, we fear "that our efforts will be ridiculed by jaded academics or will be viewed as too transparent." However, these techniques work.

As we can see, departmental chairpersons have many responsibilities. They fill a role that is at times ill-defined and murky. Many of the specific duties required of them—such as faculty evaluations, budgets, purchasing, and faculty recruitment—are dealt with at some length elsewhere in this book.

ROLES AND RESPONSIBILITIES OF DEPARTMENT CHAIRPERSONS

Department chairpersons serve as the chief administrative officer of the department, and are responsible for representing the department to the university administration, to the dean of the college, and to the department's faculty and students. The position of the department chairperson is integral to the university's central mission: the education of its students.

To Faculty

Department chairpersons report directly to their academic dean and are responsible for:

- Establishing and implementing procedures within university guidelines for the recruitment of new faculty
- Counseling and guiding faculty; encouraging outstanding teaching, research, and other professional activities; organizing faculty meetings and departmental committees to further the business of the department
- Enforcing faculty responsibilities
- Promoting faculty development, including encouraging faculty members to attend professional conferences, join professional organizations, and travel, etc.
- Protecting faculty rights, including recommendations on personnel matters such as leaves of absence, sabbatical leaves, research grants, etc.
- Giving periodic appraisal for recommending reappointment, tenure, promotion, and salary adjustments
- Fostering productive, interpersonal, professional relationships among faculty of the department

To Students

- Ensuring that proper curricular and career advisement are available to all students majoring and/or taking courses in the department
- Monitoring student-department scholarships and prizes; and, within university procedures, responding to student grievances and grade appeals
- Coordinating the recruitment of undergraduate and graduate students

To Curriculum and Programs

- Establishing department statements of mission and objectives within those of the university and periodically reviewing the department's progress in achieving them
- Establishing department policies in cooperation with faculty related to curriculum content and changes, instructional standards, evaluation methods, textbooks, and course syllabi
- Planning and presenting course schedules

- Appointing faculty members to cocurricular responsibilities and recommending released time to the dean

To Budget and Instructional Resources

- Accounting to the dean for fiscal management of departmental accounts
- Managing departmental facilities and instructional resources
- Recommending faculty and staff salaries to the dean within the limits imposed by the respective salary schedules
- Preparing, presenting, receiving, and administering the departmental budgets, which include:
  1) Annual operating and capital equipment budget
  2) Library appropriation
  3) Allocating the resources of the department so that institutional, research, administrative, and travel needs can be met equitably
  4) Fostering extramural support for and helping staff members to apply for such assistance, which may come from: federal and private agencies; business, industry, and professional groups; and alumni and friends
- Handling responsibility for departmental liaison with university offices dealing with particular fiscal activities, such as: 1) dean's office (for budgets, travel, and extramural funding); and 2) business offices (for activities relevant to purchasing, personnel, and accounting)
- Planning for long-range financing for special programs and activities
- Writing and reviewing funding proposals in cooperation with the department faculty and the appropriate academic support areas; administration and evaluation of the proposal and/or projects as the department's chief administrator
- Insuring that all budgetary operations conform to institutional and governing board guidelines and policies

To External Relations

- Conveying university and college policies, procedures, and actions to the department
- Representing the department in the college and university and with off-campus organizations
- Presenting departmental policies, procedures, and actions to the students

To Office Management

- Administering departmental facilities, hiring, supervising, and evaluating department staff and establishing the department's office procedures

To Personal Professional Performance

- Providing professional leadership and example in the department
- Maintaining and demonstrating competence in teaching, research, and professional activities including participation in professional associations and community service in accordance with standards mandated by university standards

Miscellaneous

- Carrying out other duties as assigned by the dean

You have an important role to play in the college and university. If you perform it well, you will contribute significantly to smooth operations. You can make a difference in the lives of students, faculty, and staff members. And while the financial rewards admittedly are not what they should be, your service and dedication are generally valued. Your effective efforts and talent do not go unnoticed; few would dispute one person's observation that an institution can run for a long time with an inept chief executive, but not long at all with inept department leaders.

REFERENCES

Gmelch, W. H., & Miskin, V. D. (1993). *Leadership skills for department chairs.* Bolton, MA: Anker.

Johnsrud, L. K. (1996). *Maintaining morale: A guide to assessing the morale of midlevel administrators and faculty.* Washington, DC: College and University Personnel Association.

Leaming, D. R. (1968). Personal interview with Robert Fuoss. Cincinnati, OH.

Seagren, A. T., Creswell, J. W., & Wheeler, D. W. (1993). *The department chair: New roles, responsibilities, and challenges.* Washington, DC: The George Washington University.

Tucker, A. (1992). *Chairing the academic department: Leadership among peers* (3rd ed.). Phoenix, AZ: ACE/Oryx.

Providing Leadership

To delegate effectively, the chairperson needs to know the strengths and weaknesses of each faculty member of the department.

As a department chairperson, you are expected to be a leader. You have many opportunities to demonstrate your leadership skills as you develop plans, encourage faculty development, set budget priorities, update the curriculum, recruit faculty members, encourage higher standards of teaching, resolve conflicts, serve on committees, or deal with other responsibilities.

Yet it is probable that most of you came into your positions with little training in management or leadership, and chances are good that you never even had given much time to any study of leadership. Consequently, you have had to depend on your instincts and the application of practical knowledge. You may have emulated the leadership skills of people you have worked for or have known.

Developing your own leadership style is a formidable, dynamic task. One way of establishing leadership capabilities is to make a list of the good and bad qualities of leaders you have known. This exercise can provide a picture of the kind of leader you aspire to become—as well as a list of traits to avoid.

Studies show that leadership often defies simple description. Indeed, the concept is difficult to articulate and understand. As Burns (1978, p. 2) has pointed out, "Leadership is one of the most observed and least understood phenomena on earth." Leadership is difficult to define, somewhat like the shibboleth: I can't define it, but I know it when I see it. While it may be difficult to define, for the purposes of this chapter, let's define it as the skills to motivate others to take certain courses of action, to persuade others that prescribed tasks must be done on time and in a particular way, and to garner respect of others, especially those with whom one works and/or associates.

One way of trying to understand leadership is to look at leadership theories. When these theories are applied to higher education, the more general theories of leadership tend to emphasize the behavior traits of leaders (Dill & Fullagar, 1987). "Successful academic leaders, in addition to their professional credibility, display certain characteristics, such as vigor, decisiveness, and a willingness to take chances" (Seagren, Creswell, & Wheeler, 1993, p. 20). According to Seagren et al., cognitive resource theory "is particularly relevant to higher education institutions. Cognitive theory emphasizes the need to understand the relationship between the leader's qualities and experience and the group's. For a high ability group, a nondirective leader is predicted to be more effective than a directive or autocratic leader."

LEADERSHIP QUALITIES

One theory of natural leaders is supported by research in terms of behavior traits (Yukl, 1989). It supports the idea that leaders possess certain common qualities. While Luthans (1992) shows that the existence of certain traits is likely to increase a leader's effectiveness, by no means is strong leadership certain. With that caveat, I list the following as qualities that will help you provide departmental leadership:

Not Coveting the Job

You should not covet your job as chairperson, nor should other university administrators for that matter. By covet, I do not mean to suggest that you should not want to be a chairperson. Instead, I am using the word in the sense that it goes to greed and avariciousness and where a person is willing to bend principles or ignore the truth to hang onto a job. People who thus covet a job, I contend, are unlikely to be as strong as those who are secure in their positions. If you are worried about protecting your job, you seldom make forceful or independent judgments.

Too many administrators will listen to a recommendation or idea and then say, "I agree with you, but . . ." What they do not go on to explain, of course, is that "If I support your recommendation, I may be putting my job in jeopardy, or, at the very least, I might incur the wrath of my boss."

Strong leaders look at the merits of whatever recommendations or ideas come before them. They analyze each idea or recommendation carefully. They may consult with others before giving their support, but they do not reject an idea simply because it may not please those to whom they report. If an idea has merit, and if it suggests the right course of action, you should back it. Fear of losing your position can paralyze you and make you ineffective. You will be less fearful when making decisions if you do not covet your job. And you will become a stronger, more respected administrator.

Having a Sense of Humor

Strong leaders have a good sense of humor. Those who are deadly serious about everything almost always fail at inspiring others. This does not suggest, of course, that a chairperson must possess a bag of tricks or a joke for all occasions. However, there are times when those working on a project become weary, when everyone becomes too serious. A well-timed humorous aside, even a bad pun, can accomplish much to help put everyone at ease, or to help put the task in proper perspective. More than likely the matter does not have life-and-death consequences. The world will not stop if the chairperson's task force does not reach an immediate decision or complete a routine task.

You shouldn't be afraid to laugh or smile when someone utters a comic aside. At times you may even make light of yourself. You will gain respect if you do, and there is no question that others will enjoy working with you.

Having Vision

The best chairpersons have vision. Not only do they have a vision, but they are able to articulate a vision, and they are able to convince others in the department to share their vision (Cameron & Ulrich, 1986; Maxcy, 1991). Strong leaders know what the department should become, what it should stand for, and how it can get there. They see the "big picture" and are able to assess the strengths and weaknesses of the department. They can provide a blueprint for getting resources and the wherewithal to bring about needed changes.

Chairpersons with vision stay on top of their disciplines, attend and participate in professional conferences, and are regular readers of professional journals and publications that address higher education issues. Indeed, more than likely they read just about anything they can get their hands on. Ideas absorb strong chairpersons; they fascinate and invigorate them. Ideas give them a reason for living.

Chairpersons of vision look for opportunities to share and implement their ideas. They are men and women creatively obsessed.

Staying Focused

Even after chairpersons establish goals, some fail to develop the necessary plans to see them realized. They are not focused. This can be remedied, however, by writing out the goals and plans. Responsibility for each activity should be specified. There should be a timetable that gives due dates and a method for assessing accomplishments. The chairperson should make the plans public, showing who is responsible for each task. Notices need to go out regularly to remind faculty members of due dates.

One problem related to staying focused is having too many goals, in other words, spreading oneself too thin. Even the best organized chairperson will have trouble juggling many different tasks that are tied to action plans.

There is no question that departmental goals are difficult to achieve unless the chairperson is able to give thorough attention to the details of any plans that have been developed. Stay focused!

Delegating Responsibility

As already noted, strong chairpersons have little difficulty with the delegation of departmental duties. They also delegate appropriate authority to those who have earned their trust.

To delegate effectively, the chairperson needs to know the strengths and weaknesses of each faculty member of the department. If something needs to be done, the chairperson must determine who has the talent to complete the job in a satisfactory manner. Also, the chairperson needs to know who has the time and who has shown that he or she can meet deadlines (i.e., who can and will produce).

Whenever you delegate responsibilities, you need to provide appropriate support and resources. Faculty members will become demoralized if you assign them tasks without the right tools.

Delegating responsibility is difficult for many, but it is an essential characteristic of effective leadership.

Knowing Yourself

Just as you need to know your faculty members well enough to gauge their strengths and weaknesses, you must also know yourself. To be effective, you must understand your own strengths and weaknesses.

If you know your weaknesses, you can generally get the support you need from those whose strengths match your weaknesses. Indeed, you can turn over to others those projects that demand skills you do not possess, and then concentrate your attention where your own talents are strongest.

Not Being Fearful of Making Mistakes

No matter how well you understand your duties and goals, you will at times make mistakes. If you worry unduly about making mistakes, however, your performance will suffer. All good leaders recognize the possibility of mistakes, but they are confident enough to know that their accomplishments will far outweigh their missteps.

One of the characteristics successful academic leaders display is their willingness to take chances (Seagren, Creswell, & Wheeler, 1993).

Being Self-Confident

Strong leaders are confident in their abilities and judgment. They show it in their speech and demeanor. Everything about them communicates self-assurance, yet they manage this without offending colleagues. Others do not see them as cocky or egocentric.

Self-confidence based on accumulated knowledge and preparation can do much to inspire others to support the agenda of any good chairperson. It promotes trust and respect, both of which are requisite to effective leadership.

Being Decisive

Strong chairpersons can make difficult decisions because they trust their judgments sufficiently. They don't postpone decisions that demand immediate action.

Faculty members probably complain more about indecisiveness than any other administrative weakness. Indecisiveness makes a chairperson look weak. It undermines trust and respect. Thus, decisiveness is a behavior worth cultivating.

At times, however, decisiveness can erode a chairperson's popularity. Difficult decisions are bound to generate some disagreement. If a decision is unpopular with some faculty members, they may fault the chairperson for the decision and any problems it may subsequently generate.

You, of course, must do what you believe is right, even at the risk of unpopularity. In the long run, if you are willing to make decisions, even unpopular ones, you will earn the respect of your colleagues. Most understand that you cannot please all faculty members at all times.

Accepting Blame for Failure and Sharing Credit for Success

Good leaders accept blame when things go wrong. They are not finger pointers. Instead, they regroup and establish corrective plans. They go forward.

Just as important, strong leaders see no benefit in being alone in the spotlight when success wins praise and recognition from others. They know they could not have achieved their goals without help. They are quick to acknowledge those who have contributed—even in the smallest way—to the success of any plan or program. In the process they gain respect from their colleagues, and they inspire them to work even harder the next time tasks are assigned.

Embracing Change

Change can be exciting, even intoxicating. It motivates leaders. Yet change without direction, or simply for its own sake, raises questions and engenders little enthusiasm. You should consider change carefully, and you need some assurance that it will produce positive results.

Whenever you plan significant changes, you should discuss your ideas with all faculty members, especially those who tend to cherish the status quo. They need to feel that the changes are not going to destroy their daily lives. Some faculty members seem innately opposed to virtually all change.

The effective chairperson recognizes that change is a necessary component to growth and improvement, yet it does not come without generating anxiety.

Being Sensitive and Caring

If you are to be a good chairperson you will be a sensitive, caring person. You must remember that all faculty members do not think alike. You know that professional and personal philosophies separate faculty members, and that faculty members bring these differences to many issues. Recognizing this, you should allow differing views to be expressed without fear of retribution. Moreover, you need to listen to and carefully consider those different views. In the process, you might find reasons to modify your ideas when the suggestions of others clearly have merit. Any good chairperson knows he or she does not have all the answers.

There are occasions when even the most reliable, even-tempered faculty members will have a bad day. You must know when to tolerate behavior that at other times would not be acceptable. If you show sensitivity in these moments, faculty members are likely to see the chairperson as someone they can work for willingly.

You should get to know something about the families of faculty members. Extend congratulations when they are due, and be there to console a faculty member when he or she suffers a personal or family setback. A well-timed note, a card of congratulation or condolence, or a bouquet of flowers can go a long way toward showing that you care about the well-being of faculty members and their families.

Possessing Strong Communication Skills

No matter how brilliant your plans are, you are not likely to succeed unless you can clearly communicate goals and expectations. Even if you are honest, dedicated, and a skilled leader, you will have difficulty getting others to take up your cause if you fail to make clear what it is you stand for and what hopes you have for the department.

Strong writing and speaking skills make a difference in leadership. These qualities often separate those who succeed from those who fail. Having wonderful ideas isn't enough. Unless you have the power to persuade others and cause them to buy into your ideas, you stand alone, and failure is virtually assured. On the other hand, if you can persuasively communicate ideas and provide important insights and details, even the most skeptical faculty member will likely give the plan a chance.

Providing Ideas and Being Flexible

Whenever you must deal with problems, you should develop possible solutions. It is a weak leader who calls a meeting and introduces a problem without offering possible ways of dealing with it. By the same token, you should invite others to present possible solutions. You should remain open-minded as you listen to suggestions. Rejecting ideas without fair consideration marks you as inflexible. Moreover, it does nothing to encourage others to provide ideas. It says to faculty members, "You already know what you want to do; you are only patronizing us."

Having a Good Work Ethic

You must set a good example by making effective use of time. The chairperson who comes to work late, wastes time in the office, and leaves early speaks volumes to his or her staff. This kind of behavior shows a lack of commitment. It encourages others to be lackadaisical, uncommitted, and uncaring. If you expect others to give the time and effort required to produce excellence, you must serve as a role model.

Being Honest and Fair

Chairpersons who are not honest and fair in their dealings with others are bound to fail. If faculty members are suspicious of your motives and see you acting unfairly, trust or respect cannot survive.

Being honest and forthright is not as easy as one might think. It is not pleasant to have to tell a faculty member that he or she is a weak teacher, or that assigned duties are not being handled properly. Still, it must be done. If you can learn to evaluate faculty members fairly, honestly, and forthrightly, and if you are honest and fair in your dealings with others, you will have taken an essential step toward becoming the leader every department deserves.

The qualities of leadership discussed in this chapter provide a framework on which to build. Undoubtedly there are other qualities that mark leadership. If you are willing to assess your strengths and weaknesses realistically and honestly, you can take advantage of those that are strong and work to correct your deficiencies.

Knowing When to Spend Your Political Capital

If there is anything to the truism "there's a time and place for everything," it is certainly the case when it comes to knowing when to spend your political capital. You need to ask whether the gain is worth the price you are paying. Most of us have just so much political capital, and when it's spent, it's not easily replenished. Is the issue you are faced with serious enough that you feel compelled to make a big issue over it with your dean? Is the matter involved one that is simply an irritation? Or are their principles at stake? Good leaders know that just as there are times you must stand up and fight, there are also times when you need to swallow your pride and let something pass.

It is generally believed that leadership traits are not innate, but are acquired through application and effort. This view gives all of us hope. We can become leaders if we are willing to work at it.

Stephen J. Trachtenberg (1992, p. 38) summed it up this way: "Good leadership depends on the ability to tolerate anxiety, loneliness, and the threat of unpopularity."

Some suggest that a better way to view leadership is to revise our way of thinking about leadership. In their discussion of cultural and symbolic theories of leadership, Bensimon, Neumann, and Birnbaum (1989) assert that these theories suggest that the role of a leader may be more modest—and less heroic—than is usually portrayed in education publications. The diffusion of authority and power in academe, not to mention the absence of clear and measurable outcomes, puts additional constraints on higher education leaders. Realistic managers will be less concerned with bold leadership and more concerned with making small improvements.

No matter how we choose to think about leadership, and even if we are content to forgo thoughts of bold leadership in favor of making small improvements, decisions must be made. And you must call on your best leadership skills to make them.

REFERENCES

Bensimon, E. M., Neumann, A., & Birnbaum, R. (1989). *Making sense of administrative leadership: The "L" word in higher education.* ASHE-ERIC Higher Education Report No. 1. Washington, DC: The George Washington University.

Burns, J. (1978). *Leadership.* New York, NY: Harper and Row.

Cameron, K. S., & Ulrich, D. O. (1986). Transformational leadership in colleges and universities. In J. C. Smart (Ed.), *Higher education: Handbook of theory and research,*Vol. 2. New York, NY: Agathon Press.

Dill, D. D., & Fullagar, P. K. (1987). Leadership and administrative style. In M. W. Peterson & L. A. Mets (Eds.), *Key resources on higher education governance, management, and leadership.* San Francisco, CA: Jossey-Bass.

Luthans, F. (1992). *Organizational behavior* (6th ed.). New York, NY: McGraw-Hill.

Maxcy, S. J. (1991). *Educational leadership: A critical pragmatic perspective.* New York, NY: Bergin & Garvey.

Seagren, A. T., Creswell, J. W., & Wheeler, D. W. (1993). *The department chair: New roles, responsibilities, and challenges.* Washington, DC: The George Washington University.

Trachtenberg, S. J. (1992). The apprenticeship approach to leadership. In J. L. Fischer & M. W. Tack (Eds.), *Leaders on leadership: The college presidency.* San Francisco, CA: Jossey-Bass.

Vroom, V. H. (1983). Leaders and leadership in academe. *Review of Higher Education,* 6, 367–386.

Yukl, G. A. (1989). *Leadership in organizations* (2nd ed.). Englewood Cliffs, NJ: Prentice-Hall.

5

Evaluating Faculty Performance

If you are unwilling to provide faculty members with honest appraisals of their work when it is less than satisfactory, you will face even more difficult tasks down the road.

Evaluating faculty members is one of your most important responsibilities. Evaluations must be done annually for all probationary faculty members, and tenured faculty members at most universities are evaluated regularly—perhaps every three years. You are expected to assess, as accurately and as fairly as possible, how effective faculty members are as teachers, as scholars, and as university and community citizens.

Some faculty members question the necessity of evaluations. In the perfect department, where all faculty members are outstanding teachers, productive scholars, and committed citizens, faculty evaluations might be unnecessary. Unfortunately, perfect departments do not exist.

The task of evaluating faculty members may become decidedly unpleasant when the overall evaluation is negative, as some chairpersons have difficulty telling a colleague that his or her work is not satisfactory. In the short run, giving a less than satisfactory evaluation is difficult; yet in the long run, it is a responsibility that can pay dividends. If you are unwilling to provide faculty members with honest appraisals of their work when it is less than satisfactory, you will face even more difficult tasks down the road.

Many universities are examining new models for evaluating and rewarding faculty, and a number have adopted models that offer faculty opportunities to select a focused agenda that matches their particular interest and expertise. The usual tripartite of teaching, research, and service are evaluated, though faculty are allowed to select one area of focus or a combination of the three. In *Restructuring the University Reward System* (1997), restructured models as effective agents of change are shown to have characteristics as spelled out in Table 5.1.

REASONS WHY YOU MUST EVALUATE YOUR FACULTY MEMBERS

- **Faculty members deserve an honest appraisal of their work.**

To evaluate otherwise is unfair. If you are dissatisfied with a faculty member's performance, and you do not inform the person, there is no way for that person to know that his or her performance is not meeting expectations. The kind of change you hope for is not likely to take place. Moreover, your unhappiness with the situation is likely to grow.

- **Students and faculty colleagues suffer whenever a faculty member does not perform well.**

Students deserve to have competent, dedicated teachers who bring inspiration and excitement to the classroom. Faculty colleagues most likely will have to do more than their fair share of the department's work if even one faculty member shirks responsibility.

- **Weak faculty members make weak departments.**

If you care about your department, you will want all faculty members to perform at a high level. Systematic, careful evaluations make change and improvement possible. Neglect in this area is almost certain to result in a casual attitude that breeds contempt for quality.

- **There is much documentation that shows that serious problems result from a haphazard approach to faculty evaluations.**

Weak faculty members who are given average or above-average evaluations will in all likelihood remain on the faculty; they will go on hurting students, colleagues, the department, and the university. Furthermore, it is unfair to recommend that tenure or promotion be denied to any faculty members who have not been advised that their performance is lacking. They deserve to be told what their weaknesses are and what they can do to improve their performance.

Additionally, a good annual review system promotes the health of the department. As Paul Woodruff, chair of the University of Texas faculty senate, points out, "Departments with a good annual review system are also depart-

TABLE 5.1 Characteristics of Restructured Models

- Models should have positive rather than punitive aspects.
- Models should have clearly identified short- and long-term goals reflective of administrator/faculty mutually derived individual action plans.
- Models should incorporate various ways of evaluating faculty, such as the use of professional portfolios and several incremental evaluations rather than one cumulative one.
- Administrators and tenure and promotion committees should define the purpose of evaluation. For example, is evaluation intended as a means of determining expertise or to determine how faculty members have contributed to the success or prestige of the university?
- Models should create an increased focus on teaching in the evaluation and reward process.
- Recognition and reward for research, teaching, and service in field settings should be part of the model.
- Research should be appropriate to the missions of the institution, college, and department, and to the needs of society. Furthermore, research should be applicable to current issues and significant in suggesting improved ways of meeting the needs of society as well as those of students.
- Universities should provide mentors for junior faculty who strive to become successful in each of the three traditional areas or experts in one area.
- Collaboration within and among academic departments and colleges for teaching, research, and service activities should be encouraged to construct knowledge and experiences applicable to changing perspectives of society.
- Differentiated faculty lines should be developed and offered to allow faculty to succeed in their chosen areas of expertise while maintaining some productivity in all three traditional areas.

From: Sid W. Richardson Foundation. (1997). Reprinted with permission.

ments that run well and have much higher morale than those that don't. The members know each other's work because they read their papers; they're interested in each other's work, and they have confidence in the quality. Departments that are not doing good annual reviews, on the other hand, are not as cohesive as a result" (Rosner, 1997, p. 4).

- **The legal ramifications of improperly evaluating the performance of faculty members are daunting.**

Sloppy evaluations breed lawsuits as well as departmental dissatisfaction. See Chapter 10 for a detailed discussion of what you should do to avoid litigation because of your evaluations.

Finally, it is implicit that handling evaluations is one of your specific responsibilities; you're paid to do it as fairly and as effectively as possible.

EVALUATING TEACHING

Evaluating teaching effectiveness is a complex process, but it need not be onerous. By approaching the task thoughtfully and systematically, chairpersons can do much to improve the level of classroom instruction for students. Moreover, most instructors appreciate knowing how well they are perceived to be doing and what they might do to improve their overall classroom effectiveness. This process should involve classroom visits as well as student and peer evaluations.

We should use all the tools at our disposal to evaluate teaching effectiveness, including student evaluation, classroom visits by peers, and teaching portfolios. Some faculty members are not willing to take student ratings seriously despite the fact that research shows that student evaluations are the single best measure of teaching effectiveness.

Classroom Visits

Although most faculty members will invite you into their classes, some are reluctant to have visits by any outsider. You nevertheless must visit the classrooms of all faculty members being evaluated if you are to be effective. One of the most effective ways for you to judge teaching skills is to visit classrooms periodically.

If you are alert you will, of course, receive bits and pieces of informal information on classroom performance. Student evaluations also will assist you in making your judgments. These are not good substitutes for first-hand observation, however. Any evaluation is weak and incomplete if it is based solely on student evaluations and casual comments of other faculty members and students. Faculty members who balk at inviting their chairperson into their classes often can be persuaded to allow visits if they understand the purpose of the classroom visits. Many experienced chairpersons have developed a form to complete during a classroom visit. In addition to providing a systematic method of evaluation, it lets the person being evaluated know in advance what you will use as a basis for judgment. Figure 5.1 is a typical form. This form can be modified easily to suit the nature of the subject matter or the kind of class to be visited.

Teaching Portfolios

Teaching portfolios offer a way for faculty members to share information about their teaching. Seldin (1993, p. 2) offers this definition of a teaching portfolio: "It is a factual description of a professor's teaching strengths and accomplishments. It includes documents and materials which collectively suggest the scope and quality of a professor's teaching performance." A teaching portfolio is a record of the highlights of a faculty member's teaching over a prescribed period of time. It will show what is unique about an individual's approach to teaching. It enables faculty members to evaluate their own teaching as well as that of their colleagues. "Portfolios not only have properties that enable us to illuminate deeper dimensions of teaching; they enable faculty—indeed, require them—to become more important actors in monitoring and evaluating the quality of their own work" (Seldin, 1993, p. 5).

Several institutions have developed models for evaluating teaching from portfolios. Among the institutions using this approach successfully are Murray State University (Kentucky), Miami-Dade Community College (Florida), and Dalhousie University (Canada). Seldin (1993) describes the process used by these institutions for evaluating teaching portfolios.

In recent years portfolios have become a popular way for faculty members to document their teaching accomplishments. They are worth exploring as additional ways to examine and evaluate teaching, although we need to be reminded that teaching portfolios—as with student evaluations—should be seen as a part of an overall evaluation scheme. They should be used in conjunction with student and peer evaluations and classroom visits, not as sole evaluation documents.

According to Seldin (1993, p. 6), the items in Table 5.2 are frequently found in teaching portfolios.

FIGURE 5.1 Teacher Evaluation

This form can be modified easily to suit the nature of the subject matter or the kind of class to be visited.

Faculty Member: ______________________________

Course Title: ____________________ Date: ____________

(Circle One)

1. The lecture (or other teaching approach) was well organized.	**not at all 1 2 3 4 5 highly**
2. It was obvious that the faculty member was prepared.	**not at all 1 2 3 4 5 highly**
3. The faculty member was enthusiastic about the subject matter.	**not at all 1 2 3 4 5 highly**
4. The faculty member encouraged student participation.	**not at all 1 2 3 4 5 highly**
5. The faculty member made good use of instructional cues—such as writing key points on chalkboard, telling students that certain points are important, using graphs or charts, etc.	**not at all 1 2 3 4 5 highly**
6. The faculty member projected his or her voice so that students could hear.	**not at all 1 2 3 4 5 highly**
7. The faculty member varied his or her voice to help hold students' interest.	**not at all 1 2 3 4 5 highly**
8. If I were a student, I would enjoy taking this class.	**not at all 1 2 3 4 5 highly**
9. It is likely students would rate the teacher highly.	**not at all 1 2 3 4 5 highly**
10. Overall quality of this class session:	**weak 1 2 3 4 5 outstanding**

11. The major strengths of the classroom session were:

12. The major weaknesses of the classroom session were:

13. What, if anything, could be done to improve the faculty member's teaching technique?

Additional comments:

Observer: ____________________ Date: ____________

Signature: ______________________________

TABLE 5.2 Elements of a Teaching Portfolio

- **Materials from Oneself**
  - Statement of teaching responsibilities, including course titles, numbers, enrollments, and a brief description of the way each course is taught.
  - Representative course syllabi detailing course content and objectives, teaching methods, readings, and homework assignments.
  - Description of steps taken to improve teaching, including changes resulting from self-evaluation, reading journals on teaching improvement, and participation in programs on sharpening instructional skill.
  - Instructional innovations and evaluation of their effectiveness.
  - A personal statement by the professor describing teaching goals for the next five years.
- **Materials from Others**
  - Student course or teaching evaluation data which produce an overall rating of effectiveness or suggested improvements.
  - Statement from colleagues who have observed the professor in the classroom.
  - Documentation of teaching development activity through the campus center for teaching and learning.
  - Honors or other recognition such as a distinguished teaching award.
- **The Products of Good Teaching**
  - A record of students who succeed in advanced study in the field.
  - Student publications or conference presentations on course-related work.
  - Testimonials from employers or students about the professor's influence on career choice.
  - Student scores on pre- and post-course examinations.

From: Seldin, P. (1993). Reprinted with permission.

Student Evaluations

Many departments have instituted some form of student evaluations. These range from highly quantifiable questionnaires that are machine scored to ones that ask students to write detailed answers to open-ended questions. In some departments the chairperson sees these evaluations; in others they are seen only by the faculty member.

FIGURE 5.2 Teaching Evaluation

Instructor's Name: ______________________________

Course Title: ____________________ Date: ______________

Use the scale below to rate your instructor on the items listed below.

YOUR INSTRUCTOR WILL NOT SEE THIS EVALUATION UNTIL FINAL GRADES ARE TURNED IN.

Do not put your name on this sheet. This evaluation will be seen only by your instructor and the chairperson of the department. Thank you.

1 — Extremely low, negative
2 — Below average
3 — Average, acceptable
4 — Above average
5 — Exceptionally high, positive

______ Knowledge of subject matter
______ Ability to share knowledge
______ Prepares adequately for class
______ Organizes class meaningfully (with syllabus, course outline, etc.)
______ Rapport with students
______ Availability and/or willingness to assist students
______ Fairness in grading
______ Reasonable in making assignments
______ Makes assignments clear
______ Makes assignments which are meaningful and worthwhile
______ Encourages questions from students
______ Inspires students to learn
______ Values student opinions
______ I would be inclined to take another course from this instructor

What are the instructor's major strengths?

What are the instructor's major weaknesses?

I expect to receive the following grade in this course: ______________

Regardless of the kind of student evaluations used, both you and the faculty member should see them. Faculty members should see them so that they can benefit from student perceptions and comments. You need to review student evaluations of all faculty members in your department. This provides some feel for the overall quality of teaching within the department, and it helps identify faculty members who seem to be doing the best job of teaching and those who appear to be weak. If there are trouble spots, they are likely to show up in student evaluations that are done on a regular basis.

If evaluations by students are to be effective, safeguards must be instituted to assure students that their comments are anonymous and can have no effect on their grades. Otherwise, it is not likely that student comments will be honest or helpful.

The following procedures provide these safeguards:

1) Faculty members must be out of the classroom when students do the evaluating.
2) Graduate assistants may be assigned to go into the various classes and handle the mechanics of getting the forms completed and turned into the department chairperson. If the department does not have graduate assistants available, members of a student advisory council may be assigned to supervise the student evaluation procedure.
3) Students must be told that faculty members will not see the completed evaluation forms until after grades are reported. (The sample evaluation form on page 46 also carries such a statement.)
4) The faculty evaluation forms should be placed in a large envelope that is sealed after students complete and return them. The sealed envelope should then be given to the department chairperson to hold until after grades are turned in.

Figures 5.2 and 5.3 are sample evaluation forms for student use.

EVALUATING ADVISING

An increasing number of universities are giving attention to student advising, and as chairpersons we are asked to demonstrate that faculty members are performing this task as expected. To get a glimpse at how well students believe their faculty advisers are doing their job, you might want to have students complete the evaluation shown in Figure 5.4.

FIGURE 5.3 Evaluation of Faculty Performance

1. The lecture (or other teaching approach) was well organized.
   (a) almost always (b) usually (c) rarely (d) never (e) not applicable
2. Instructor answers student's questions effectively.
   (a) almost always (b) usually (c) rarely (d) never (e) not applicable
3. Instructor presents material clearly.
   (a) almost always (b) usually (c) rarely (d) never (e) not applicable
4. Instructor is accessible to students on course matters outside of class.
   (a) almost always (b) usually (c) rarely (d) never (e) not applicable
5. Class sessions are relevant to course subject matter.
   (a) almost always (b) usually (c) rarely (d) never (e) not applicable
6. Course requirements are clear.
   (a) almost always (b) usually (c) rarely (d) never (e) not applicable
7. Grading criteria for the course as a whole are clear.
   (a) almost always (b) usually (c) rarely (d) never (e) not applicable
8. Considering the type of exams, the results are reported by the instructor within a reasonable amount of time.
   (a) almost always (b) usually (c) rarely (d) never (e) not applicable
9. Considering the type of assignments, the results are reported by the instructor within a reasonable amount of time.
   (a) almost always (b) usually (c) rarely (d) never (e) not applicable
10. Instructor treats students in a courteous and/or professional manner.
    (a) almost always (b) usually (c) rarely (d) never (e) not applicable
11. The class begins at scheduled times.
    (a) almost always (b) usually (c) rarely (d) never (e) not applicable
12. The class usually ends:
    (a) on time (b) early (c) late (d) not applicable
13. What is your current class status?
    (a) fresh. (b) soph. (c) junior (d) senior (e) graduate (f) other
14. What is your current cumulative grade point average?
    (a) below 2.0 (b) 2.00–2.49 (c) 2.49–3.00 (d) 3.00–3.49 (e) above 3.49 (f) none yet
15. What grade do you expect to receive in this course?
    (a) A (b) B (c) C (d) D (e) E (f) Pass / Fail
16. Main reason for taking course:
    (a) general requirement
    (b) interested in subject
    (c) course in major
    (d) easy course
    (e) recommended by another student
17. Approximately how many classes have you missed in this course?
    (a) 0–3
    (b) 4–7
    (c) 8–15
    (d) more than 15
    (e) went only for exams

EVALUATING RESEARCH AND SCHOLARLY ACTIVITY

You will find that evaluating research and scholarly activity is generally easier than evaluating teaching. Problems occasionally arise, however, when faculty members do not know what is expected of them in this area, or when they have misconceptions about how much weight is given to different kinds of activities.

In departments that have good written promotion and tenure guidelines, the evaluation process is much easier. The more precise the guidelines, the more helpful they become. They will specify exactly what counts as research and/or scholarly activity, and how much weight is attached to the various activities. They will provide faculty members with answers to such questions as how research and publication done as a joint project is weighed; the weight to be given to writing or editing a textbook; and credit for popular articles or book reviews.

Obviously the promotion and tenure guidelines must be thorough and up-to-date, and the decisions they incorporate should not be made by chairpersons without faculty input. While in the final analysis you must be the one who approves the department guidelines concerning research and/or scholarly activity, all faculty members should have some part in their development and periodic review. A copy of the guidelines should be given to each new faculty member on the day he or she joins the department.

There are two examples of departmental promotion and tenure guidelines in the appendix of this book. Both provide systems for evaluating research and/or scholarly activity.

EVALUATING SERVICE ACTIVITIES

Service activities to be evaluated include university, college, and department committee work. Also included are such extracurricular involvements as supervision of student activities and participation in community affairs. We generally describe the latter as "participation in extramural activities that may serve directly or indirectly the best interests of the university."

In recent years, community service has come to mean those activities where one uses his or her education and training to assist a worthy community group or organization when a professional relationship can be demonstrated. Faculty members are expected to use their expertise in providing leadership for the community. Thus, for example, a faculty member in geography would be credited with service for providing leadership if he or she mapped an area that had been designated for historical preservation. The same faculty member would not be credited with service for coaching a little league baseball team.

A nastier problem associated with community service develops when faculty members are paid as consultants. For example, what if you have two faculty members in geography who do community service using their expertise, and one of them receives pay as a consultant? Should the faculty member

FIGURE 5.4 Advisor Evaluation

Advisor's Name: ______________________________

Department: ____________________ Date: ______________

Use the following scale to rate your advisor on the items listed below.

5 — Strongly agree
4 — Agree
3 — Neutral
2 — Disagree
1 — Strongly Disagree
0 — Does not apply

_____ 1. Keeps his or her office hours as posted.
_____ 2. Is familiar with my academic background.
_____ 3. Helps me select courses that match my interests and abilities.
_____ 4. Knows the university and department policies.
_____ 5. Helps me explore careers in my field of interest.
_____ 6. Seems to enjoy advising.
_____ 7. Is willing to discuss personal problems.
_____ 8. Helps me to examine my needs, interests, and values.
_____ 9. Encourages me to talk about myself and my college experiences.
_____ 10. Encourages my interest in an academic discipline.
_____ 11. Encourages my involvement in extracurricular activities.
_____ 12. Is knowledgeable about courses outside my major area of study.
_____ 13. Is approachable and easy to talk to.
_____ 14. Shows concern for my personal growth and development.
_____ 15. Keeps personal information confidential.
_____ 16. Is flexible in helping me plan my academic program.
_____ 17. Is a helpful, effective advisor whom I would recommend to other students.

who is paid receive the same service credit as his colleague whose service is donated? For many chairpersons this is an increasingly serious issue and one that may become a pivotal issue when promotion and/or tenure are being considered.

Faculty members are expected to serve on department, college, and university committees. They also receive service credit for their contributions to local, state, or national professional organizations. Thus, by holding an office or serving on committees within such organizations, a faculty member would be credited with service. To assist faculty members in understanding service expectations, departmental guidelines should provide a precise definition of service as well as the level of service expected.

Evaluating Job Performance in Carrying Out Departmental Assignments

Faculty members are also expected to undertake certain responsibilities assigned by the chairperson. You in turn are expected to provide resources and support so that the faculty member can complete the assignment in a professional manner. As timely completion of the assignment is generally important, expected outcomes with specified due dates should be made clear at the time the assignment is given.

The use of a performance log can help you keep a record of assignments and how they are handled. Figure 5.5 is an example of such a performance log.

FIGURE 5.5 Faculty Performance Log

Name ______________________ Date: ______________

Assignment: ________________________________

____

____

Use the following scale to rate the task handled.

5 — Exceptionally well
4 — Well
3 — Average
2 — Below average
1 — Not at all

Met deadlines: yes / no

Comments: ________________________________

____

____

FIGURE 5.6 Evaluation of Cooperativeness

Faculty Member ____

Department: ________________________ Date: _________________

Use the following scale to rate your colleague's character, attitude, and commitment to programs and students of the department and/or university.

5 — Agree enthusiastically
4 — Tend to agree
3 — Neutral
2 — Tend to disagree
1 — Disagree emphatically

_____ 1. Is the kind of person I can trust

_____ 2. Has a positive attitude, which encourages me to want to work with him or her

_____ 3. Is personable and enjoyable to be around

_____ 4. Is a valuable colleague

_____ 5. Is a good addition to our faculty

_____ 6. Works hard trying to get along with others

_____ 7. Is strongly committed to students

_____ 8. Takes an active role in discussion about college policies and activities

_____ 9. Is a truthful, honest person

_____ 10. Is interested in improving the department and college and its programs

_____ 11. Works and gets along well with others

_____ 12. Is supportive of peers

_____ 13. Assumes fair share of departmental duties

_____ 14. Should be promoted / tenured (circle one)

Additional comments:

Signature of evaluator: ________________________ Date: _____________

If the log sheets are completed each time an assignment is given to a faculty member, it soon becomes apparent which faculty members are doing superior work and which are letting the department down. You should keep the completed log sheets in folders maintained for each faculty member. They become a helpful paper trail should it become necessary to document that a faculty member's work has been less than satisfactory, and they also verify excellence (i.e., they help you evaluate faculty performance).

If a faculty member does not complete work assigned or does the job inadequately, the chairperson needs to meet with him or her to see what can be done to correct the deficiency. You need to put the faculty member on notice that timely, professional work is always expected.

Evaluating Cooperativeness

While the idea of evaluating collegiality is often controversial, nonetheless some universities evaluate faculty on this quality. As Whicker, Kronenfeld, and Strickland (1996, p. 13) point out, "Tenure criteria are sufficiently vague, and the standards applied to each criteria are sufficiently evolving in most institutions that grounds for rejecting all but the most brilliant candidates can be found. You plainly do not want to be perceived as unpleasant, venal, unethical, or unprofessional by current department and institutional standards." The following, for example, is taken from a university's promotion and tenure policy.

". . . evidence of character, attitude, and personality that ensure cooperation with colleagues and commitment to programs and students of the department, college, and the university."

Figure 5.6 is the instrument many chairs have completed in an attempt to get some objective measure of how cooperative a colleague is.

PEER EVALUATIONS

The participation of other faculty members in the evaluation process can be especially helpful. In a small department, most faculty members have a good feel for the kind of work done by all of their department colleagues. Even in a large department, a number of faculty members can generally be called upon to evaluate those whose work they know.

Peer evaluation committee members often evaluate the teaching of all probationary faculty members. They visit classes and provide you with an

FIGURE 5.7 Faculty-Peer Evaluation

Faculty Member: ____

Evaluator: ______________________________ Date: __________________

Use the scale below to rate the faculty member being evaluated on the items listed. Return the completed evaluation to the department chairperson.

1 — Extremely low, negative
2 — Below average
3 — Average, acceptable
4 — Above average
5 — Exceptionally high, positive

A. **Teaching.** Complete this section only if you have observed the faculty member's teaching.

_____ 1. Ability to share knowledge
_____ 2. Rapport with students
_____ 3. Classes seem to be well organized
_____ 4. Good preparation is evident
_____ 5. Inspires students to learn
_____ 6. Encourages students to ask questions
_____ 7. Teaching ability compares favorably with other members of this department

Summarize the strengths/weaknesses of this faculty member's teaching skills:

B. **Research / Scholarly Activity**

_____ 8. Level of activity meets departmental expectations
_____ 9. Faculty member's activity in this area is meaningful
_____ 10. Publications are relevant and should count toward promotion and/or tenure
_____ 11. Work in this area compares favorably with other faculty members of this department

Summarize the strengths/weaknesses of this faculty member's research/scholarly activity:

C. **Service**

_____ 12. Willingly accepts assignments
_____ 13. Level of activity in this area is what is expected
_____ 14. Acts responsibly, professionally
_____ 15. Is a good representative for department/university
_____ 16. Work in this area compares favorably with other faculty members of the department

Summarize the strengths/weaknesses of faculty member's service:

assessment of the teaching skill of the person being evaluated. Other departments have some form of peer evaluation which functions most notably when faculty members are asked to make decisions regarding promotion and tenure.

In peer evaluations, specific information about performance should be sought. The form shown in Figure 5.7 provides a way to gather useful assessments.

Peer reviews ought to go beyond simply visiting a colleague's class, completing an evaluation form, and turning it in to the department chairperson. If we are going to be fair in evaluating our peers, we need to gain a thorough knowledge of their special talents; understand their teaching philosophy; know something about their knowledge in the content area; understand their approaches to teaching, student learning, and achievements; and be familiar with their contributions to the profession and to the campus.

PROBLEM EVALUATIONS

What to Do if the Evaluation Is Unsatisfactory

Occasionally you must evaluate faculty members who are not performing at the expected level. When you complete an evaluation that is unsatisfactory, you should take the following steps:

1) Set goals with the faculty member. This is best done by working jointly with the faculty member.
2) Describe direction and suggestions to assist the faculty member in accomplishing the agreed-upon goals.
3) Set timelines for the faculty member to accomplish the desired changes.
4) Be certain to spell out the consequences of not taking corrective action.

Terminating a Faculty Member

It happens from time to time that a faculty member must be terminated. It is important that a lot of effort go into hiring quality faculty—those you are going to want to promote and award tenure. Occasionally, however, you will find that no matter what you do, someone whom you have hired does not work out. The sooner you determine that, the better. A lot of attention should be given to evaluating first-year faculty and terminating those who are not performing at the expected level.

In counseling with those you must terminate, you need to be sympathetic. If faculty members have access to legal counsel, advise those you are terminating to seek legal advice. Most legal advisers will tell faculty members who are being terminated that they shouldn't try to fight back. "When a faculty member who's been targeted comes to me, I tell him not to be a bug on the windshield," said Eileen Wagner (1996), an attorney in Richmond, Virginia, who works with faculty members who have been asked to leave their institution. "The hardest part of my job as a counselor," she said, "is to convince him not to fight but to negotiate and leave voluntarily" (Wagner, 1996, p. 1).

Evaluating faculty performance is a burdensome task, and I know of few chairpersons who look forward to the task. Yet if used properly, evaluations can help faculty members understand what's expected of them, and they can use your evaluation as a guide for personal development. Certainly those chairpersons who take faculty evaluations seriously will soon recognize their value.

REFERENCES

Seldin, P. (1993). *Successful use of teaching portfolios.* Bolton, MA: Anker.

Sid W. Richardson Foundation. (1997). *Restructuring the university reward system.* Fort Worth, TX: Sid W. Richardson Foundation Forum.

Rosner, F. (1997, May). Post-tenure review: Accountability in Texas. *Academic Leader,* 13 (5).

Wagner, E. (1996, August). Termination: When a faculty member must go. *Academic Leader,* 12 (8).

Whicker, M. L., Kronenfeld, J. J., & Strickland, R. A. (1996). *Getting tenure.* Newbury Park, CA: Sage.

Budgetary Matters

One thing that does not change from one institution to another is the need for faculty to be involved in the budget process.

Taking care of the department's money consumes much of a chairperson's time. Financial decisions are difficult, especially in times of scarce resources, so chairpersons often face difficult decisions. Even as faculty members want and need more funds to support their professional activities, the costs of goods and services continue to increase at a rate much higher than the funding for higher education. "Between 1990 and 1993 public spending on higher education in the United States declined by $7.76 billion (including budget cuts and inflationary losses)" (Munitz, 1995, p. 9).

Monitoring the budget—that is, knowing at any given time how much money the department has and how much it owes—has always been an important function. Today, however, the chairperson must manage department resources with precision. For example, the chairperson must decide who gets travel funds when there is not enough to meet all faculty travel requests. Wise and careful equipment purchase decisions are necessary when equipment needs are far greater than funding.

ALLOCATION OF FUNDS

After funds are allocated to public universities, they are parceled out to various parts of the university. The provost or vice president for academic affairs gets money for the university's academic sector. In turn, he or she apportions that money to the various colleges and often to campus units that report to him (admissions, registrar, library, etc.). The provost will use some kind of formula for distributing these funds. It may be a sophisticated formula that takes into account many different pieces of information (student credit hours produced, number of majors, value of equipment inventory, etc.). On the other hand, the formula may be one that is quite crude. For example, it may be based simply on what each college has received in the past. If that is the case, you may want to lobby for a change because such formulas generally fail to take into account many changes, and growing, progressive programs can be penalized.

At some universities, the provost will allocate funds to all spending units in the various colleges. At other schools, the deans will allocate funds to the departments that report to them. Once again, the dean will use some formula, and it can likewise be sophisticated or crude. Figure 6.1 shows a typical funding formula.

Analyzing this formula, one can see that 10% of the total allocation is earmarked to support the college office. The department base is 4.99%, which means that 4.99% of the total allocation is set aside for the academic departments. In this particular college there are 14 departments, so 1/14 of the amount is set aside for each of them. To help with understanding of the formula, let's use a hypothetical example for distributing funds for the category "faculty."

FIGURE 6.1 College Funding Formula

Current Expense	
College Office	10%
Special Needs	25%
Department Base	4.99%
Student Credit Hours	
(.125% basic)(.875% other)	26.69%
Major Programs	4.55%
Majors	10.85%
Faculty	17.92%

Equipment: Formula Based on Department Size

$4,433	Large Depts. (16 or more faculty members)
$2,980	Medium Depts. (5–15 faculty members)
$965	Small Depts. (1–4 faculty members)

Travel: Based on projected recruitment needs for the year. A certain percentage is held by the college with the balance divided by the number of faculty members and distributed to departments.

If you look at faculty in the current expense section, you will see the figure 17.92%. For purposes of illustration, let's assume that the total allocation for the college is $200,000. To find what the category "faculty" means, first determine what 17.92% of $200,000 is; it comes to $35,840, obviously. If we divide $35,840 by the total number (117) of faculty members in the college, we will then know how much to distribute to the various departments for each of their faculty members. Dividing $35,840 by 117 gives us $306.32. Thus, a department with eight faculty members would receive $306.32 x 8, or $2,450.56. This amount would be added to money allocated to that department from other parts of the formula.

ALLOCATING DEPARTMENT FUNDS

At many universities, funds allocated to departments are designated as "current expense" and "equipment." Travel funds may or may not be merged into the "current expense" category. If they are merged, you will have the flexibility to increase or decrease travel funding depending on the travel needs of the faculty. If, for example, in a given year faculty members, for whatever reason, do not plan to travel as much as in other years, you may decide to increase the current expense and/or equipment budget and decrease the travel allocation.

You should be precisely aware of your equipment needs. As you put together your department's annual budget, ask each faculty member to provide a list of equipment needs. The list should be specific as to price, specifications, justification for purchase, recommended vendors, etc. After all faculty members have turned in their equipment recommendations, you should develop a master list that establishes purchase priorities. By doing so, you will be prepared to make prompt decisions on how to spend the equipment allocation.

In order to develop budget plans, you should also consult faculty members to see if extraordinary supplies will be needed for the upcoming year. These costs are paid for out of the "current expense" and "equipment" funding line items, which must be stretched to cover :

- All supplies, including paper, pens, note pads, calendars, paper clips, staples, duplicating fluids, etc.
- Telephone expenses

- Postage
- Faculty travel
- Honoraria

PURCHASING SUPPLIES, EQUIPMENT, AND SERVICES

Public universities generally vest purchasing authority in a director of purchasing and his or her staff. At many universities, purchases made by other individuals are unauthorized and will not be approved retroactively. Individuals may be held personally liable for purchases they make. This is true regardless of the source of funds.

You are charged with initiating all requisitions. After you have signed a requisition, it must be signed by the dean of the college. When the requisition reaches the purchasing office, a purchase order number is assigned, and accounting verifies that the department has sufficient funds to pay for the goods or services. The requisitions are then competitively bid or approved by a procurement officer and mailed to the vendor. A copy of the requisition is then sent back to the department.

At most universities, if the purchases are below a certain dollar value, competitive bids are not required unless deemed appropriate by purchasing or the department. Purchases over the designated amount require competitive bids that are handled by the purchasing department based on specifications provided by the department. After bids are received by purchasing, orders are generally awarded to the lowest responsible bidder who meets the specifications.

One caution here to chairpersons new to the job: At most universities it is a violation of university policy to obligate the university for amounts exceeding a certain designated amount (e.g., $500 at many institutions). Don't try to get around this by permitting a vendor to talk you into purchasing something for $1,996.00, let's say, and billing your institutions $499 at separate times so that you can immediately get what you want. If you must have a costly item in a hurry, ask your purchasing office for help.

Many schools have established alternative purchasing methods through which a department can obtain nearly all goods and services in advance of the department's needs. You should remember that at many institutions payment will not be made for "after-the-fact" purchases.

Routine Orders

If the cost of a purchase is under the established dollar amount, and bids are not required, submit a requisition, and an order will be mailed to the vendor. At some universities, requisitions are orally bid by purchasing or the department. If the purchase is over the specified dollar amount, written bid requests go out with a deadline for their return. Generally, it takes about 18 days to confirm bids and mail an order to the successful vendor.

Contracts

Most departments can purchase many commonly used items from state and university blanket contracts. The advantage is convenience for the department and the knowledge that requisitions do not have to be bid. Carpeting, furniture, chemicals, laboratory supplies, computers, and copiers are a few of the items usually available in this manner.

Agreements

These special orders allow the department to contract for such things as technical and professional services, engaging consultants or lecturers, or paying accreditation services. Generally, they are noncompetitive. The advantage for the department is that the vendor simply submits an invoice as services are rendered. Individual purchase orders are not required after the agreement has been approved.

Office Supplies

These may often be obtained from your campus bookstore, or an intrauniversity voucher form, or from other office suppliers.

COMPLETING PURCHASE ORDERS

Preparing a purchase order or an intrauniversity departmental transfer voucher is relatively easy. Look at past purchase orders to assist you, or call someone in the purchasing office for assistance.

Once the purchase order or voucher is filled out, you will need to sign the form and forward it to your dean's office. When the dean approves and signs the purchase order, he or she sends the form directly to purchasing. Purchasing in turn sends the order to the vendor and returns a copy to the department. The department may check the status of an order with the vendor. However, changes to the order may not be made unless they are coordinated with purchasing.

DIFFERENT BUDGETING APPROACHES

Budgeting and purchasing practices vary from university to university, so it is difficult to provide advice that is not general. If you are new in your job as chairperson, it is wise to talk to personnel in the budget and purchasing office, consult with veteran chairpersons on campus, and listen to your secretary.

One thing that does not change from one institution to another is the need for faculty involvement in the budgeting process. Share a copy of the total departmental budget at the beginning of the fiscal year, and then provide updates at least every quarter. Get faculty input when sending through your funding and budget by having faculty members submit their projected financial needs for the coming year. Not only should your efficiency in allocation improve with faculty input, but also the overall faculty morale will increase as well.

Be an advocate for adequate funding for your department. Your "goal is at minimum to maintain the department's current resource base, and at best to acquire as many additional resources as possible" (Meisinger, 1994, p. 50). Your faculty will think you are not an effective chairperson if you request fewer resources than are currently available. And they will be especially pleased with your leadership if you are successful in getting increased funding for your department. "Advocates often ask for more resources than they really need because they know that the cutters will reduce budgets regardless of the amounts requested. The cutters will reduce budget requests, knowing that the requests are padded and that by cutting the budgets there is little danger of injuring programs. This behavior demonstrates the built-in pressure for expansion that characterizes the budget process" (Meisinger, 1994, p. 51).

Universities have different approaches to budgeting, and understanding these may be helpful to you in your role as chairperson. The essentials of these approaches are described briefly here, though you should keep in mind that they are not mutually exclusive.

Incremental Budgeting

Lindblom (1959) described this approach as the science of muddling through. It focuses largely on increases and decreases rather than on the budget base.

With this approach, departments and other spending units will have their budgets increased or decreased depending on what amount of money is available to the university. For example, if the state allocates fewer dollars to the university, your department will likely have its budget reduced incrementally. Whatever allocation model has been used for funding, your department will not be altered from year to year when this budgeting model is used.

Planning, Programming, and Budgeting Systems

This approach to budgeting calls for examining the costs and benefits of programs and activities and links the planning process to the allocation of resources. A program budget will provide information about the costs and benefits of its activities. It calls for sophisticated—and often expensive—information gathering, and detailed analyses of policy alternatives.

Zero-Base Budgeting

This approach focuses on examining all programs and activities during each budget cycle. It assumes no budget from previous years, and so each year's budget is begun from a base of zero. In other words, it assumes no budget history.

Performance Budgeting

This approach focuses on measures of program performance. It attempts to improve efficiency and improve outcomes. In recent years, some states have mandated some funding through this approach, though often it is an add-on feature rather than an integral part of the budgeting. When this is used, specific outcomes measures are generally defined in both qualitative and quantitative terms.

Formula Budgeting

This approach focuses on some type of distribution that attempts to achieve a "fair share." Quantitative measures are established and funds are allocated on those measures, as seen in the formula presented earlier in this chapter.

Responsibility-Center Budgeting

This approach—sometimes called cost-center budgeting—focuses primary responsibility on colleges and schools for the management of resources, which become revenue and cost centers. Your department would be expected to count on revenue tuition dollars, research funds, gifts, etc., and to include salaries and expenses for operating as costs. It also would likely be assessed something for its share of indirect costs of operating and maintaining the university.

As you might imagine, there are strengths and weaknesses to each of these budgeting approaches. Some are especially bothersome for those of us in academia as they often focus too much attention on the "bottom line" to the expense of academic performance.

Budgeting can give you a lot of headaches, especially if you do not have an experienced secretary or administrative assistant. The more you learn about the budgeting and purchasing processes at your school, the better off you will be. Certainly you will be less frustrated with your job.

REFERENCES

Lindblom, C. E. (1959, Spring). The science of muddling through. *Public Administration Review,* XIX, 79–88.

Meisinger, R. J. (1994). *College and university budgeting.* Washington, DC: National Association of College and University Business Officers.

Munitz, B. (1995, Fall). Wanted: New leadership in higher education. *Planning for Higher Education,* 24.

Recruiting Students

Recruiting and retaining students will become an increasingly important activity for departments that expect to maintain current enrollment.

Developing effective student recruitment programs is becoming increasingly important as the number of potential students declines. It is likely that you will either have to become an active, effective recruiter or face increasing declines in enrollment.

Many student recruitment programs are quite inexpensive and require little time and effort to administer. One relatively common and cost-effective approach to student recruitment is to write personal letters to all students who have expressed an interest in a particular field of study. Your admissions office should receive lists of people who, when taking the ACT or SAT tests, indicate your university as an institution of choice. These tests also ask what the individual intends to study and provides his or her test scores. Thus, you can get the names and home addresses of genuine prospective students. If the chairperson wishes to be selective, letters can be sent only to those persons who score at a predetermined level.

USING ALUMNI TO HELP RECRUIT STUDENTS

If your department has alumni who have become well known, their support can be enlisted to help your recruiting efforts. Here is how they can be of special assistance:

1) Identify those students who have test scores at or above a predetermined level. For example, you might decide that all those students who have composite scores of 25 or above on the ACT and who have expressed an interest in your school and your discipline should be sent letters.

2) Draft a letter, then share it and the recruiting concept with a well-known alumnus or alumna to see if he or she is willing to let you prepare letters on his or her letterhead.
3) After letters are prepared, signed by the alumnus or alumna, and returned to your office, mail them to the persons you are trying to recruit.
4) Here is the beginning of a sample letter:

    Mr. Joseph Stillwell
    121 Mt. Savage Lane
    Ashland, KY 60511

    Dear Joseph:

    I am pleased to learn of your interest in Midwest University, and I am particularly pleased to hear that you are thinking about majoring in English. As one who studied English at Midwest University, let me tell something about its courses, programs, and faculty.
5) Invite alumni to make personal contact or write letters to prospective students who live in their geographical area.

Subscribing to a clipping service to get the names of high school students who engage in certain activities or receive special honors can provide another means of student recruitment. For example, if your department sponsors a forensics program, from newspaper clips you can get the names of students who participate in and win awards in forensics. A congratulatory letter from you, along with information about the department, might be just the thing to persuade a student to think positively about attending your university.

Incidentally, simply monitoring the education section of selected newspapers will provide much of the same information. Many publications list awards, honors, and scholastic activities, generally in Sunday editions.

The illustrations of recruiting activities in this chapter are mainly related to journalism. Most would work just as well for other academic programs, however.

THE SCHOLASTIC JOURNALISM PROGRAM

This program is intended to give a taste of college life to high school students who plan to study journalism. Selected students spend three days on campus, living in a dormitory, attending classes, and working on publications or other student activities.

The program began several years ago when announcements were sent to journalism teachers and principals at high schools throughout West Virginia and in parts of Ohio and Kentucky. The announcements explained the purposes and procedures of the program, and were accompanied by student application forms.

Two Scholastic Journalism Program students of the same sex are brought to campus at the same time. They share a dormitory room, and each is assigned a college companion who is either a junior or senior journalism major. When the students arrive, they are first given a tour of the School of Journalism. They then check into their dorm rooms, and thereafter attend classes with their assigned companion. The schedule allows time for the high school student to work on a story for the campus daily newspaper. The student receives a story assignment from the managing editor and is guided through the process of writing the story on one of computers in the newsroom. The students are assisted by either a faculty member or a newspaper staff person.

The schedule includes more than classwork. If there is an artist series activity, a sports event, or a special lecture, high school students attend with their companion. Whenever there are no special events taking place, participating students may be taken to a movie or visit the Huntington Museum of Art, or even the Huntington Mall.

While the schedule is full, it is kept flexible enough to accommodate a student's special interests. For example, if a student is interested in band, we set up an appointment with the band director, and if a student expresses concern over financial aid, we make arrangements for the student to talk with an appropriate university representative.

The program brings 20 to 30 high school students to campus each year. Because of the good response to the program, the School of Journalism has been able to be highly selective. It looks for students who have a strong commitment to studying college journalism and those who have superior academic ability.

An assessment made after the first years of the program indicates:

- By the time high school participants leave campus, they feel at home at Marshall University.
- After spending several days with a student from another high school, a college companion, and students working on the campus daily newspaper, solid friendships are established. Indeed, several of the participants

correspond regularly with their new friends, and faculty members have observed that those who were together in the program are often seen together after they become college students.

- Those who have been through the program become active in student publications even as college freshmen, which at Marshall University is unusual.

Getting all faculty members in the School of Journalism involved is especially important. Every effort should be made for participants to meet all faculty members sometime during their campus stay. Also, selecting the right kind of college companion is important.

Except for time, the program costs very little. Arrangements are made through the university office of admissions to get dorm rooms at no cost. The participants pay their own travel expenses except in special financial need circumstances. The school pays for some special activities such as artist series events, but costs are minimal.

The application form calls for the usual kinds of information. The applicants describe what high school journalism experiences they have had and tell why they want to participate in the program, and each is expected to sign a statement affirming his or her interest in studying journalism at the college level. Applicants must be nominated by either their high school journalism teacher or their high school principal.

Faculty members, as well as participants, have responded favorably to the program. The following letter, received from a student shortly after his campus visit, is typical:

> Dear Dr. Leaming:
>
> Thank you for the letter that I received this week. Also, thank you for allowing me to participate in the Scholastic Journalism Program. I truly enjoyed every minute of my stay, and I especially enjoyed working on the Parthenon staff. Betsy, my two college companions, Dave Jenkins and Eric Rinehart, and those I came into contact with during those three days made it so much fun that I really hated to leave. I believe that I have made a few friendships that I cannot possibly forget, while at the same time, I learned more in three days than I could have hoped to imagine.
>
> As for my future, I have firmly decided that Marshall University and the W. Page Pitt School of Journalism will be seeing me after I graduate from East. Its credentials and atmosphere are just what I want in my

college education. I am now counting down the days when I can begin my college at Marshall.

Again, I thoroughly enjoyed being on campus, as I am sure that Pat Sanders did also.

Sincerely,

(signed) Danny Adkins

As a side note, Danny did enroll at Marshall, as did the other participant, Pat Sanders. Both went on to earn journalism degrees.

We took pictures of the students in various activities while they were on campus, and we mailed to their hometown newspapers stories that told of their participation in the program as well as something about the program itself.

THE AMBASSADOR PROGRAM

The Marshall University School of Journalism also developed the Journalism Ambassador Program to get current students involved in student recruitment. It is designed to help spread the word of Marshall journalism to high school students.

Journalism majors apply to become "ambassadors" to the high school from which they graduated. Those selected return to their schools during university breaks, where they visit a journalism or English class to speak about Marshall journalism.

Training sessions help ambassadors plan and carry out recruitment responsibilities. Each is asked to write a letter to a former high school teacher asking to visit a class during a break from university studies. Sample letters are provided to the students. Instruction on making presentations before a high school class is provided. Moreover, information such as courses of study, enrollment, and special features is given to the ambassadors. They also are given brochures and pamphlets to pass out to the high school students.

An effort is made to select at least one ambassador from each high school represented in the applications. After each ambassador makes a visit, he or she provides the department with a visit report, providing names of interested students. Often high school students inquire about other academic disciplines at Marshall, and representatives of other departments are asked to respond to those inquiries.

In conjunction with these programs, the School of Journalism instituted two simple campaigns aimed at providing identity for Marshall journalism. Out of private funds, Marshall journalism window decals were purchased. They were given to students, faculty members, alumni, and friends. Special Marshall journalism sweaters were made up in school colors and sold or given away to more than 150 individuals.

Other activities to recruit and gain support from alumni and friends for Marshall's School of Journalism are also pursued. The school publishes a regular alumni newsletter and has established a Wall of Fame to recognize outstanding alumni. The school formed a Marshall Journalism Alumni Association whose members have helped raise funds and recruit students.

WORLD WIDE WEB SITES

In recent years, universities have begun to take advantage of the Internet to provide information to prospective students. "Increasingly . . . the (World Wide Web) pages have evolved into marketing and recruiting vehicles that are being tested for their ability to attract new students to campus" (Weinstein, 1996, p. 17).

The value of the computer in recruiting students is as yet uncertain. Nevertheless, we do know that thousands of colleges and universities now have home pages and use them to provide information to prospective students. Many have evolved into marketing and recruiting vehicles that are quite sophisticated.

It is too early to tell how much we will come to depend on the computer to lure students to our campus, but as David Merkowitz, spokesman for the American Council on Education, said, "The Internet represents another recruiting tool colleges can't afford to ignore" (Weinstein, 1996, p. 31).

Anyone who has browsed the Internet and examined university web sites knows that while some are attractive and provide useful information, many others are dreadful. If you are going to have a home page for your department, it should be good. You should see to that. Here are some guidelines:

- Seek the optimal balance between visual sensation and graphic and text information.
- Use shape, color, and contrast to give visual impact to your home page. Otherwise it will be graphically boring.

- Design a good contrast between foreground and background elements. I have seen many pages that are especially difficult to read because there is little contrast between the type and the page. Dense text documents without the contrast and visual relief offered by graphics and careful page layout and typography are more difficult to read, especially on the low-resolution screens of today's personal computers. Black text on a white background is the easiest to read.
- Keep information on your home page timely. Web sites should be updated regularly.
- Keep the pages uncluttered and clean. Many pages are too busy and lack a strong dominant focal point. The page should be a well-organized composition.
- While photographs and graphics are attractive, remember that the more of these are used the longer it takes to open a file, and many viewers may not be willing to wait the time it takes to open your page. Be judicious in the use of graphics and animation.
- Provide easy to follow links and "hot spots."
- Be interactive. Good interactivity engages the user and makes your site memorable.
- Make logical use of type styles and sizes.
- Design for the "lowest common denominator." This speaks to what type of computer the end user has, platform type, power, color capability, size of monitor, etc.

A recent study reveals what college-choice characteristics important to students bound for either private or public institutions. The top ten characteristics are listed in Table 7.1.

As you develop your recruiting strategies, make sure that you emphasize the college-choice characteristics that students value most. You also should know what the bottom ten college-choice characteristics are. Table 7.2 presents this information.

The study done by Sevier and Kappler (undated) reveals that students are especially interested in information that will validate the institution's cost. "Students and parents want to know that for the money paid, the college or university will deliver the degree—and by extension the opportunity—that it says it will." Your recruiting materials should emphasize what your graduates

TABLE 7.1 Top Ten College-Choice Characteristics

Students Bound for:			
Private Institutions		Public Institutions	
Quality of faculty	7.89	Safety	8.06
Availability of specific majors	7.86	Availability of scholarships	8.02
Safety	7.80	Cost after financial aid	7.88
Quality of academic facilities	7.73	Availability of specific majors	7.85
Availability of scholarships	7.69	Cost before financial aid	7.81
Quality of residence life	7.66	Quality of faculty	7.74
Cost after financial aid	7.55	Opportunity to hold job while attending	7.72
Friendliness	7.52	Friendliness	7.60
Teaching emphasis	7.52	Teaching emphasis	7.56
Academic reputation	7.43	Quality of academic facilities	7.54

Scale: 1 = not important, 9 = very important.
From: Sevier, R. A., & Kappler, S. D. (Undated). Reprinted with permission.

are doing, what jobs and careers they have, what graduate schools they attend, and what opportunities they are realizing.

Another important finding in the Sevier and Kappler study is that high school counselors have a lot of influence over where students attend college. Also, they found that the following recruiting strategies were the most effective with students:

1) Campus visit
2) Scholarship brochure
3) Spending a night on campus
4) Financial aid brochure
5) Letter from admissions representative
6) Catalog

While a good bit of time and effort have gone into establishing and carrying out recruitment activities, you should be equally concerned with keeping students. You should get to know students, and faculty should take their advising responsibilities seriously. Faculty members need to provide special activities for currently enrolled students. One such example is the effective Leaving

TABLE 7.2 Bottom Ten College-Choice Characteristics

Students Bound for: Private Institutions		Public Institutions	
Academic support	6.18	Beauty of the campus	6.23
Location	6.12	Campus leadership opportunities	6.19
Campus leadership opportunities	6.14	Opportunity to study abroad	6.13
Guidebook recommendation	5.47	Opportunity for three-year BA	5.86
Proximity to large city	5.45	Location	5.84
Magazine recommendation	5.29	College guide recommendation	5.38
Ethnic diversity of students	5.20	Proximity to large city	5.21
Opportunity for three-year BA	5.00	Someone I know attends	5.08
Someone I know attends	4.53	Magazine recommendation	4.89
Religious reputation	4.06	Religious reputation	3.55

Scale: 1 = not important, 9 = very important.
From: Sevier, R. A., & Kappler, S. D. (Undated). Reprinted with permission.

the Nest program. It is a series of seminars designed to assist students in finding and succeeding in jobs upon graduation.

The seminars are scheduled over a five-day period. The first provides instruction on putting together a résumé. The second deals with finding job openings. At the third seminar, interviewing for a job is discussed. The fourth features tips on coping in the workplace. The last seminar is a wrap-up session presented by the director of Marshall's Career Planning and Placement Office, who provides his own tips on getting and keeping jobs and explains the services of his office.

DEVELOPING RETENTION PROGRAMS

Working to keep students in school is just as important as recruiting them. If we lose a high percentage of those we recruit, then our recruiting efforts have proved to be costly.

Before developing a retention program, it's a good idea to learn what research shows us about why students drop out of college. Table 7.3 shows what the typical male and female college dropout profiles look like (Edwards, Cangemi, & Kowalski, 1990).

TABLE 7.3 Male and Female Dropout Profiles

Male College Dropout Profile

- Not committed to the institution
- Middle or low GPA
- Not satisfied with being a student
- Does not consider education to be contributing to personal development
- Considers life repetitive
- Is not aware of institutional, social, and academic rules
- May live with parents

Female College Dropout Profile

- Not committed to the institution
- Poor performance in high school
- No membership in campus organizations
- Little faith in employment value of degree
- Perceives an opportunity to transfer
- Does not believe that education leads to self-improvement
- No commitment to earning a bachelor's degree
- Not satisfied with instruction
- Does not participate in decision-making
- Does not feel she was being treated fairly
- Does not meet with staff and faculty members informally

From: Edwards, M., Cangemi, J. P., & Kowalski, C. (1990, Fall). Reprinted with permission.

Noel (1995) reported the top ten reasons students stay in college, as shown in Table 7.4.

Universities that truly care for students and are willing to spend money to try to keep them can certainly develop effective retention programs. By looking at what research tells us about why students drop out and why they stay in school, it would not be difficult to develop the appropriate kinds of support systems that would make a difference in the lives of students. You have a special responsibility to work with your faculty to see that they understand the importance of caring for students and showing students that they care. Also, they need to understand how important quality teaching is to keeping students in school. Obviously, you also need to emphasize quality advising.

TABLE 7.4 Why Students Stay in College

- Caring faculty/staff
- High-quality teaching
- Adequate financial aid
- Student involvement in campus
- High-quality advising
- Excellent counseling services
- Excellent career planning
- Concern about student/institutional "fit"
- Admissions geared to graduation
- Early alert system

From: Noel, L. (1995, August). Reprinted with permission.

Most other areas that influence students to stay in school are outside of your area of control, but you can use your influence to see that the university knows what needs to be done to see students through to graduation.

Recruiting and retaining students, as noted in the beginning of this chapter, will become an increasingly important activity for departments that expect to maintain current enrollment. While the direct purpose and benefit are evident, recruitment and retention activities have the additional potential of cementing relationships among students, alumni, and faculty. They also cause faculty members to assess their department's program and activities and to think about its overall mission and how it is being fulfilled.

REFERENCES

Edwards, M., Cangemi, J. P., & and Kowalski, C. (1990, Fall). The college dropout and institutional responsibility. *Education,* 111 (1), 107–115.

Noel, L. (1995, August). Don't cut back retention with cutback management. *Recruitment & Retention in Higher Education,* 9 (8), 5.

Sevier, R. A., & Kappler, S. D. (Undated). What students say. White paper no. 3. Cedar Rapids, IA: Stamats Communications.

Weinstein, B. (1996, November 3). Newest recruiting tool is on-line. *The New York Times Education Life,* 17.

8

Recruiting and Hiring Faculty Members

One thing that can change your department more than anything else is the hiring of excellent faculty.

Faculty recruitment is time-consuming, costly, and at times frustrating. When it ends with the hiring of a highly qualified individual, you are an exultant chairperson. However, if a mistake in hiring occurs—as is bound to happen occasionally—you face months, or even years, of tribulation. To achieve positive results, you must give undivided attention to hiring faculty members; you must not overlook even the smallest detail of the process.

BE PROACTIVE IN RECRUITING FACULTY

Recruiting and hiring excellent faculty can change the culture of your department more than almost anything else you do as chairperson. If, for example, you are unsatisfied with the quality or quantity of research by your current faculty, you should try to hire faculty members who have strong research records. Here are some things you can do to develop a proactive faculty recruitment program:

- Decide before you advertise exactly what kind of person you are hoping to hire. What primary and secondary competencies are you seeking?
- Do more than advertise to reach potential candidates. You should know who is out there and contributing to your field so that you can seek them out whenever you have an opening. More than likely your faculty will be acquainted with potential candidates. You and your faculty should get on the telephone and urge outstanding individuals to apply at your school. If you are not acquainted with potential candidates, call around to some of the leaders in the field to get names of people to contact.

- Make your advertisement say something. Describe in your advertisement what makes your university and your department unique. Sell whatever you have to sell. What attracted you to the university? It may be that the same thing would attract others.

You will need to take the lead in recruiting and hiring new faculty members. At most universities, individual colleges have established procedures that must be carefully followed. The procedure assures the department chairperson that he or she has met all legal requirements and completed the required paperwork. Here is an example of the steps (obviously modified to meet specific campus requirements) that the College of Science uses.

DEPARTMENT CHECKLIST FOR RECRUITING FACULTY

1) Chairperson sends a letter to the dean requesting approval to recruit.
   - Letter must include a justification.
   - The provost will notify the dean when request is approved/disapproved.
   - The dean will notify the chairperson.
2) Chairperson will complete and submit to the dean the recruitment authorization form.
   - Notice of vacancy (ad) must be attached.
   - College liaison will approve/disapprove.
   - Recruitment authorization form will be approved/disapproved by the provost and forwarded to the personnel office.
   - Dean will receive a copy of the approved recruitment authorization form and send a copy to the chairperson.
   - Chairperson or personnel will place advertisement(s). The chairperson should complete and submit the appropriate requisition.
3) Chairperson will submit the completed recruitment sources form to the dean.
   - College liaison will approve/disapprove.
4) Chairperson will appoint search committee.
   - The search committee will include at least one female and representation from a minority group.

- The college liaison and the affirmative action officer should be invited to the first committee meeting.
- The chairperson of search committee will be elected/selected.
- The department chairperson will submit in writing to the dean the names of the search committee members and the name of the chairperson.
- The college liaison will approve/disapprove.

5) Chairperson of search committee handle the following activities.
   - Maintain up-to-date applicant flow data sheet.
   - Mail affirmative action postcards to applicants.
   - Follow all steps as stipulated in guidelines.
6) When screening is completed, the chairperson of the search committee and the department chairperson will submit an applicant flow data sheet to the dean with the names of the best qualified candidates.
   - The college liaison will approve/disapprove.
   - The affirmative action officer will approve/disapprove and return the form to the dean.
   - The dean, in consultation with the chairperson, will determine candidates to be interviewed.
7) When final selection is made, the department chairperson will submit the following items: the proposed faculty appointment form, the affirmative action recruitment checklist, and a certification statement.
   - The chairperson will notify unsuccessful applicants in writing.
   - The college liaison will approve/disapprove.
   - The dean will forward documents to the provost and affirmative action officer for approval/disapproval.
   - The dean will notify the chairperson when approved.
8) Department chairperson will determine salary recommendation.
   - Consult with the office of institutional research to determine salary.
   - Send the dean a memorandum detailing salary agreement and rank with a request that an offer letter be prepared.
9) Dean will prepare offer letter for appropriate signatures.

Copies of all curriculum vitae and related documents submitted by those applying for faculty positions should be kept for a period of three years. These records should be regarded as confidential.

While this procedure must be followed to assure conformance with university policy, it clearly cannot assure that quality faculty members will be hired. You must assume that responsibility. It is a fact that many universities are handicapped in their recruiting efforts because of salaries, teaching loads, and location. Even so, every effort to recruit quality faculty members must be made. You should conduct careful, extensive background checks. It is important to contact individuals who can comment on and evaluate personal and professional qualifications of those who are being seriously considered. Contacting only those who are listed as references is insufficient. (Applicants are not likely to list as references those who have anything negative to say.) When interviewing a prospective faculty member, you also must be candid about what is expected of the applicant if he or she accepts an offer to join the faculty. Such candor will enable the candidate to determine whether he or she will be a good fit with the department and will serve well the department chairperson, the department, and the candidate.

Once you receive permission to recruit, you should begin by reviewing the college recruitment procedures (see Chapter 3). Early on, you will need to appoint a search committee.

THE SEARCH COMMITTEE

Search committees should reflect the race and gender makeup of the university. Beyond that, you should use your judgment regarding committee composition and size. Some universities require that women and minority faculty be represented on each search committee, which can become a vexing problem if your university has so few of either that the same ones are called on over and over again to serve on search committees. Those individuals can quickly come to resent being asked to serve.

The nature of the position being filled undoubtedly will have a bearing on faculty members who are chosen to serve. If, for example, an anthropologist is being sought by the department of sociology and anthropology, it makes sense for you to name to the search committee faculty members whose specialty is anthropology.

Once the search committee is formed, its members should meet to discuss search procedures. At this first meeting, members should elect a chairperson, unless you have chosen to name a faculty member to serve in that capacity. The affirmative action—or equity, as it is sometimes called—office should be consulted to discuss affirmative action requirements and procedures, and to sign off on certain forms at some universities. The affirmative action officer can also offer suggestions for reaching qualified minority and women candidates.

The chairperson of the search committee is responsible for maintaining some kind of applicant flow data sheet, for mailing affirmative action cards to all applicants, and for following steps stipulated by college guidelines (see Chapter 3).

SCREENING APPLICANTS

When applications begin coming in, the department secretary should keep them together in a secure, confidential file. The applications should be available for search committee members to review as their time permits.

Shortly after the closing date, the search committee chairperson or you should examine each application to see if the candidate meets minimum requirements as advertised for the position. Those who meet minimum requirements for the position as announced should remain in the pool to be evaluated by all members of the search committee. Applicants who are going to be considered should be invited to submit letters of reference, usually three to five, depending on what the search committee considers adequate.

Some departments request letters of reference from all persons who apply. I oppose this procedure for several reasons. Why would the search committee members want to be burdened with paperwork on individuals who do not meet minimum requirements for the position or who, for one reason or another, will not be considered seriously? Furthermore, the time of those who write the letters is wasted. It seems abundantly more appropriate to ask for reference letters only from applicants who the committee decides are worthy of further consideration.

Reference letters should be read carefully so that they can be accurately interpreted. Kenneth E. Eble (1978, p. 106) says, "Letters of recommendation abound in simple and complex evasions of truth." He points out that what is written is not necessarily what the writer meant to say. For example, he says that a "mature scholar" likely means "one who entered graduate school late, has been there a long time, and will likely go into retirement before evincing any youthful spark or brilliance. Some signs of immaturity probably means that the person has hardly developed since puberty" (Eble, 1978, p. 106). The point of all of this is that we should be careful when evaluating candidates on letters alone, and we should scrutinize letters for exactness of evidence.

Search committee members should be assigned to make reference calls. By dividing this task, the calls can be completed within a few days without unduly burdening one or two members.

Each caller should be instructed to ask essentially the same questions. Here are some suggestions:

Telephone Reference Check Questions

1) How long have you known the applicant? In what capacity?
2) How would you rate his or her teaching ability?
3) How does the applicant get along with students? With faculty colleagues?
4) How willing is the applicant to contribute to the department's work outside the classroom?
5) Is the applicant responsible?
6) Would you judge the applicant to be an ethical person?
7) Why do you think the applicant might be interested in joining our university?
8) What are the applicant's major strengths? Weaknesses?
9) How would you evaluate the applicant's potential for growth?
10) Does he or she have any problems we should know about?
11) Is there anything I have not asked that you could add to give me a clearer picture of what the applicant is like?
12) If you were in my position, would you recommend that this candidate be hired? If not, why?

The person making the telephone check should type notes that provide answers to these questions. The notes should indicate the person giving the information and the date and time of the call. These notes should then be turned over to the search committee chairperson.

Should calls be made to persons other than those whose names are provided by the applicant? While some might disagree, I believe such calls must be made if valid evaluations are to be obtained. Few people applying for a job will list as references any acquaintances who are likely to have anything negative to say. Most often those listed as references will be friends, and even the most probing reference check is not likely to turn up anything but a positive assessment. One must, of course, honor the request that an applicant's employer not be contacted unless the applicant gives permission. Still, there are other ways to get names of individuals who can provide an honest assessment of an applicant's personal and professional qualifications.

After all reference checks are completed and letters of reference received, a meeting should be called to narrow the list to those whom the committee wishes to consider further, perhaps five to ten names. Teleconferencing with the top candidates then should take place to narrow the list of those you wish to bring to campus. I have seen many instances when teleconferencing was not done, and candidates who simply were not suitable were brought to campus, a situation that could have been avoided by a teleconference with the candidate and members of the search committee. After the teleconferences have been completed, the search committee is in a good position to recommend candidates for campus interviews.

After the search committee reaches agreement on the most qualified candidates, the search committee chairperson reports that information to you, the department chair. You then present the applicant flow data sheet, along with the names of the most qualified candidates, to your dean. Affirmative action officers must usually give their approval, after which the dean, in consultation with you, determines which candidates actually will be invited to campus for interviews.

The committee chairperson next needs to call candidates to set up times for their visit. One important point to remember is that at most universities the candidates pay their travel expenses and are then reimbursed by the university. The committee chairperson will, of course, need to know each candidate's travel schedule so that arrangements can be made to meet each candidate at the airport or other point of arrival.

THE CAMPUS VISIT

Candidates usually spend two days on campus. Their schedules include interviews with individual faculty members, the search committee, student groups, the department chairperson, the college dean, the dean of the graduate school, and the vice president for academic affairs.

Arrangements for pickup and lodging should be completed prior to the visit, and the schedule for the candidate should be prepared well in advance and sent to the candidate. You might also prepare a kit of attractive materials to send, that could include, for example, documents to show what faculty development opportunities exist on your campus, or a strategic planning document, or materials about the community that you can get from the local chamber of commerce. Applicants can call the department chairperson to clear up any questions they may have. Figure 8.1 is a sample of the schedule for a candidate to be interviewed.

What is not shown in the schedule, though typically included at many universities in a campus visit, is the allocation of time for the candidate to teach a class. Asking the candidate to teach is a good way to assess his or her classroom capabilities. It can demonstrate how a prospective faculty member

FIGURE 8.1 Interview Schedule for John M. Doe

Wednesday, May 8	
9:50 PM	Arrive Locker Airport on Delta 3016. Met by department chairperson.
Thursday, May 9	
8:00 AM	Breakfast, Holiday Inn.
9:00 AM	Tour of department facilities.
9:30 AM	Meet with Dr. Jane Smith, Dean, College of Liberal Arts, Smith Hall 165.
10:00 AM	Meet with Dr. Roscoe Handy, Professor, and Dr. Ruby Twoshoes, Assistant Professor, Smith Hall 332.
10:30 AM	Meet with Dr. Ron Davis, Professor and Dr. Jim Arnold, Professor, Smith Hall 332.
11:00 AM	Meet with Dr. Edward Knight, Associate Professor, Smith Hall 319.
11:30 AM	Tour of campus. Free time.
12:00 PM	Lunch with search committee,* Oliver's Restaurant.
2:30 PM	Meet with Dr. Robert Jones, Associate Professor, and Dr. Susan Quell, Assistant Professor, Smith Hall 332.
3:00 PM	Meet with Dr. Mary Harvin, chairperson, and take tour of city.
4:30 PM	Taken to Locker Airport by Mrs. Sally Kay, Administrative Aide.
6:55 PM	Depart on Delta 849.

Dr. Doe is interviewing for the position now held by Dr. Ron Galloway. Dr. Doe's résumé is attached.

* Search committee members need to inform Dr. Harvin of availability for lunch. Breakfast is an option if lunch isn't possible.

responds to students, how he or she prepares for a class, and how well the candidate approaches the subject matter. It provides still another dimension which can be useful in evaluations.

INTERVIEWING CANDIDATES: QUESTIONS TO AVOID

You and others on campus will ask each faculty candidate certain questions during his or her campus visit. To avoid legal problems, it is important that you know that certain questions should not be asked.

Questions about race or ethnic heritage. What is your race? What is your lineage, ancestry, national origin, or descent? What language do you commonly speak? What was your maiden name? What is your birthplace or citizenship?

Questions about religion. What is your religion? Does your religion prevent you from working weekends or holidays?

Questions about personal data. How old are you? What is your birthdate? Are you married, divorced, or single? Do you have children? Are you pregnant? With whom do you reside?

Medical questions. What is your height and weight? Are you disabled? How often will you require time off because of your disability? Have you ever filed a workers' compensation claim? Have you ever been treated for any conditions or diseases or been hospitalized? Do you currently take any prescription drugs? Have you ever been treated for drug or alcohol addiction?

Other miscellaneous questions. Do you still owe on the loans taken out during school? Do you own your own home or rent? Who should we contact in case of emergency? Have you ever been arrested? What are the dates of your military service?

There is almost no aspect of faculty recruitment that is not restricted by federal and state laws and regulations. Statutes regulating employer conduct include Title VII of the Civil Rights Act of 1964, as amended (Title VII), the post–Civil War Civil Rights Act, the Age Discrimination in Employment Act (ADEA), the Immigration Reform and Control Act of 1986 (IRCA), and relevant state statutes that prohibit employment discrimination. Moreover, the recently enacted Americans with Disabilities Act (ADA) presents employers with additional pre-hire considerations and occasionally conflicts with other employer policies.

Also, applicant screening measures may be challenged under the theory that certain measures violate the individual's constitutional or common law right to privacy or under contractual theories that rely on employee handbooks or collective bargaining agreements.

INTERVIEWING THE CANDIDATE: EVALUATIONS

Each faculty member, administrator, and student involved in the interview process should provide a written evaluation of each candidate. Evaluation sheets should be turned in to the search committee chairperson after the candidate's visit is concluded. Figure 8.2 shows a sample evaluation sheet.

THE SUCCESSFUL CANDIDATE: DETERMINING RANK AND SALARY

The search committee should meet to evaluate all candidates after campus visits have been completed. Members of the committee then should recommend to you which candidate they feel should be made an offer. In most departments, a faculty meeting follows so that faculty members can discuss each candidate and the recommendation of the search committee. They also need to discuss the matter of rank and salary that they want the department chairperson to recommend to the dean of the college.

You should review policy guidelines for determining rank for incoming members of the faculty. Most universities have a written policy that addresses this matter. For example, policy may stipulate that a terminal degree is required for appointment to certain ranks. It also may require that a person must have had a number of years of full-time teaching to be eligible for appointment to a given professorial rank. I have encountered faculty members who tell me that their university does not have such policy, that instead the vice president for academic affairs or dean determines rank and salary based upon current market conditions.

You will need to know all faculty salaries so that you do not create inequities within your department, providing this is a concern of the department and/or university. Generally, new faculty members should not be employed at salaries higher than those being paid to current members of the

FIGURE 8.2 Interviewer's Worksheet

Applicant's name (last-first-middle):

____

Date: ______________________

Personal qualities. Observe applicant; write several adjectives or descriptive phrases:

Evaluation:	Outstanding	Excellent	Good	Adequate	Unsatisfactory
Appearance and poise:	Outstanding	Excellent	Good	Adequate	Unsatisfactory
Oral communication/ expression of ideas:	Outstanding	Excellent	Good	Adequate	Unsatisfactory
Educational background:	Outstanding	Excellent	Good	Adequate	Unsatisfactory
Experience in administrative/ academic area:	Outstanding	Excellent	Good	Adequate	Unsatisfactory
Leadership potential:	Outstanding	Excellent	Good	Adequate	Unsatisfactory

Willingness to hire applicant. Use the following scores to rate applicant:

Score:

1–2	Prefer not to hire this person
3–4	Satisfactory
5–6	Be pleased to hire this person
7–8	Prefer this person to most
9–10	Particularly like to hire this person

Comments: A summary statement is required. Ratings of OUTSTANDING or UNSATISFACTORY or 0 or 10 should be amplified in this space.

Potential worth to Northern State University:	Outstanding	Excellent	Good	Adequate	Unsatisfactory

Remarks: (Supplement or qualify motivation and potential ratings as appropriate)

Recommendation:

___I recommend further consideration

___I do NOT recommend further consideration

Evaluator's Signature: ______________________________________

staff whose credentials are like those of the person being hired. Some universities require faculty members who are negatively affected to sign off giving their consent. This, as we might expect, can be a contentious issue. Matters of this sort ought to be discussed long before you have to deal with it while trying to hire a faculty member. At such times, the issue is more likely to become emotionally charged.

Once you have established a salary and rank to recommend, you will either inform the dean or make an offer, depending on policy at your university. Often you will need to send a letter to your dean along with a proposed faculty appointment form, an affirmative action recruitment checklist, and a certification statement or something similar.

After salary approval by the affirmative action officer and/or the vice president for academic affairs, notify the candidate that an offer is forthcoming. Either the dean or you then prepares an offer letter that often is signed by the vice president for academic affairs and the university president. It includes conditions of employment: rank, salary, and indication of whether the appointment is probationary or temporary.

Make a special appeal to your candidate. For example, you might have each faculty member write to tell the person how much he or she would like to have him or her as a colleague. Keep in touch by letter and telephone to see if the person you want to hire has any questions or concerns that you can address. The candidate usually must accept within a designated number of days. When the offer is accepted, the search is completed.

The final task then remaining for the search committee chairperson is to write letters to all unsuccessful candidates. You must see that all search records are kept for a period of three years to meet guidelines of affirmative action and the Equal Employment Opportunities Commission.

As noted earlier, the process of filling a faculty position is time-consuming and requires meticulous record keeping. It is an important task. All involved can take pride in their effort when the new faculty member turns out to be a prized addition to the department.

REFERENCES

Eble, K. E. (1978). *The art of administration: A guide for academic administrators.* San Francisco, CA: Jossey-Bass.

Perlman, B., & McCann, L. I. (1996). *Recruiting good college faculty: Practical advice for a successful search.* Bolton, MA: Anker.

9

Dealing with Sexual Harassment

It has been my experience that many students who voice complaints are reluctant to file formal charges, yet they want someone in authority to be aware of the situation.

As a chairperson, you must fully understand your university's policy on sexual harassment, as you have the duty to see that it is enforced. Moreover, it is your responsibility to see that all faculty and staff members in your department are familiar with the policy. They need to know that you take the matter seriously and that you will not tolerate sexual discrimination or harassment in any form. Your responsibility is to set the appropriate tone of the department; i.e., to establish an atmosphere of professionalism where men and women interact with trust and respect. Turning a blind eye to offensive behavior constitutes bad judgment, if not malfeasance.

A DEFINITION

Sexual harassment is a form of sex discrimination prohibited by Title VII of the Civil Rights Act of 1964 and by Title IX of the Education Amendments of 1972. Moreover, it is prohibited in both employment and public accommodation contexts by laws in most, if not all, states. It is defined as unwelcomed behavior of a sexual nature or with sexual overtones. Sexual harassment takes two legal forms:

1) ***Quid pro quo.*** This form of sexual harassment is a "this for that" demand for sexual favors in exchange for some job benefit.
2) ***Hostile environment.*** A hostile environment refers to conditions or behaviors that interfere with the individual's job performance or that create an intimidating or offensive work environment. Employers are liable for this form of sexual harassment when they know, or should know, about the harassment and fail to take prompt and reasonable remedial action.

Within these two general categories, many different behaviors or conditions can constitute sexual harassment.

BEHAVIOR THAT MAY CONSTITUTE SEXUAL HARASSMENT

A wide range of conduct can be considered sexual harassment, and men as well as women can be victims. Title VII forbids any harassment in which one, some, or all the employees of one sex suffer significantly unfavorable treatment on the job because of their gender. Federal courts have identified some of the following examples of sexual harassment:

Unwelcome sexual advances. A coworker repeatedly asked a female employee for dates and wrote love letters to her after she rejected his overtures. An employee who is repeatedly propositioned by a supervisor or coworker who is trying to establish an intimate relationship can sue the employer for sexual harassment. Some specific examples of unwelcome advances may be:

- any form of subtle pressure for sexual activity
- physical actions such as unnecessary physical brushes or touches, obscene or suggestive gestures, leering or ogling, physical aggression such as pinching or patting
- verbal comments such as disparaging sexual remarks, humor and jokes about sex or male/female relationships, sexual innuendoes, or remarks about a person's clothing, body, or sexual activities

Coercion. A female employee was repeatedly asked by her boss to "do something nice," with the understanding that a favor would be bestowed or a reprisal made. In another case, two male employees were forced to engage in sexual activity with the boss's female secretary with the threat that they would be fired if they refused.

Favoritism. When employees who submit to sexual favors are rewarded while others who refuse are denied promotions or benefits, the employer may be liable for hostile environment sexual harassment.

Indirect harassment. An employee who witnesses sexual harassment can sue the employer. For example, a nurse complained that a doctor grabbed and fondled other nurses in her presence, causing an offensive sexually hostile environment.

Offensive physical environment. Graffiti and displays of nude or pornographic pictures can be sexual harassment for which the employer is liable.

The National Advisory Council on Women's Educational Programs provides this definition of classroom harassment: "... harassment in which the faculty member covertly or overtly uses the power inherent in the status of a professor to threaten, coerce, or intimidate a student to accept sexual advances or risk reprisal in terms of a grade, a recommendation, or even a job."

Even with the definition and examples of sexual harassment provided, many disagreements still exist as to what constitutes sexual harassment. As Black and Gilson (1988, p. 70) point out:

> The law, whether legislative or judge-made, cannot fully define sexual harassment. It can provide a framework for examining claims, but it cannot produce a comprehensive list of do's and don'ts. Evaluation of any given campus circumstance involving claims of harassment depends partly on established standards, partly on a 'reasonable person' test. That is, would a reasonable person find the alleged behavior offensive? Common sense, along with the legal framework, determines the standards from which campuses should draw their policies and actions.

Black and Gilson (1988) cite a charge of sexual harassment that occurred at Vanderbilt University where an exchange of remarks through a computer system led to sexual harassment allegations. A female student filed a complaint with the school and the U.S. Department of Education, saying she was "electronically gang-raped" by offensive remarks directed at her during a classroom computer conversation.

She said the instructor was advised in class about the remarks, but allowed them to continue. According to the complaint, the instructor subsequently printed the remarks and laughed about them during another class session.

During the demonstration, students at individual keyboards could simultaneously and anonymously send messages to others. The remarks directed at the complaining student dealt with sexual matters and became more explicit until she finally left the room in disgust.

Whether this rises to the level of sexual harassment either in the eyes of Vanderbilt officials or the courts has yet to be determined. At the very least, however, the instructor was guilty of insensitivity and poor judgment in encouraging behavior that made a student uncomfortable. Also, it is an example of the kind of problem we are likely to see more frequently in higher education in years to come.

There are many unanswered questions: When does an innocent flirtation become sexual harassment? How serious is one incident? How do you determine culpability? Once you do, what do you do about it? Because the personal and professional lives of individuals are involved, great care and thought must be given to handling the situation.

Sexual harassment often is in the eye of the beholder. Friendliness and thoughtless or innocent remarks can be misread. The Equal Employment Opportunities Commission (EEOC) published guidelines in 1988 stating that "a single incident or isolated incidents of offensive sexual conduct or remarks generally do not create an abusive environment unless the conduct is quite severe." The commission quotes the U.S. Supreme Court: "The mere utterance of an ethnic or social [or sexual] epithet that engenders offensive feelings in an employee would not affect the conditions of employment to a sufficiently significant degree to violate Title VII."

Most universities have a sexual harassment policy and procedures for dealing with complaints. You are obligated to deal with any such complaints that come to your attention; failure to do so can result in disciplinary action against you.

University policies generally state something to the effect that at the discretion of the president, corrective and/or disciplinary actions, ranging from a warning up to and including termination, will be taken against any academic or administrative supervisor who failed to take corrective action when there is probable cause to believe that he or she knew, or should have known, that one of the persons protected by this policy was or had been subjected to sexual harassment by one of his or her guests, employees, or contractors.

On most campuses, the office of affirmative action handles sexual harassment complaints. Employees who feel they have been sexually harassed should contact their immediate supervisor; students should contact their academic dean for counseling and other appropriate action. If the complainant feels this is not appropriate, she or he should contact a member of the equal opportunity grievance panel or the office of affirmative action. The latter office can provide the names and telephone numbers of members of the equal opportunity grievance panel.

HANDLING SEXUAL HARASSMENT COMPLAINTS

It has been my experience that many students who voice complaints are reluctant to file formal charges, yet they want someone in authority to be aware of the situation. Some may complain to a faculty member they trust, or they might bring their complaint to you, expecting you to see that the offensive behavior stops. In counseling a student or faculty member who complains to you, you should follow these guidelines:

1) Listen carefully and sympathetically without being judgmental.
2) Advise the complainant never to be alone with the person he or she claims is doing the harassing.
3) Tell the complainant that she or he should let the person doing the harassing know that the behavior is not appreciated and that it must stop. The complainant should say, for example, "Stop it. I don't like what you are doing. It makes me very uncomfortable." "I have no wish to see you socially." "Please stop making sexual remarks or jokes around me." These and similar statements clearly indicate that the behavior is unwelcome. Pushing away an offensive person, showing annoyance through facial expressions or other such nonverbal behaviors also show that the advances are unwelcome. However, in unequal power situations, nonverbal behavior of this kind may be inadequate. A more direct verbal response might be called for.
4) Advise the complainant to keep a journal of time, place, date, and description of each incident. List the names of any witnesses.
5) Suggest that the complainant write a private letter to the person doing the harassing. The letter should state the facts, describe how the complainant feels about the harasser's action, and indicate the complainant's expectations. A copy of this letter should be kept by the complainant.
6) Suggest that the complaining person keep a small, hidden tape recorder on his or her person that can be activated if the harasser's actions continue, provided surreptitious recording is not prohibited by law in your state. If you have any questions regarding this, you should contact your campus legal affairs office.

7) Suggest that the complainant talk to fellow students or coworkers to find out if others have been harassed by the same person, and try to determine if they will support the complainant if he or she decides to take action.

You should keep a record of the meeting and advise the affirmative action officer of the situation. Also, you should talk to the person accused of sexual harassment to advise him or her that a complaint has been filed, emphasizing the seriousness of the matter. Even if no formal complaint is made, you must advise him or her to avoid any behavior that could be construed in any way as sexual harassment. If the accused person is a faculty member, you need to remind him or her to review a copy of the university's sexual harassment policy statement, which is something you should distribute to all faculty and staff at the beginning of each academic year. Finally, you should keep notes of this meeting as well, specifying when it was held and exactly what was said. This course of action is grounded in the legal protections you need in your role as chairperson. To prevent being held liable for the acts of other people, you need to investigate claims of sexual harassment thoroughly. Section 1604.11c of the EEOC Guidelines on Sexual Harassment say:

> An employer . . . is responsible for its acts and those of its agents and supervisory employees with respect to sexual harassment regardless of whether the specific acts complained of were authorized or even forbidden by the employer and regardless of whether the employer knew or should have known of their occurrence.

If the complainant chooses not to file formal charges, and if the matter described seems of relatively minor consequence, all that is needed to prevent employer liability for sexual harassment is for you to take prompt action to end the harassment.

PREVENTING SEXUAL HARASSMENT

The best way to deal with sexual harassment is to do everything possible to prevent it. As indicated earlier, you should establish a tone for the department that does not give comfort to misconduct of any kind. If you shrug off complaints, a suggestion that you will turn a blind eye to this type of behavior has been clearly given. On the other hand, if you bring up the matter in faculty meetings, handle complaints seriously and expeditiously, and make it clear that sexual harassment will not be tolerated, you will have taken the first step toward preventing this type of behavior.

While men and women alike can be victims of sexual harassment, generally the matter involves a man harassing a woman. Table 9.1 offers some tips for faculty on avoiding situations where harassment complaints could arise.

You can help educate your faculty and staff members if you are knowledgeable about the many issues related to sexual harassment. A book edited by M. Paludi (1990) of Hunter College, *Ivory Power: Sexual Harassment on Campus*, offers worthwhile insights about defining and measuring harassment, its impact on victims, and methods of handling complaints. In addition, there is an extensive appendix that lists involved organizations, audio/visual resources, sample workshop materials, staff training guides, and other materials.

A videotape created by Augsburg College's Center for Faculty Development can be used in workshops for either faculty or students. The videotape, *Is This Harassment?*, consists of five vignettes:

- A professor discusses a rape image in a John Donne poem
- A student objects to her advisor about a required course taught by a professor who makes sexist jokes and calls only on men in class
- A theater director is rehearsing *Romeo and Juliet,* when she becomes aware that the male lead enjoys his physical contact with the female lead
- A professor touches a student several times during an office visit
- A faculty member who is dating a student now has that student in class

After each vignette, the facilitator can stop the tape and lead a discussion based on questions that appear on screen. [Those interested in purchasing the videotape should contact the Center for Faculty Development, Augsburg

TABLE 9.1 Tips to Help Faculty Members Avoid Sexual Harassment Complaints

Faculty Should

1) Not meet behind closed doors with students or colleagues
2) Avoid making sexual remarks of any kind
3) Keep their hands off students and colleagues
4) Make certain that all encounters with colleagues and students are professional in every aspect
5) Avoid double-entendres
6) Go out of their way to avoid any behavior that might be misconstrued as attention of a sexual nature

College, 2211 Riverside Avenue, Campus Box 97, Minneapolis, MN 55454; telephone (612) 330-1330.]

TABLE 9.2 Ways to Discourage Sexual Harassment

1) If possible, keep the door open when you visit your professor or advisor. When the door of a small office is closed the atmosphere sometimes becomes "cozy" rather than professional. If you feel uncomfortable when the door is closed, you can always say, for example, "Excuse me, but I'd prefer to have the door open" without going into any long explanations.
2) Dress neutrally in class and when visiting professors or advisors. Clothing does not cause sexual harassment. However, some men may perceive low-cut tops or skimpy shorts as a sexual invitation even though that is not what it means to the woman wearing such clothes. It might also encourage some men to think of women physically instead of intellectually.
3) Avoid any kind of flirtatious behavior with professors. Remember, too, that it is always possible for some men to misinterpret friendly behavior as an indication of sexual interest. Professors are no exception. You are generally better off to keep conversations businesslike, rather than personal, especially when you are first getting to know your professor.
4) Beware of threats of retaliatory law suits. There have been instances in which women who brought formal accusations of sexual harassment against someone were subsequently threatened with a libel suit by the harasser. (In all instances the suits were later dropped.) Our goal always is to protect those who might be harassed. There are additional reasons to be especially attentive to this problem, however; not the least of these is the legal costs that can grow out of charges of sexual harassment. Moreover, problems of sexual harassment are time-consuming, and they tend to become divisive. The matter of evidence—since sexual harassment often involves surreptitious actions—is troubling and complex. Innocent parties can be hurt, and the pain does not go away quickly.

Taking an active position against sexual harassment will do much to insure a positive, professional climate in your department. Only in such a climate can all individuals give all their efforts to what matters most—education.

From: Hughes, J. O., & Sandler, B. (1986). Reprinted with permission.

A publication, *In Case of Sexual Harassment: A Guide For Women Students* (Hughes & Sandler, 1986), recommends ways to discourage sexual harassment. These are outlined in Table 9.2.

BEING SENSITIVE TO WOMEN IN THE CLASSROOM

It seems appropriate to include in this chapter a reference to the need for sensitivity toward women in the classroom. While it does not deal directly with sexual harassment, it nonetheless speaks to the broader issue of helping all students—men and women alike—get the best education possible by creating the right kind of environment for learning.

To address this matter, we must first acknowledge that in the past too many teachers have been insensitive to female students. This issue was addressed by Bernice Sandler, Director of the Project on the Status and Education of Women, Association of American Colleges. In a presentation to Marshall University academic deans she noted, for example, how some teachers often unknowingly mistreat women by tending to ask women "who" or "what" questions that require little in-depth knowledge. On the other hand, she said, they would be more likely to ask male students "how" or "why" questions that provide an opportunity to explore more in-depth knowledge.

Sandler reminded us that we often interrupt women students and help them with their responses, while our behavior is different with male students. We typically give male students the opportunity to discuss questions without interruptions even when their responses may be off the mark. Moreover, she added that we often fail to call on female students even when they wish to make a contribution, or that we often give nonverbal signals of inattention or disapproval, such as furrowing the brow or even scowling.

Sandler's observations are worthy of consideration. Along with the more complex matters of sexual harassment, legal and otherwise, they should be topics for discussions at faculty meetings. By being sensitive to these matters, we have a better chance of creating a positive learning environment in our departments.

Sexual harassment must be a topic of genuine concern for every chairperson and educator. Ignoring it in hope that it will go away is irresponsible. If we believe that sexual harassment won't or can't happen, we are hiding from reality. Studies show that 20% to 30% of all female college students experience some form of sexual harassment. Two percent of all female students experience direct threats or bribes for sexual favors. While 2% does not sound like a great number, it in fact translates to hundreds of students at even mid-size universities. In addition to the personal anguish it causes, sexual harassment has an adverse effect on the learning and working climate. That alone is reason enough to require us to deal with the problem.

REFERENCES

Black, D. R., & Gilson, M. (1988). *Perspectives and principles: A college administrator's guide to staying out of court.* Madison, WI: Magna.

Hughes, J. O., & Sandler, B. (1986, April). *In case of sexual harassment: A guide for women students.* Washington, DC: A publication of the Project on the Status and Education of Women, Association of American Colleges.

Paludi, M. (Ed.). (1990). *Ivory power: Sexual harassment on campus.* Albany, NY: State University of New York Press.

Sandler, B. (1991). *Being sensitive to women in the classroom.* Discussion with academic deans, Marshall University.

The campus climate revisited: Chilly for women faculty, administrators, and graduate students. (1986, October). Project on the Status and Education of Women. Washington, DC: Association of American Colleges.

Avoiding Legal Problems

One protection is to develop a sensitivity to legal concerns, so that a figurative red flag goes up each time you must make certain kinds of decisions.

Much of what we do in our jobs these days is subject to examination and questioning by others. And chances are that sometime during your career, you will need legal counsel. We live in a litigious age. As a department chairperson, you make decisions every day that have the potential of being challenged in a court of law. What can you do to avoid legal problems? One protection is to develop a sensitivity to legal concerns, so that a figurative red flag goes up each time you must make certain kinds of decisions. It warns you to be particularly cautious and to take into account the consequences of your actions.

SOME QUESTIONS TO CONSIDER

To help you develop this legal sensitivity, I have assembled a number of questions that have legal ramifications. These are real questions, taken from life.

1) *Is it possible to dismiss a faculty member who routinely refuses to do what I instruct him to do?* Yes, though it might not be easy. A faculty member who refuses to obey orders is guilty of insubordination, which is cause for dismissal. Insubordination should relate to a repeated refusal to obey reasonable institutional rules or administrative directives. Before you make a charge of insubordination, you should warn the offending faculty member, in writing, that his or her behavior is inappropriate and must be corrected. If, subsequently, the behavior does not change, you have reason to proceed with the insubordination charge. Before taking that step, however, be sure to discuss the matter with your dean and the university's legal counsel.

2) *I have been told to keep a "paper trail" on faculty members who regularly present problems. What is a "paper trail," and is this good advice?* A paper trail

is nothing more than a written record of specific events related to the problems under consideration.

For purposes of illustration, let's assume that faculty member John Doe refuses to attend department faculty meetings. You call Professor Doe into your office to discuss the matter. After he leaves your office, you should make notes to show what transpired during the meeting, especially covering the following:

- Date and time of the meeting
- Reason for the meeting
- The main points discussed
- Any agreements reached
- Any instructions or orders given
- Any unresolved points of disagreement

It is a good idea to follow up the meeting with a note to Professor Doe outlining the results of the meeting. If Professor Doe fails to attend the next departmental faculty meeting, file a copy of the minutes that show he was absent. Send him a written memorandum in which you note his absence and your disappointment and disapproval.

In brief, you should keep a written record of any discussion that pertains to the problem. This is the paper trail, and it will prove critical to your case should you decide to go forward with a charge of insubordination.

3) *During an interview with a finalist for a teaching position, it seemed to me that the candidate was withholding information. He seemed evasive; something didn't seem right. How much checking on his past should I do, and is it permissible to call references he has not listed? In doing a background check, are there precautions I should take?* You are obligated to see that a thorough reference check has been conducted for all candidates you invite to campus as finalists for a position. Indeed, you may face legal problems if you don't. The failure to do an adequate reference check can cause the university to be sued for negligently putting someone inappropriate for the job into a position where he or she can injure or otherwise endanger other people.

There are other points to consider, however. You should remember that it is easier to do a thorough reference check and make a decision not to hire someone than it is to recommend against reappointment or tenure of someone who should never have been hired in the first place. If you are going to get an accurate picture of a candidate, you must expand your reference checking beyond the list of references the candidate provided. The number of calls you need to make depends on what you learn from your initial calls. If you don't get answers to your questions, or if you get contradictory responses, keep seeking until you get a thorough profile of the candidate.

You should write down the responses you get to questions during reference checks. Also, it is important to remember that questions you must avoid in candidate interviews must be avoided in reference checks as well. For example, just as you would not ask a candidate his or her age, you cannot ask for that information during a reference check. Questions must pertain to matters directly related to job performance. You should treat all reference checks as confidential and provide the information only to those individuals who have a role in the hiring process.

4) *What are my responsibilities if I receive reports that a faculty member in my department is engaging in sexual harassment? What action should I take, if any?* Sexual harassment is against federal and state laws, and universities generally have policies that forbid it. As a university administrator, you have the responsibility to inform those in your unit of the policy and to see that it is enforced. Thus, it is your responsibility to investigate carefully any reports you get regarding sexual harassment. They must not be ignored. On the other hand, you cannot take any specific action until someone complains about a particular individual.

What you can and should do is remind all faculty and staff members in your department on a regular basis that the university has a policy that forbids sexual harassment. Circulate the printed policy dealing with sexual harassment, and let everyone know that you take the matter seriously and that you will not tolerate sexual harassment in your department. You may want to invite a spokesperson from affirmative action to a faculty meeting once a year to discuss the matter of sexual harassment. Also, you may want to show your faculty a videotape, *Sexual Harassment: Issues and Answers.* It defines sexual harassment and outlines an employer's legal responsibility for prevention. The tape also depicts realistic situations to advise administrators on how to react to and resolve sexual harassment complaints. (The video is available from the College and University Personnel Association, 1233 20th St., NW, Suite 503, Washington, DC 20036; telephone (202) 429-0311.)

As has been pointed out by a number of lawyers, to avoid damages—personal and monetary—the best course is thorough understanding, planning, and education.

If a student complains to you that she or he has been sexually harassed, you should make arrangements for the student to see someone in affirmative action. You also should advise the student to:

- Tell the harasser to stop, making clear that the behavior is unacceptable.
- Keep a written record detailing the offensive behavior: a description of the behavior, where it happened, and when.
- Avoid being alone with the harasser.
- Wear a small, hidden tape recorder that can be activated in the event the offending behavior continues (see the caveat spelled out in Chapter 9).
- Report to you immediately if the offending behavior continues.

Sexual harassment is a problem that has far-reaching implications. If you take the steps just outlined to familiarize those in your department with your university's policy on sexual harassment and its importance, you will have taken a positive step toward minimizing sexual harassment problems.

5) *May I legally remove a student from a class if he or she causes disturbances in the classroom?* A faculty member faced with this problem should be advised to contact the university officer responsible for student affairs. At most universities, he or she has been given the authority by the university president to remove a student from a class. At one such university, the authority is covered under an emergency action policy which states, "Emergency action is a special category that may be used by the president or his/her designee when, on special occasions, he has the authority to impose the sanction, inter alia, of suspension to a student or group of students from school or from a residence hall who act or refuse to act, the result of which conduct is to interfere with the rights of others and which conduct is nonpeaceful or is disruptive or which conduct constitutes a danger to health, safety, or property of others or his/herself provided that a hearing is held within 72 hours of the decision."

6) *What precautions should I take when providing information about a former employee?* You have no worries about this if you simply give accurate information that is related to job performance. Avoid questions about age, physical or mental disabilities, previous discrimination complaints, or periods of unemployment.

There is a growing tendency to give only dates of employment and nothing more. Society is poorly served if we feel constrained from sharing proper information. I would encourage you to be helpful—and legally safe—by providing references that are accurate and limited to job performance. Thus, you can comment on a former employee's punctuality, attendance, classroom effectiveness, etc.

In a recent case, *Olsson v. Indiana University Board of Trustees,* 571 N.E. 2d 585, (1991), a university instructor was asked to write a letter of recommendation for a student seeking a teaching position. The faculty member did not believe the student was adequately prepared to teach and said so on the recommendation sheet.

The principal who interviewed the student for the job revealed the recommendation. The student did not get the job, and subsequently sued the instructor, claiming defamation.

The state's court of appeals supported the school, ruling that the student could not collect damages because:

- The instructor had shown no "malice or reckless disregard" for the truth.
- The instructor had not written the letter in "bad faith." The letter had been seen only by the person it was intended for; the instructor was a supervisor of students, so evaluation was her responsibility.
- Others submitted negative evaluations of the student.

In *Olsson v. Indiana University Board of Trustees,* the court ruled that letters of recommendation, written in good faith and appropriately distributed to a limited audience, are protected from defamation damages.

7) *The college has mandatory advising. Suppose during the course of an advising session a faculty member—the student's adviser—pays little attention to the courses the student has decided to take. Suppose further that by taking these courses and not taking others the student will have to spend an extra semester in school. What are the legal ramifications?* Bad advice can end up in court—and advisement questions do make it to court quite often. If the information provided a student is in fact wrong, the legal system may decide responsibility and assess damages. Courts often apply contract theory in the situation. They find that an agreement was made, and each party is bound to uphold its side of the bargain. Thus, faculty members who sign registration sheets indicating approval of a schedule need to examine carefully what they are signing. Signing off as an adviser is serious business and should be approached seriously by all who are assigned to serve as student advisers.

You may consider having regular training and updating sessions for all faculty who do advising, and you probably have in place some systematic means for spot checking student folders to see that advisers are maintaining adequate records for each advisee.

8) *If I know that a faculty member in my department has a drinking problem, what should I do? Am I legally responsible for any harm he may do while drinking on the job? What should I do if I suspect that a faculty member has a drinking problem, though I have nothing to support my suspicions?* If you have reason to believe that a faculty member has a drinking problem and you do nothing about it, you may find yourself in a position of having to explain why you did nothing. You may indeed bear some legal responsibility for not taking action.

What should you do if you suspect a drinking problem? Investigate; attempt to determine whether or not the problem exists. You can learn how to go about this by contacting professionals skilled in counseling alcoholics. They also can help you learn how to approach the individual to see that he or she gets help. Keep a written record of any action you take.

Individuals with drinking problems often are skilled at hiding their problem and deceiving others. You may come away from an early meeting with an alcoholic convinced that there is no problem whatever. See Chapter 11 for a complete discussion on how to deal with this problem.

9) *Are faculty members protected by the First Amendment in any public criticisms they make of the university, or of me as department chairperson, or of faculty colleagues?* Until the 1950s, courts generally took the position that public employees agreed to suspend their rights to criticize their institutions in exchange for employment. When matters pertaining to loyalty oaths and organizational affiliations came up in the 1950s and 1960s, however, courts extended the constitutional free speech protections granted others to public employees, including college instructors.

Early court cases ruled that faculty members have the right to criticize their employers when they are commenting on matters of public concern. Since then the courts have been kept busy with employer-employee free speech disputes. Defining what "matters of public concern" includes has proved to be difficult.

In *Connick v. Meyers,* 461 U.S. 138, (1983), the court defined "matters of public concern" as those "relating to any matter of political, social, or other concern in the community."

As Black and Gilson (1988) point out, courts have tended to give considerable weight to employers' decisions on employee free speech. They have done so because they believe employers must be able to maintain some control over employee conduct. Black and Gilson add, "The closer the speaker stands to the object of the criticism, organizationally, the greater the emphasis courts will place on this factor. Put another way, courts are more willing to listen to complaints of disruption (due to criticism) from coworkers than from more distant administrators such as presidents or trustees" (p. 80).

Faculty members do have the right to criticize, provided they speak out on public concerns. Courts have upheld the right of universities to dismiss faculty members in instances where the faculty members' criticisms have been viewed as personal in nature.

10) *Can you insist that faculty and staff get permission before speaking with reporters?* It depends. Obviously, I would not think that any college or university would want to impose such a restriction, but officials at the University of Mobile (Alabama) believe otherwise. The president and the board of trustees there recently approved a policy that permits "only individuals designated by the president or board of trustees to release written or verbal statements to any member of the media concerning the University of Mobile's mission, policies, procedures, activities, events, or information pertaining to students, faculty, or administrative staff, or the board of trustees" (Gag Order, 1997).

The policy also says that "Any faculty or staff member contacted by a reporter must be referred to the office of public relations. Contacts with any trustee must also be referred to the public relations office" (Gag Order, 1997).

The University of Mobile is a private, sectarian institution, and First Amendment rights for faculty and staff at such universities and colleges are less clear than those at public institutions. Still, there is legal precedent for calling into question whether the University of Mobile will be able to restrict its employees in the manner stipulated by the policy. *Marsh v. Alabama* ruled that "A privately owned town could not restrict literature distributed on its streets and that ownership does not always mean absolute dominion" (Gag Order, 1997).

11) *A faculty member in my department wants to copy a chapter from a book to distribute to students in his class? Is this legally permissible?* To answer this question, we need to examine carefully the agreement on guidelines for classroom copying shown in Table 10.1 that was in both the House report and the Conference Committee report. It demonstrates a purposeful sheltering of educational copying to a greater degree than we would find in other fair-use situations.

12) *Suppose I learn that a faculty member in my department is having an affair with a student who is in his or her class. What, if anything, should I do? Is this any of my business (or the university's)?* The faculty member's behavior in this instance is inappropriate, and you should say something to him or her. You are likely to be told by the faculty member that both the student and the faculty member are of legal age and what they do in their private lives is of no concern to you or the university. However, it is not that simple. There is a matter of conflict of interest and professional ethics to be considered. Both provide reasons for a faculty member not to be sexually involved with a student in his or her class.

13) *What should I do if I think the university is going to be sued?* Advise your academic dean and the university's chief legal counsel of the situation. The latter will advise you on what you should do, if anything. He or she also will look after the university's interest by deciding what course of action the university must take to defend itself against a lawsuit.

14) *What are my responsibilities if I receive reports or otherwise have reasons to believe that a faculty member in my department is using department equipment, supplies, or facilities for nonuniversity-related or nonuniversity-sanctioned activities?* It is against the law for any state employee to use state equipment, supplies, or facilities for nonofficial business. Faculty members need to be reminded of this from time to time. Certainly all new faculty members need to be informed.

If you have any reason to believe that a faculty member is using equipment, facilities, or supplies for nonuniversity-related purposes, you need to investigate and put a stop to the practice if you discover it is indeed contrary to policy or law. If you believe that a serious problem exists, talk to your academic dean and the university's chief legal counsel. Even if you believe the problem is not serious, you should keep a written record on the matter.

15) *A professor in my department routinely ignores the regulation requiring all faculty members to provide their students with a course syllabus. What recourse, if any, do his or her students have in such a case?* Most universities have a policy that deals with course syllabi. A typical one says, "During the first two weeks of semester classes (three days of summer term), the instructor must provide each student with a copy of the course requirements which includes the following items: 1) attendance policy, 2) grading policy, 3) approximate due

TABLE 10.1 Agreement on Guidelines for Classroom Copying In Not-for-Profit Educational Institutions

With Respect to Books and Periodicals

The purpose of the following guidelines is to state the minimum standards of educational fair use under Section 107 of H.R. 2223. The parties agree that the conditions determining the extent of permissible copying for educational purposes may change in the future; that certain types of copying permitted under these guidelines may not be permissible in the future; and conversely, that in the future other types of copying not permitted under these guidelines may be permissible under revised guidelines.

Moreover, the following statement of guidelines is not intended to limit the types of copying permitted under the standards of fair use under judicial decision and which are stated in Section 107 of the Copyright Revision Bill. There may be instances in which copying which does not fall within the guidelines stated below may nonetheless be permitted under the criteria of fair use.

I. **Single copying for teachers**

A single copy may be made of any of the following by or for a teacher at his or her individual request for his or her scholarly research or use in teaching or preparation to teach a class:

A. A chapter from a book
B. An article from a periodical or newspaper
C. A short story, short essay or short poem, whether or not from a collective work
D. A chart, graph, diagram, drawing, cartoon or picture from a book, periodical, or newspaper

II. **Multiple copies for classroom use**

Multiple copies (not to exceed in any event more than one copy per pupil in a course) may be made by or for the teacher giving the course for classroom use or discussion; provided that:

A. The copying meets the tests of brevity and spontaneity as defined below; and,
B. Meets the cumulative effect test as defined below; and,
C. Each copy includes a notice of copyright.

Definitions

BREVITY

(i) Poetry: (a) A complete poem if less than 250 words and if printed on not more than two pages or, (b) from a longer poem, an excerpt of not more than 250 words.
(ii) Prose: (a) Either a complete article, story or essay of less than 2,500 words, or (b) an excerpt from any prose work of not more than 1,000 words or 10% of the work, whichever is less, but in any event a minimum of 500 words. (Each of the numerical limits stated in "i" and "ii" above may be expanded to permit the completion of an unfinished line of a poem or of an unfinished prose paragraph.)
(iii) Illustration: One chart, graph, diagram, drawing, cartoon, or picture per book or per periodical issue.

(iv) "Special" works: Certain works in poetry, prose, or in "poetic prose" which often combine language with illustrations and which are intended sometimes for children and at other times for a more general audience fall short of 2,500 words in their entirety. Paragraph "ii" above notwithstanding, such "special works" may not be reproduced in their entirety; however, an excerpt comprising not more than two of the published pages of such special work and containing not more than 10% of the words found in the text thereof, may be reproduced.

SPONTANEITY

(i) The copying is at the instance and inspiration of the individual teacher; and

(ii) The inspiration and decision to use the work and the moment of its use for maximum teaching effectiveness are so close in time that it would be unreasonable to expect a timely reply to a request for permission.

CUMULATIVE EFFECT

(i) The copying of the material is for only one course in the school in which the copies are made.

(ii) Not more than one short poem, article, story, essay, or two excerpts may be copied from the same author, nor more than three from the same collective work or periodical volume during one class term.

(iii) There shall not be more than nine instances of such multiple copying for one course during one class term. [The limitations stated in "ii" and "iii" above shall not apply to current news periodicals and newspapers and current news sections of other periodicals.]

III. Prohibitions as to I and II above

Notwithstanding any of the above, the following shall be prohibited:

A. Copying shall not be used to create or to replace or substitute for anthologies, compilations, or collective works. Such replacement or substitution may occur whether copies of various works or excerpts therefrom are accumulated or reproduced and used separately.

B. There shall be no copying of or from works intended to be "consumable" in the course of study or of teaching. These include workbooks, exercises, standardized tests, and test booklets and answer sheets and like consumable material.

C. Copying shall not:

a) substitute for the purchase of books, publishers' reprints, or periodicals;

b) be directed by higher authority;

c) be repeated with respect to the same item by the same teacher from term to term.

D. No charge shall be made to the student beyond the actual cost of the photocopying.

These guidelines were developed by three organizations: The Ad Hoc Committee of Educational Institutions and Organizations on Copyright Law Revision; the Authors' League of America, Inc.; and the Association of American Publishers, Inc.

dates for major projects and exams, and 4) a description of general course content."

Obviously, the faculty member who fails to provide students with a course syllabus is violating university policy. Students should be advised to take up the matter with the department chairperson. If the problem is not corrected, the academic dean should be consulted.

16) *Suppose a faculty member is conducting a field trip off-campus. He is driving a university vehicle, and several students are with him. An accident occurs, and occupants of the car are injured. An investigation shows that the faculty member was negligent. What are the legal ramifications?* States carry insurance for their vehicles and employees. The insurance covers the student passengers riding in the university automobile. The insurance would generally cover any legal costs arising out of the accident, although some states may have the discretion on whether the involved faculty member will be represented by the state.

17) *Do I have the right to insist that a faculty member cut back in the hours being given to a second job if I determine that the teacher is not getting university work done?* The university has a right to require disclosure of outside employment and place limits on it. Consider the case of *Cook County College Teachers Union v. Board of Trustees,* 481 N.E. 2d 40, (1985). The school limited outside employment by full-time faculty members and required them to complete extensive disclosure forms and report all outside income and benefits. One faculty member challenged the school. A state court ruled in favor of the school and supported the principle that schools could limit outside activities that interfered or conflicted with campus employment.

18) *Can the university restrict what an instructor says in class, or does a person's right to free speech and academic freedom override the university's authority?* At the University of Alabama, administrators tried to convince an instructor to stop discussing his Christian views in the classroom (Staff, 1993). The instructor refused, claiming his rights to free speech and academic freedom would be violated if he were forced to stop such discussions. The case went to court. A district court initially ruled for the instructor. But the 11th Circuit Court of Appeals decision said that the University of Alabama could limit religion in the classroom without violating the instructor's free speech or academic freedom. The instructor then filed an appeal. The appeals court ruled that the school, not the instructor, controls the classroom, and that the school can limit the individual free speech rights of instructing employees.

19) *What legal problems can arise from evaluating faculty and staff?* The performance evaluation can give rise to charges of defamation, illegal discrimination, negligence, invasion, and breach of contract.

To avoid legal problems, be fair and honest, and be able to document everything in writing. Be careful to avoid evaluating anything that does not track the essential functions of the job. In other words, you should be cautious not to evaluate a faculty member's performance on factors that are not job-related.

Rely as much as possible on objective criteria and avoid those that are subjective. Don't say, for example, that "I receive lots of complaints from students about Professor Jones' teaching." Instead, say "This semester 14 students complained to me about Professor Jones' teaching."

Also, you should make certain that faculty members know what is expected of them. For example, courts are likely to support complaints when a faculty member can show that he or she was not told the specific requirements relating to publication until tenure was denied.

Whatever you do, be extremely careful in maintaining confidentiality throughout the evaluation process. You may discuss the evaluations only with those with a "need to know." This means you are permitted to discuss a faculty member's evaluation only with those up the chain of command or those serving on review committees.

20) *Can you ask a woman about pregnancy, childbearing, or child care during a job interview?* A few years ago, a major airline company asked an applicant about pregnancy and childbearing. The applicant, Donna Sales, took the company to court alleging sex discrimination. A federal court of appeals ruled that the applicant had shown clearly that the airline had discriminated against her in its hiring process by conducting her interview differently from the way it conducted others. The airline, on the other hand, could not demonstrate that its questions about child care and childbearing were in any way job-related. The court ruled that the airline was liable for violating Title VII merely in terms of its hiring process.

21) *Can you search a professor's office?* It all depends. A faculty member is entitled to a degree of privacy in a campus office, but there are circumstances where you may search a professor's office without his or her permission, though before you take it upon yourself to do this, you should make certain that your dean and the university's legal counsel agree to this course of action.

Moreover, you would be well advised to think long and hard before searching an office.

In *O'Connor v. Ortega* (Black, 1997), the Supreme Court ruled that while public employees may have legitimate expectations of privacy in their offices, administrators have a competing need for "supervision, control, and the efficient operation of the workplace." It left open the possibility that a work-related search could be legally justified. The suit came about after the Napa State Hospital placed a staff psychiatrist on administrative leave over alleged misconduct. Administrators were concerned about the status of state property and in turn searched his office, seizing certain items.

Ortega sued, claiming the search, which was conducted without a warrant—violated his Fourth Amendment rights. In making its decision, the Supreme Court considered the reasonableness of both the inception and the scope of the intrusion.

This is an area in which universities would be well advised to develop policies and procedures. Santa Rosa Junior College in California (Leatherman, 1997, p. A11) apparently had no such policy when it was determined to find out who had written a flyer and five anonymous letters disparaging its president.

The college hired a private investigator and a handwriting expert who delved into personnel files of 10 faculty and staff members, entered 13 faculty offices, and tapped into 50 computers in an effort to find the responsible person. A tenured professor was identified as the offender and was fired. That professor in turn sued, claiming defamation and a violation of her right to free speech.

Santa Rosa's lawyer has made it clear that he plans to rely on *Connick v. Meyers* (see previous discussion in question 9) in developing legal strategy to defend against the faculty member's accusation that it violated her free-speech rights.

22) *A tenure-track faculty member in the third year of his probationary period requests a two-month unpaid leave to help his wife take care of their newborn twins. Must you grant his request?* The Family and Medical Leave Act of 1993 requires you to grant the leave, providing certain conditions are satisfied. It requires covered employers to provide up to 12 weeks of unpaid, job-protected leave to "eligible" employees for certain family and medical reasons.

- Eligibility requirements:

  1) The employee must have worked for a covered employer for at least one year, and for 1,250 hours over the previous 12 months.

2) There must be at least 50 employees within 75 miles.

- Reasons for taking leave:

  1) To care for the employee's child after birth, or placement for adoption or foster care;

  2) To care for the employee's spouse, son or daughter, or parent, who has a serious health condition.

  3) For a serious health condition that makes the employee unable to perform the employee's job.

23) *What are the major causes of faculty litigation?* According to a report by Baez and Centra (1995), the leading causes of faculty litigation are those outlined below:

Poor Training On the whole, key academic leaders from academic vice presidents to department chairs, have not been instructed on the motives underlying most personnel disputes. As a consequence of this unknowingness, these key institutional leaders may respond in a manner which puts the institution at risk.

Violation of Written Agreements The first area of concern to the courts is that once an agreement is made, it is faithfully executed. Most faculty disputes occur because the institution has failed to uphold its agreement with the individual. This agreement could be found as part of the faculty contract or could be a part of the policies that govern the institution (e.g., faculty code or personnel procedures).

Violation of Basic Rights The second area of concern to the courts is that the rights of the individual be protected from the oppression of governmental agencies or impersonal organizations. These basic rights are detailed in federal and state constitutions and in the various nondiscrimination federal regulations.

Inconsistent Enforcement of Procedures One concept of nondiscrimination is that everyone is treated the same. Therefore, policies and procedures that are applied inconsistently are considered by the courts to be inherently unacceptable.

Faculty Perception of Being Treated Unfairly Poor communication and a sense of not being appreciated may be all it takes to motivate a faculty member to sue. Litigation of this type may be few in number, but it does take up a significant percentage of the time spent by the college counsel.

The best thing you can do to avoid legal problems is to be familiar with the university's policies and to carry them out. Beyond that, you must think about the consequences of your decisions. If they are negative, you should act carefully and seek advice from your dean, academic vice president, and university attorney. If you feel your actions may result in a lawsuit, ask for permission to discuss the matter with the university's legal counsel.

REFERENCES

Baez, B., & Centra, J. A. (1995). *Tenure, promotion, and reappointment: Legal and administrative implications.* ASHE-ERIC Higher Education Report No. 1. Washington, DC: The George Washington University.

Black, D. R. (1997). *Maintaining perspective: A decade of collegiate legal challenges.* Madison, WI: Magna Publications.

Black, D. R., & Gilson, M. (1988). *Perspectives and principles: A college administrator's guide to staying out of court.* Madison, WI: Magna Publications.

Connick v. Meyers, 461 U.S. 138, (1983).

Cook County College Teachers Union v. Board of Trustees, 481 N.E. 2d 40, (1985).

Gag order. (1997, June). *Academic Leader,* 13 (6) 7-8.

Leatherman, C. (1997, June 6). A college is riled after administrators search faculty offices and computer files. *The Chronicle of Higher Education,* pp. A11–12.

Staff. Religion and the classroom don't mix. (1993, January). *Perspective,* p. 3.

Staff. *Olsson v. Indiana University Board of Trustees,* 571 N.E. 2d 585, (1991).

11

Dealing with Difficult Faculty

Many faculty members who are difficult to get along with are honestly surprised when they are told they are being obstinate or that their behavior creates problems for others.

As with most chairpersons, I came into my job quite unprepared. I knew next to nothing about the important job of managing a budget and little more about managing people. I soon discovered, as most of us have, that managing people would be my biggest challenge. It would occupy most of my time and present me with the most vexing problems. Dealing with budget problems, no matter how frustrating, is easy when compared to dealing with people problems.

While handling some personnel problems is relatively simple (e.g., making arrangements for classes to be covered for a hospitalized faculty member takes time but little else), many other personnel problems are both time-consuming and troublesome; some even defy resolution. In this chapter, we will look at problems that fall into the latter category—the really tough ones.

Most faculty members do not make a conscious effort to make life difficult for others and for their chairperson. I said most, not all. Likewise, many faculty members who are difficult to get along with are honestly surprised when they are told that they are being obstinate, or that their behavior creates problems for others. Their view is that others are difficult to get along with; they are not. I remember some years ago talking to a faculty member and telling him that he was argumentative. He argued long and hard that he was not.

It may be trite to suggest that people are hard to understand and that most have no idea at all why they act as they do. However, it bears mentioning because people are complex. They behave as they do for a multitude of hard-to-understand reasons. While we often cannot explain the perverse behavior of others, almost nearly as often, even the perverse individuals themselves have difficulty explaining their actions and attitudes. Unfortunately, there are few simple solutions to the problems they cause that you must try to resolve.

REMINDERS ABOUT DEALING WITH FACULTY

Let's begin this human relations investigation by looking at some reminders for dealing with all faculty members.

A good administrator must be a good listener. Many faculty members who complain a lot just want someone to listen to them. It's obvious, of course, that we cannot respond to the needs and concerns of faculty members when we don't hear what they are saying.

When we listen to complaints, we are tempted to engage in conversation, to respond with logical arguments, to judge, or to criticize. Generally, it is better to listen silently, doing little more than showing concerned interest.

Always allow others the opportunity to save face. It is human nature to want to crush those who attack us. Despite this instinctive reaction, everyone is better served if difficult faculty members are given a way to save face. This is one of the reasons to avoid public reprimands of faculty or staff. Permitting a person to save face makes perfect sense to me, though I occasionally run into those who question such a practice with comments like, "You had your chance to get even; why didn't you do it?" or something similar. Good leadership is not about getting even.

As dean, I have on occasion had to ask a chairperson to step down. Providing the opportunity of resigning from the position can save face. On occasion, I've had someone across campus say to me that the deposed chair had said that I had begged the chairperson to stay on, which does not trouble me, even though that has not been the case. If this provides a suitable face-saving defense for the chairperson, that's well and good.

Don't make snap judgments. People often behave the way they are expected to behave. If we make the judgment that a particular faculty member is difficult to work with, chances are he or she will see to it that our judgment is validated.

Keep an open door. By talking with faculty members regularly, you may be able to head off problems, contain them, or keep them from escalating. Once individuals have become entrenched, they may be less inclined to listen to suggestions for dealing with a problem. Faculty members will feel better about dealing with you when there is a problem if they interact with you when there is not a problem.

When you make a mistake, admit it. All of us make mistakes, and when we do, we should be willing to admit to them. The expression "Be big enough to admit mistakes" has real-life meaning.

Look for ways to compliment faculty members. Even the weakest faculty member has qualities that permit a compliment from time to time. Yet often we fail to let others know that we appreciate their efforts. As a department chairperson, set aside time to observe what others are doing and to let them know that you are interested in their work—and that you appreciate the good that they do.

You are in a better position to point out problems if you can open a discussion with, "Well, Jim, you know how much I appreciate all the good things you do for the department . . ." If you never tell Jim that you appreciate his good work, however, you can't use these mollifying words.

Treat everyone honestly and fairly. One of the hardest jobs of administrators is telling others that their work does not meet expectations. It's tough, too, to give a faculty member a poor performance appraisal. But everyone loses—the department, students, staff, and other faculty members—if we are less than honest in dealing with such matters.

The best thing to do today to become a better department chairperson tomorrow is to vow that you will be open, honest, and fair.

Write things down. Not only is it important to write down reminders to avoid forgetting important things to do, but it is also important to write down any agreements that you make with faculty members. If you don't do this, you will find yourself in arguments with faculty members about what you actually said. Writing memos to yourself helps avoid conflicts.

Compromising is not necessarily a sign of weakness. There are times when the advantages of compromise far outweigh the advantages of holding firm. You need to look at each situation carefully and determine what would serve best—now and in the future. Many chairpersons view negotiating as a sign of indecisiveness. They should remember the words of John F. Kennedy: "Compromise need not mean cowardice."

Remember that you are "their" chairperson, but they are not "your" faculty. You serve as chairperson to enable faculty members to do their jobs, yet the reverse of that is not true. Certainly faculty members can do much to make your job easier, but their primary responsibility is to teach, engage in scholarly activity, and provide service. On the other hand, your chief responsibility is to make it possible for faculty members to fulfill their responsibilities.

Remember that a faculty member is not necessarily wrong just because he or she sees things and behaves differently from the way you do. This notion was brought sharply to my attention not long ago when a colleague pointed out that he finally understood why he often was at odds with another person. "When I rode with her to the airport not long ago and she came upon a parking area that was closed, she simply got out and moved the cones," he said. "I am the kind of person who would back up and find another parking place. But she moves the cones! I think that speaks volumes about how different our approaches to many things in life are," he concluded.

Sure enough, you will have to deal with cone movers, along with those who turn away from cones. And those who must put off important projects until the last minute, or insist that giving a student an incomplete in a particular situation where it is something you would not do. We each view things from our own unique vantage point, and while we often insist upon doing things our way, it may be all right to accept other ways of doing things as well as other perspectives on problems or solutions.

I am reminded here of how L. T. Anderson, a West Virginia newspaper columnist, used to deal with those who would write letters disagreeing with his point of view. He would return their letters after stamping them with a special message he had made up. In large letters it read: You May Be Right.

Even if you are effective in your relationships with most faculty members in your department, you will still be faced at times with some who are difficult to deal with. They will try your patience and cause you to question your administrative skills. Let's look at some of these difficult people and consider how they might be dealt with.

THE FACULTY MEMBER WITH A SUBSTANCE ABUSE PROBLEM

What should you do if you learn that a faculty member in your department is drinking, or otherwise abusing any substance, on the job, and that his substance abuse makes him ineffective?

This is not an easy problem, nor is it one you can ignore. The problem is exacerbated by the fact that it is covered under the Americans with Disabilities Act (ADA). You cannot approach a person with a substance abuse problem by being confrontational. Instead, you must observe the person's performance relative to objective standards. If a faculty member's work suffers in comparison to those standards, deal with that fact, and do not accuse him or her of anything.

If you accuse a faculty member of being an alcoholic, you run the risk of being sued for defamation. Drinking alcohol is not illegal, though it becomes your concern if a person is caught drinking while at work. If you catch a faculty member in the act, you then have a basis for challenging his or her alcohol use.

If you believe that drinking is affecting the faculty member's work, you should call the person in for a conference to discuss his or her performance and your expectations. If you know he or she has been drinking on the job you can say so, though you should expect that the faculty member will deny that a problem exists.

"Sure, I have a drink now and then, but it's not a problem," he will say (we'll use a male as an example). He then will go on to say that he doesn't have to drink, that he could quit anytime he wants to, and that you shouldn't be concerned.

You have to be insistent. Tell him that if it really is not a problem, he has nothing to be concerned about. You, of course, also must tell him that you will not tolerate any drinking on the job, and that if you see any evidence of it, then you will insist that he get help. That is probably all you should expect to achieve in the first meeting: putting him on notice.

Alcoholics are good at deceit; they have a lot of practice at it. The drinking probably will continue, and it will present more problems no matter how much the drinker schemes and covers up. As soon as you have evidence that he is still drinking and that it is interfering with his work, you need to take the next step: Insist that he get professional help. Your involvement from this point will depend in part on the seriousness of the problem. If the professional insists on treatment requiring extended confinement, you will have to help make arrangements for a leave of absence, and, of course, further arrangements to assure that classes and other responsibilities are covered. Additionally, you should stand ready to provide other support that the faculty member and his family may need. This could be something as simple as expressing personal concern, or it could extend to arranging for additional support systems.

Once treatment is complete and the faculty member is back on the job, you would be wise to seek professional guidance on dealing with the recovering alcoholic. The more you learn about problem drinkers, the better you will be in keeping the faculty member on the job of coping with alcoholism. Your effort may be time-consuming and frustrating. Setbacks seem to be the rule rather than the exception. However, the rewards that come with seeing a faculty member recover and lead a productive life are enormously gratifying.

The Obstinate Faculty Member

Stubborn faculty members who insist on doing everything their own way can create problems not only for you but also for other faculty and staff members. They often are not persuaded or impressed by logic. They will insist that they have the answers to just about everything, and imply that suggestions that run counter to theirs are stupid and useless.

One way to deal with this person is to look around to find if there are others who can work easily with him or her. If you identify such a person, try to find what special techniques that person uses that you don't. Ask yourself honestly if you are doing something to cause the kind of reaction you are getting from Dr. Obstinate. If you are at fault, then you must be prepared to modify your own behavior or to accept the reaction you get.

You should be prepared to talk candidly with the difficult faculty member about his or her behavior, explaining the problems it creates. Ask if there is anything you can do to get cooperation. There is a chance—perhaps slim, but nonetheless a chance worth hoping for—that you will find that the obstinate person is reacting to something you are doing.

If all else fails, you may have to resort to explaining the consequences of the unwanted behavior. If it comes to this, you will probably need to point out that you have the final say on setting the priorities and direction for the department and on how resources for the department are to be used. You also need to let the person know that getting along is much better than quarreling. Moreover, explain that you don't have time to waste on dealing with such distracting behavior.

The Weak Classroom Teacher

It is not at all uncommon to have to deal with a faculty member who is not performing up to the expected level in his or her classes. You should begin by establishing as best you can the causes for it. Does the person have the pedagogic skills? Is the faculty member preparing adequately? Are personal problems involved?

If the faculty member is new, these may not be easy questions to answer. On the other hand, if the faculty member has been around awhile, you will be able to answer these questions quickly.

Once you've determined the reason for the faculty member's inability to perform at the level you expect, you can decide how best to respond. Regardless of the problem, you will have to talk about the matter directly with the faculty member.

If pedagogic skills are lacking, you may assign the person to work closely with an experienced faculty member whose skills are recognized. In addition, you might try the following:

- Have the faculty member videotape his or her classes. By studying the tape, areas for improvement can be identified. Follow-up videotaping can show if any improvement is noticeable.
- Have experienced teachers make classroom visits and supply their recommendations on teaching style.
- Suggest that the faculty member ask students to suggest areas for improvement.
- Have the person sit in on other faculty members' classes.
- See if your department or college of education has courses that might benefit a struggling classroom teacher.

If the problems are not related to pedagogic skills, your challenge is even more complex. Certainly you will need the cooperation of the faculty member if significant changes are to be made.

The Department Gossip

The department gossip is an interesting, complex person. He or she gets pleasure out of passing on disparaging information about colleagues, especially if the information is sensational.

Isolating the gossip is probably the best response. If you can persuade other faculty members that gossip is hurtful and shouldn't be tolerated, then they may take the next step and tell the gossip they don't want to hear about others. If you really want to stop a gossip short, just say, "I would rather not hear about it. I don't like to talk about others." I also have found it effective to tell the person spreading the gossip that I feel uncomfortable talking about a colleague who isn't present. "Why don't we call Joe in and hear his side?" Usually that will stop the talk abruptly.

Most of us enjoy sharing news with others. We take some delight in passing on something that others have not heard of, yet most of us stop short of making up things or passing on unsubstantiated bits of information, and we take special care not to pass on information that is hurtful to our colleagues. The department gossip, however, is not governed by the same rules of conduct. Gossips will make the lives of their colleagues miserable if given the slightest opening. Typical gossips need a bit of truth from which to spin their juicy tidbits. Suppose, for example, that Sydney Smith, a new faculty member who is ABD, has to delay his dissertation defense due to scheduling conflicts of some members of his committee. The department gossip might tell a colleague, "It's too bad Smith couldn't defend his dissertation. I understand some of his committee members have real problems with the way he gathered his data." By the time this passes through a couple of more gossips in the department, poor Smith—according to the stories being told—is about to be kicked out of his doctoral program!

A little sunshine is a good antiseptic, so say advocates of open meeting and records laws, and so will you when dealing with the department gossip. Simply making the truth known will help to kill rumors that department gossips start or spread. If, for example, you distribute a Monday morning memo, you might insert something like: Because of unanticipated scheduling conflicts with members of his dissertation committee, Sydney Smith has had to reschedule his defense. He says that it looks now as if all his committee members will be able to convene near the end of this month.

The Department Snitch

There are faculty members who have a need to run to the dean, the vice president, or the campus newspaper with every departmental problem. This behavior is particularly frustrating when it is a problem you are not even aware of, and you feel especially rankled that you have not been given an opportunity to try to solve it. Moreover, you discover that talking with the faculty member about the advantages of keeping problems "within the family" doesn't work. Try the following strategies.

Bring the problem before the faculty. Suppose you have a faculty member who has complained to your dean about the way you have allocated travel funds. At the very next faculty meeting after learning about what he or she has discussed with your dean, you might say something like, "John has complained to the dean about the formula we use for distributing travel funds in our department. I think this is something that we should discuss. What are your feelings about our travel fund use?"

You must take care to let John know that this is something he could have put on the agenda without complaining to the dean. If you don't make that clear, he and others may come to believe that the best way to get something on the faculty agenda is to complain to the dean or others.

Create a special committee (department welfare committee?) for department problems. And have the one who likes to complain chair the committee. Furthermore, I would appoint to the committee others in the department who enjoy complaining. There are probably some advantages in creating a legitimate forum for the complainers, but I wouldn't stop there. I would charge the committee with coming up with possible solutions to problems they identify. Oftentimes they will see—we hope—that while it is easy to complain, it is a lot more difficult to come up with workable solutions that will satisfy others in the department.

The Loud, Abusive Faculty Member

If you've not yet had to deal with a loud, abusive faculty member, just wait. Your time will likely come. Some faculty have learned that they can accomplish certain things by being loud and abusive, and they seem to relish getting chairpersons in their cross hairs. "What gives you the right to schedule a faculty meeting whenever you want without consulting faculty! Any idiot can see that I have classes to take care of for crying out loud. I am damned tired of imbeciles playing chairman, and if you think I'm going to take this without talking to the dean, then you've got another think coming." And on and on he screams, getting louder and more abusive with each new breath. What do you do? Here are some suggestions:

First of all, hold your ground. Whatever you do, try not show that you can be intimidated in these kinds of situations. Try maintaining your position. If you are sitting down at your desk, remain seated. Remember, you can hold your ground without becoming combative. Indeed, I've found that by being calm, the loud and abusive attacker will often become unsettled and less certain, which then gives me an edge.

Keep control of yourself. The worst thing you can do is to lose your self-control. If that happens, you and your attacker will likely be yelling at each other, which will accomplish nothing. Let the out-of-control faculty member go on with his or her tirade while you take a deep breath and think about what you might want to say or do.

When the blasting stops, speak calmly. You might want to say, with the calmest voice you have, "Is there anything else you want to say?" If he comes back with another attack, wait until he finishes and then ask, "And is there anything else?"

Whenever he's finished his attacks on you, seize the opportunity to summarize what he's said and what you can do to deal with his concerns. If you've been accused of something about which you are wrong, you need to acknowledge it and indicate how you will prevent a recurrence. On the other hand, if you have not done anything wrong, you need to calmly set the record straight.

Use this opportunity. Let the faculty member know how you like to deal with disagreements. For example, you might say "Jim, I know you are upset, and I would like us to work out our differences, but that's not possible when you are yelling. I hope in the future you will be calm and rational when you come to me with complaints. That way, we may be able to deal with our problems. You should know that from now on I will not talk to you when you are loud and abusive. It's not a productive way to deal with problems." A warning here: It may take several minutes to get this message out. My experience tells me that about the time you say "calm and rational," the attacker is likely to let go with another volley. "What do you mean calm and rational? Are you suggesting that I am not rational? Who gives you the right to sit in judgment of me?" And so it goes. You have to be persistent in letting him know how you feel and how you expect to deal with his anger and frustration.

Interrupt if you must. Do this by saying his name over and over until you get his attention and he quits talking. Remember, too, that you have to adjust to the situation.

Know that you can dictate the terms on which you will speak. Several years ago when I was chairperson, I had a faculty member who was given to loud and abusive assaults. One day he came into my office screaming and swearing loudly at me as I was seated at my desk. I slowly stood up, pointed my finger at him, and ordered him out of my office. I told him that when he calmed down and could speak to me rationally, I would be happy to discuss his complaint with him.

The next day I called him into my office and told him that I expected more mature behavior from him. His emotional outburst had given way to calmness in the passing hours, and while he was still upset with me, I had the upper hand. After all, he was in my office at my invitation. It allowed me to set the terms of how we could disagree without losing control of our emotions.

More recently, when I came into a new situation, I was warned about a faculty member who tends to become loud and abusive. In my first such encounter with him, I asked, "Do you always have trouble controlling your emotions?" It did not immediately help me in dealing with him, but it led to our calm discussion about how we ought to respond to differences of opinion. I have always been a strong advocate of expressing differences of opinions on professional matters, where there is a lot of room for differences. But we must learn how to do this without making our "professional" differences "personal."

A word of encouragement is in order here. Most faculty members are courteous and easy to get along with, and you don't have to be a street fighter to be an effective chairperson. Nonetheless, from time to time, you will have to let faculty members know that you will stand up to them if they attack you. How can you learn to do this if it's not in your nature? Here are some suggestions:

Role play. Have a friend play the role of the loud and abusive faculty member. If you make the situation as real as possible, you will get some of the feelings of being attacked. As with any role-playing situation, you want to learn from it and get to a point where you are performing in a way that makes you feel good.

Lay out your expectations, publicly. At a faculty meeting, talk about what can be gained by having calm and reasonable discussions about differences, pointing out how it is impossible to accomplish much of anything by yelling at each other. Let faculty members know that they can expect to be treated this way by you, and you, in turn, expect to be treated the same way.

Treat others with respect, always. Above all else, treat others with respect, and do all you can to command respect. Faculty members are not as likely to beat up on you verbally if they respect you.

The Lean, Mean Venting Machine

There are some people who seem to take pleasure in hurting others. These are the nasty, cruel faculty among us. Those who believe that our modern society promotes this kind of behavior describe it as a "get even" society of inappropriate frankness and rudeness that rules. They note the recent revival of prisoner chain gangs, rap music's debasement of women, and "theater of humiliation" radio and television talk shows that degrade and exploit.

As chairperson you will have to protect others from this kind of person. Most often, he or she will engage in "trickle down" nastiness, taking it out on the individual one rung down the social ladder. Hence, students, junior faculty, and staff members are often the targets of this person's meanness. Nicolaus Mills, a professor of American studies at Sarah Lawrence College, maintains that the interplay of biology and environment is a critical part of determining how mean we are. He says "[t]oday's corporate Darwinism has fostered such circumstance, creating a lifeboat ethic, the notion that the country can't support everyone and that if you have to shove more vulnerable folks out of the lifeboat for self-preservation, well, so be it" (Kelleher, 1997, p. 8F).

You must be on the watch for this type of behavior and let those who exhibit it know that it won't be tolerated. You should make it clear that you will take the side of those being abused.

The High Maintenance Faculty Member

Some faculty members, for whatever reason (and there are many), demand a lot of a chairperson's time. They need to feel needed and loved. They need to be reassured. But how much of your time are you willing to give them? How much do you have to give? What is the cost to you and to others (remember that time you give to high maintenance faculty is time you do not have for others)? Answering these questions will help you to see more clearly what your role as chairperson is and how well you can deal with that role.

While the high maintenance faculty member is not necessarily difficult in the usual meaning of the definition, he or she nonetheless can become a difficult problem for you. Faculty members of this kind will use every excuse to take up your time, and you may have to have a direct talk with them about what this does to your schedule. The ideal way of dealing with such a faculty member is to find a way to provide reassurance without having to spend an inordinate amount of time in the process. While normally I've had an open-door policy, I at one point changed to deal with a couple of faculty members who would walk into my office five or six times a day. I purposely made it difficult for those faculty members to see me and in the process weaned them of their need to take up so much of my time.

The Unmotivated Faculty Member

Faculty members who have lost their enthusiasm and who are no longer energetic and productive require special attention. The work they are not doing falls to others in the department, and morale problems ensue. You cannot ignore this kind of problem for long.

Performance evaluation sessions provide a good opportunity to discuss this matter with the unmotivated person. You must listen carefully and try to understand what's behind the troubling behavior. If the faculty member was once productive, what's changed? A good way to begin discussion is to start with something like, "Where do you see your career going?" Or ask the faculty member to talk about his or her goals. Regardless of the approach, you are likely to pick up on some helpful clues if you listen carefully. This is how the conversation might go:

"So, Joe, tell me about your short-term goals, and then we will talk about where you see yourself going 10 or 15 years from now."

"That's really hard for me to discuss. I guess I just want to be here teaching the same classes that I now teach."

"Well, maybe you would like to try some new courses. We are going to need someone to teach another section of Urban American History next term, and I remember how you used to inspire students to learn. Perhaps you can get that old feeling back by taking on a course you haven't taught for a long time."

"It sounds as if you're suggesting that I don't now have enthusiasm for what I'm teaching."

"Well, I think that's something we should talk about."

There are other ways, of course, to approach this problem. If merit money is available, you can certainly reward those who are performing at a high level and send a message to those who aren't. Weak student evaluations oftentimes will get the attention of unmotivated faculty members. However, some simply will rationalize their poor showing.

Faculty development can provide opportunities to challenge the unmotivated person. Support for faculty development shouldn't be perceived as a reward for weak performance. Even so, progress is possible if the right agreement is made for providing the unmotivated teacher with released time, travel funds, or other faculty development support. You can be forthright about this by explaining that a higher level of performance will be expected in the future. Further, the faculty member needs to be told that evaluation follow-ups are in order until his or her performance meets your expectations.

None of these approaches will work, however, unless the root of the problem is identified and dealt with. If the faculty member is having personal problems, his or her lack of motivation will undoubtedly be evident so long as these problems persist. Likewise, if the faculty member's behavior is caused by a lack of respect or trust in you, then lack of motivation will likely persist until you can win back respect and trust.

Sometimes it makes sense for unmotivated faculty members to get a fresh start. You might want to see what you can do to find another teaching post for them. Frankly, I've never had much success with this, though I have known faculty members who discovered for themselves a need to start over. In more than one instance, I have heard that they were able to get their old energy and motivation back.

The truth of the matter, though, is one we ought not ignore: Given our current demographics in higher education, we have—and will have—an increasing number of faculty members who have had long and distinguished records of good work. Some of them will begin to slow down, to mark time. I have seen it. And if you haven't, you probably will. I have found this to be especially painful when outstanding classroom teachers don't have what they used to, but they refuse to retire. Students make fun of them, complain that they are not learning, or believe that the faculty member doesn't understand modern day society and how it relates to the subject matter he or she teaches. Sadly, you come to believe that the faculty member's teaching is lacking, and because you have had so much respect for him or her or because you are a personal friend, you hurt.

The foregoing assumes the faculty member is approaching retirement, but that may not always be the case. Faculty members like this are often powerful in their own departments, even though they have quit learning and have grown stale. They are often good people who have done good work and who are secure in their jobs. Seasoned chairpersons find them difficult to deal with, and new, incoming chairpersons know they cannot afford to make them angry. We are tempted to ignore them. But can we? Should we?

Each such situation is different. Still, you might try the following, depending on the nature of the situation:

Talk to family members. This is a delicate area, and one that you should not engage in without careful contemplation and discussion with appropriate campus officials. You should not give the appearance of "running an end-run" on the faculty member in question or suggesting that you are pressuring the faculty member to retire. With those considerations in mind, it might nonetheless be possible for you to talk with a caring family member and tell him or her that "John is having real problems in the classroom," giving specific examples of what he is doing. Of course, your reason for talking with the family is to see if it can help devise strategies to assist the faculty member with taking direct action for dealing with the problem, which may mean retirement.

Talk to campus officials. It is possible that the university would be willing to develop some arrangements so that the faculty member could teach less by taking on other responsibilities. If money is a problem, finding some way for the faculty member to handle the problems will be critical.

Get to know the faculty member better. The problem may not be age, though we are quick to blame it on that if a faculty member's performance declines. In addition to money problems, there may be many other kinds of concerns or worries that have surfaced. Perhaps the faculty member would like to retire, but she is reluctant to because she can't deal well with a husband who makes life miserable for her when she is at home. Or it may be that the faculty member is having to take care of elderly parents. If your relationship with the faculty member is strictly professional, you are not likely to learn about his or her concerns.

We often forget that our colleagues may not have anyone in whom they can confide. Can you make it comfortable for them to share with you some of the personal things in their life that trouble them? Do you want to play that role? If you can and are willing to accept that as a part of your responsibility as a chairperson, you may be able to help faculty members who are not performing well to work through their problems. Not all of us can do that, of course.

Difficult faculty members are a challenge. Dealing with them can be especially time-consuming, and can create a feeling of failure. There are few times that you will walk away from dealing with difficult faculty believing you have forever solved some problem. Chances are you will have it all to deal with it again . . . and again. Moreover, there is no magic potion to help us. We can read book after book and attend conferences and workshops on the subject, only to discover that we cannot easily put faculty members in neat categories that seem to be represented here. The obstinate faculty member may also be the department gossip. Moreover, we soon discover that a strategy that works for one will not necessarily work for another faculty member who exhibits a lot of the same behavior. If I could sum up my advice in just a few words, it would be: Listen carefully, have a good sense of humor, and get to know and be comfortable with yourself so that you can be secure.

REFERENCES

Kelleher, K. (1997, June 22). We're lean, mean venting machines. *The Tennessean,* p. 8F.

12

Building and Maintaining Morale

The confidence the faculty have in their leaders decreases with the distance the leaders are from the faculty.
— Linda Johnsrud

While a faculty morale problem is something that can do great damage to a department, it is seldom something that chairpersons deal with systematically or formally. Little attention is given to building and maintaining morale as a major responsibility of chairpersons. One reason for this is that morale is a vague and complex concept. Moreover, many administrators believe that it takes money to deal with all morale problems, and they believe that if they don't have money there is nothing they can do about morale—even if it is bad and getting worse. In thinking this way, they ignore low-cost and no-cost responses to faculty morale problems. This chapter examines ways to assess and talk about faculty morale and ways to deal with it.

Johnsrud (1996, p. 1) defines morale as "the level of well-being that an individual or group is experiencing in reference to their worklife." She makes several others observations relative to the meaning of morale and our attempts to assess and deal with it.

- The factors that administrative staff and faculty perceive as having an effect on morale can be measured.
- Morale exists in individuals and groups.
- Morale matters. This is based on the evidence that demonstrates that morale affects performance (Johnsrud, 1996, pp. 4–5).

CAUSES OF LOW MORALE

The causes of low morale are virtually unlimited. Moreover, they may have to do with factors beyond your control, such as personal or family problems.

Some of the most cited causes that are strictly work-related include the following.

Salary and related matters. Given the reduced level of support for higher education in the United States in recent years, salary increases seldom exceed the increases in cost of living. Faculty members are understandably concerned over this. Johnsrud (1996, p. 31) points out that "salaries that are perceived as being unfair lead to long-term dissatisfaction and can have a great effect on the faculty members' morale and effectiveness." Salary by itself is not the only issue. Fringe and retirement benefits matter. Faculty members expect support for professional development.

Leadership. Many faculty members do not have good feelings about their university's leadership. Johnsrud (1996, p. 34) says that "the confidence the faculty have in their leaders decreases with the distance the leaders are from the faculty (i.e., they have the most confidence in their chairs, less in their deans, even less in vice presidents and presidents, etc.)." Indeed, most studies show a definite decrease in confidence from chairs through board of trustees.

Collegial relations in the department. This area represents the kind of relations faculty members have with their chairperson. It also represents how well faculty members feel that they fit into the department intellectually and socially. Obviously how well faculty members get along and the kind of support they have for each other factor into collegial relations. Faculty members who are difficult to get along with and who are themselves unhappy can create low morale for a complete department.

Professional worklife. Teaching, advising, and committee responsibilities all make a difference in how faculty members assess their professional worklife. Moreover, the kind of support—whether clerical or technical—bears on this. Even the parking situation can make a difference in a faculty member's professional worklife well-being.

Faculty governance. Faculty members want and expect to have some input both at the department level and the college and university levels. They want some say about budgets and personnel matters. They also expect clear protection of their academic freedom.

Reward and evaluation system. Faculty members look for rewards when their productivity in teaching and research increases. They also want clearly stated promotion and tenure expectations. Faculty members who are not praised for doing a good job or who feel that tenure guidelines are ambiguous are unlikely to have high morale. Rosner (1997, p. 3) notes that according to the University of Texas faculty senate president, "[D]epartments with a good annual review system are also departments that run well and have much higher morale than those that don't."

Quality of students. Students at all levels who have ability and a strong work ethic make a difference in the way faculty members feel about their professional worklife.

Support service. A good library provides support for faculty as do the offices of research, faculty development, and computing. Even duplicating/printing facilities make a difference in the way faculty members assess their morale.

The erosion of working conditions and the public's dissatisfaction with higher education also factor into the morale equation. As we know, the public is demanding greater accountability, complaining about our workload, and questioning the tenure system. Many believe that faculty members are arrogant, out-of-touch, and undeserving of higher salaries or additional support. Moreover, many of those outside the academy—including our elected representatives—believe that we are not doing a good job of educating students.

In recent years we've seen tenure come under attack. We've seen the relevance of our research questioned. We also have been criticized for expanding programs and increasing tuition, and many states have developed policies intended to reduce program duplication. We look for support from some of those legislators who have been there for us in the past, but they are listening to their constituents. Unfortunately, many of their constituents are angry taxpayers who insist that taxes be lowered. Moreover, legislators have found that cutting higher education funding and diverting money to such things as building prisons, improving roads, and fighting drug problems causes little public outcry. Whether justified or not, many nonacademics—including a fair number of legislators—believe that higher education wastes taxpayers' dollars with its layers of administrators and watered-down curriculum. Those same people perceive that college faculty lack a work ethic (in other words, we have soft jobs) and that we are overpaid, given the hours they perceive that we work. Kerlin and Dunlap (1993) found that:

> Retrenchment activities in higher education learning institutions in the U.S. has seriously undermined the morale of faculty members. There has been a notable deterioration in both education quality and faculty morale as a result of austerity measures initiated by administrative officials of educational institutions. Retrenchment and reorganization measures have also increased the incidence of occupation-related stress and overall job dissatisfaction among faculty members.

IMPROVING FACULTY MORALE

The following are things that you can do to improve morale in your department:

Communicate, communicate, communicate. Faculty members want to know what's going on; they want to be made to feel a part of things. Faculty members should know how money is allocated to the department and how it is spent. Keeping faculty members in the dark regarding budget matters contributes to their low morale. Having regular faculty meetings and communicating in other ways on a regular basis helps morale.

Let faculty members know that they are appreciated. As a chairperson, you must be ever alert for the accomplishments of faculty so that you can congratulate them and let them know how much you appreciate their efforts. If a faculty member does an especially good job of supervising a project or chairing a committee, tell that individual how much you appreciate that time and effort. Congratulate faculty when a job is well done.

Involve faculty members in the governance of the department. All major policy decisions made at the department level should have faculty involvement. For example, if the department is expected to have a merit salary plan, faculty members should help to develop one. Likewise, departmental promotion and tenure guidelines should grow out of faculty committee work. Indeed, the more ways in which you can involve faculty in the major affairs of the department, the better off both you and faculty morale will be.

Budget decisions should be made public, and faculty members in your department should be asked for their input regarding academic program priorities and how funds should be spent. Most faculty members are aware that difficult choices have to be made, but they resent not being included in the decision-making process.

Establish a positive tone of cooperation. If all faculty members work to cooperate with each other, department morale will be enhanced. As chairperson you should let faculty know that cooperation is expected. When a faculty member is ill or must be away from campus, do other faculty members willingly cover his or her classes? Are they willing to share equipment?

Address the issue of high starting salaries. Very often these days, salary increases are small and mandated, which leaves you with little say or flexibility regarding salary increases. However, when you hire a new faculty members you often have some latitude regarding their starting salary. I believe that you should stretch this to the limit by providing the best beginning salary possible. If you do this, however, you will want the support of current faculty. If you independently create inequities, you will do much to create morale problems.

Don't permit small amounts of money for merit raises to divide your faculty. I don't know whether you've been faced with this or not, but I have on several occasions—and on more than one campus. A small salary increase has been approved, and you are asked whether you want to provide across-the-board salary increases or to provide merit increases. If the amount is small and you have a choice, I believe you ought to favor across-the-board increases. Merit increases may not be worth the tensions they cause when the dollars are less than the cost-of-living increases.

Establish clear policies and distribute them widely. Faculty have every right to be upset and dissatisfied with their professional worklife when policies are unclear and shifting. Whether these policies have to do with promotion and tenure or travel funds, faculty members need to know what the ground rules are. Moreover, it is especially important that you are consistent with policy application and interpretation.

Treat all faculty members fairly and without favoritism. There always will be the temptation to reward some faculty members and punish others. This, of course, is permissible providing we reward and punish within acceptable and known policies. We shouldn't be governed by ad hoc policies.

Look for opportunities to provide faculty members with consulting. In your position as chairperson, you often are called to recommend faculty for consulting. By recommending our faculty on the basis of their competence—rather than on how we feel about them personally—and by spreading these opportunities around, you can help with faculty morale.

Work to develop positive relations with members of the community. If you can develop a special tie to the local community, this special relationship will enrich the lives of individual faculty members.

Treat all faculty members as professionals and with respect. You will find that you can have a positive influence on faculty morale if you treat all faculty members with respect and as professionals. Faculty members need to be told precisely what is expected of them and then left alone to do their jobs so long as they are fulfilling expectations.

No one likes to have another person looking over his or her shoulder, and if appropriate leadership is provided, most faculty members will not need excessive supervision. Generally, faculty members will work better and be more productive if they are treated as professionals.

Spread the work around. While it is tempting to assign work to those you know will do the job well and on time, doing so penalizes the good workers and rewards the slackers. Moreover, such behavior can create an unhealthy work environment that can produce low morale. Make certain that all faculty members know that you expect them to do their fair share of departmental work.

Avoid the unilateral contract. Partin (1991) asserts that the unilateral contract can be one of the most insidious causes of low faculty morale. He says that a unilateral contract is "an unwritten, unspoken agreement between two parties—only one of whom is aware of its existence" (Partin, 1991, p. 1). Most chairpersons have had to deal with this problem at one time or another. We've all had faculty members who will take on almost any assignment in the department. They are on virtually all department committees, they teach those night classes that must be covered, and they work hard at recruiting students. But they are not doing research or publishing: They are not doing those things that they must do to get promoted. When they are not promoted, they want to know why you have not lived up to your end of the bargain.

We must make certain that faculty members do those things that will increase their chances of getting promotions and tenure and that they do not spend an inordinate amount of time on other assignments. Counsel those who are not making appropriate progress toward promotion and tenure.

Work to create a supportive culture. A chairperson who listens to faculty and discusses their concerns without being judgmental goes far to create a supportive culture. Other supportive actions include finding funds for faculty travel, covering for faculty when they are ill, or taking an interest in their research projects.

Make a habit of meeting regularly with faculty members to see how they are, to find out what they need, or to listen to their concerns. Faculty members like to talk about their work, and it boosts morale for the chairperson to say occasionally, "Tell me how your classes are going."

Do what you can to provide an environment and structure that adequately satisfies the human needs of your faculty and encourages new ideas, risk-taking, and creativity. It should be an exciting, reinforcing environment that encourages faculty members to engage in professional activities and meet new challenges.

Tolerate differences. A university ought to be a place where ideas are challenged. Faculty members should be encouraged to voice their disagreement with ideas advanced by other department faculty members. They should be reminded that debate is invigorating and healthy. Likewise, they should be reminded that while professional differences of opinion are to be expected, the differences should not be carried over into their personal lives.

Faculty members, for the most part, love their jobs, but they are worried. "The rewards for their jobs are eroding; their autonomy to define their work priorities is under attack; and they do not see the current leadership or system of governance capable of protecting their personal and professional interests" (Johnsrud, 1996).

LOW-COST AND NO-COST BOOSTS TO FACULTY MORALE

You can do your part to enhance faculty morale by implementing low-cost and no-cost responses to faculty morale issues. Johnsrud (1996, pp. 118–120) recommends the following:

Leadership. The lack of confidence in the leadership of the institution is a major morale issue that demands a creative and sensitive response. Confidence in leadership can be enhanced with increased understanding of the pressures confronting campus leaders. The more faculty know and understand the goals, values, and priorities of senior administrators, the more they are likely to trust their leadership.

Reward and evaluation system. The anxiety expressed by all faculty regarding tenure and promotion is not unique to this campus but is an issue that contributes to alienation and frustration. Unclear and/or shifting expectations seem to be the primary source of the problem. The teaching, advising, and service load of faculty should be monitored. Departments should be required to support the efforts of faculty to meet tenure and promotion criteria by allocating workload appropriately.

Institutional support. Although salary is the most frequently cited economic need by all faculty, other forms of support or compensation also are needed. The equitable distribution of resources is vital to morale. Deans and chairs should be held responsible for ensuring that faculty at all ranks receive support and assistance.

Faculty governance/departmental relations. The primary locus of faculty governance is at the department level. Although faculty governance per se did not have a negative effect on faculty in this study, relations between the department and faculty were viewed as very important to morale.

Collegial relations. Positive relationships among colleagues contribute to positive morale. Senior administrators need to support efforts to build collegiality and maintain community. Deliberate steps can be taken to enhance the social and intellectual interaction within the departments and schools. For example, faculty colloquia designed to challenge thinking, invigorate participants, and improve the sense of academic collegiality can be fostered.

FACTORS THAT PRODUCE HIGH MORALE

Rice and Austin (1988) found four key features that produced high morale at ten liberal arts colleges. They discovered, first of all, that the colleges where high morale exists had distinctive organizational cultures that are carefully nurtured and built upon. They also found that those colleges have strong, participatory leadership that provides direction and purpose while conveying to faculty the empowering conviction that the college is theirs. Third, all of the colleges where high morale exists have a firm sense of organizational momentum. They were colleges "on the move." Finally, the faculty at the ten colleges studied have an unusually compelling identification with the institution that incorporates and extends the other three characteristics contributing to high morale.

Rice and Austin (1988, p. 58) list the following characteristics of high-morale colleges:

- High involvement of faculty in decision-making
- Environment that supports faculty and their work
- Collaborative environment
- Risk-taking encouraged
- New ideas likely to be tried
- Anticipatory long-range planning
- High proportion of faculty attended liberal arts colleges
- Narrow gap between perceived and desired involvement in decision-making
- Individual career orientations likely to be accommodated by the organization
- Administrators and faculty have similar views about the academic workplace

Morale can be a problem if you fail to respond quickly and fairly to faculty conflicts. Honest differences of professional opinion always exist, and when differing viewpoints are expressed with civility they can be healthy. Debate—

devoid of personal attack—causes faculty members to think and respond to ideas. You often can deal effectively with such problems by getting the involved faculty members together to talk about the problems and to see if differences can be resolved.

REFERENCES

Johnsrud, L. K. (1996). *Maintaining morale: A guide to assessing the morale of mid-level administrators and faculty.* Washington, DC: College and University Personnel Association.

Kerlin, S. P., & Dunlap, D. M. (1993, May/June). For richer, for poorer: Faculty morale in periods of austerity and retrenchment. *Journal of Higher Education,* 64 (3).

Partin, B. L. (1991, Fall). The unilateral contract: A faculty morale nightmare. *The Department Chair,* 2 (2).

Rice, R. E., & Austin, A. E. (1988, March/April). High faculty morale. *Change,* 20 (2).

Rosner, F. (1997, May). Post-tenure review: Accountability in Texas. *Academic Leader,* 13 (5), 3.

Understanding the Americans with Disabilities Act

It is no longer merely an act of compassion to help disabled students; we are required by law to assist them.

Colleges and universities that are recipients of federal funds have been required to make their programs, services, and facilities accessible to disabled individuals since the passage of the Rehabilitation Act of 1973. Section 504 of the Act states: "No otherwise qualified handicapped individual in the United States . . . shall, solely by reason of his handicap, be excluded from the participation in, be denied the benefits of, or be subjected to discrimination under any program or activity receiving Federal financial assistance."

The Americans with Disabilities Act (ADA) has become law, reinforcing the mandate of section 504 and expanding it to all institutions of higher education, regardless of whether they receive federal financial assistance.

In this chapter we will examine how ADA affects your role as the chief administrator of an academic unit, with particular emphasis on the implications of ADA on hiring faculty and staff members and on the academic programs within your department. We'll also look at what faculty members must know about the law as they deal with those students covered by ADA. It is no longer merely an act of compassion to help disabled students; we are required by law to assist them.

WHAT IS ADA?

First, it is important to understand who is protected by the ADA. According to the law, every person is covered who either has, used to have, or is treated as having a physical or mental disability. The law protects any person with a "physical or mental impairment" that "substantially limits one or more major life activity." This definition includes people:

- with mobility impairments, such as those who suffer from paralysis or use wheelchairs, crutches, or walkers
- who have lost one or more limbs
- who are blind or have vision impairments
- who are deaf or hearing impaired
- who have mental or psychological disorders, including mental retardation, emotional and mental illness, and learning disabilities
- with any number of different psychological disorders, including depression and post-traumatic stress syndrome
- with cosmetic disfigurements, such as burn victims
- with serious contagious and noncontagious diseases, including AIDS, AIDS-related complex, epilepsy, cancer, and tuberculosis
- who have suffered from drug addiction in the past (people currently using illegal drugs are not protected)
- suffering from alcoholism (but they can be required to conform to the same standards as others)
- with learning disabilities if the learning disability "substantially limits one or more" of the major life activities of the student. The ADA specifies that the ability to learn is a major life activity. Each student's disability must be viewed as unique and handled on a case-by-case basis.

The following conditions are not covered:

- Eye color, hair color, height, weight (except in unusual circumstances where obesity is the result of a medical condition)
- hearing loss, arthritis, and Alzheimer's disease associated with advanced age
- temporary impairments or illnesses
- minor impairments that do not limit a major life activity
- pregnancy

Further, it is important to recognize that if you consider a person to be disabled, the ADA applies and protects him or her even if that person does not meet the statutory definition. This would include, for example, an individual who has an impairment that the employer erroneously perceives is substantially limiting; or an individual with an impairment that is only substantially limiting because of the attitudes of others (e.g., an employer that discriminates against a burn victim because of potentially negative reactions of others; or an individual with no impairment who is erroneously regarded as having an impairment). The inclusion of coverage for persons regarded as disabled means that if an employer rejects an applicant because he or she has a physical or mental condition, this may be enough to bring the person within the definition of disability.

IMPLICATIONS OF ADA IN HIRING AND SUPERVISING

You cannot discriminate in hiring, review, promotion, demotion, discharge, or other aspects of employment against any applicant or employee with a disability, on the basis of the person's disability, if the person is qualified and able to perform the "essential functions" of the job with "reasonable accommodations."

The rules against nondiscrimination require providing all disabled employees with equal or equivalent access to all benefits of the employment, in an integrated setting, that would be available to a similarly situated employee, unless doing so would be an "undue hardship." This could include the use of cafeterias, employee lounges or smoking areas, company cars, drinking fountains, and bathrooms.

Employers can discriminate if there is a "substantial probability" that a person's disability would pose a "significant risk" to the health and safety of others. This decision cannot be based on assumptions, stereotypes, or past experience.

Employers cannot refuse to hire someone simply because it might cause workers' compensation or health insurance rates to increase, and in most cases cannot refuse to provide at least some insurance to disabled employees if insurance is provided to other employees.

Employers may set minimum qualifications for applicants or employees where the qualifications have a legitimate relationship to the job in question and the qualifications relate to essential functions of the job.

If you have any questions regarding the effects of ADA on hiring or supervising faculty and staff, you should contact your university's ADA compliance office, a position required by law.

IMPLICATION OF ADA ON ACADEMIC PROGRAMS

The ADA does not seek to change your fundamental methods of ensuring a sound education and successful completion of an academic program. Instead, it is designed to ensure that students with disabilities have equal access to your academic programs and can successfully complete their studies. It is very important that your university clearly identify the essential requirements of the educational program. The ADA does not require us to "take any action that would result in a fundamental alteration in the nature of a service, program, or activity, or in undue financial and administrative burdens."

Although the ADA strongly emphasizes physical access, there is an equally important aspect of nondiscrimination for academic access. People with disabilities must meet the same criteria of admission as the nondisabled. However, once they have decided to pursue a certain study, students with disabilities are entitled, under both section 504 and the ADA, to reasonable accommodations, placement in the most integrated setting feasible, and enjoyment of all campus activities to the extent appropriate. It is important to remember that just because a student claims a disability, it does not follow that he or she is disabled, and that you must therefore make accommodations. Those with learning disabilities, for example, must be able to document that they qualify to be covered under ADA. If faculty members have any doubts regarding a student's claim, they ought to contact the office of disabled services. Indeed, it is probably not wise to make accommodations for students claiming to have learning disabilities until they are verified by the appropriate campus official. Faculty rarely have the expertise to be able to make a determination on the matter, and it is better left to those who are experienced in making such evaluations.

Here are some of the accommodations you may have to make for students covered under ADA:

- providing more time to take tests
- providing special equipment; e.g., if a student with a disability is taking a course requiring the use of a computer, you may have to provide adaptive equipment to overcome a barrier. If the student is blind, you may have to equip the computer with a Braille keyboard and a voice response system.
- giving different kinds of assignments. For example, if you require an oral presentation, you may have to substitute another kind of assignment for the student with a speech impairment.

- modifying academic requirements. An example of this might be providing an alternative to replace the required foreign language requirement for students who are hearing impaired or who have auditory processing problems. Some schools will permit students to take American Sign Language in the place of a foreign language.
- providing special services. Students with auditory processing problems may need help with notetaking in those courses where concise and accurate notetaking is required. Some universities use student volunteers or work-study students as in-class interpreters. If you do this, however, you must ensure that these students are qualified sign language interpreters.
- providing additional instruction time. A student who is learning disabled may need more instructional time than other students. Again, student volunteers or work-study students may be able to provide this.
- modifying class attendance requirement. While establishing a maximum number of classes that can be missed before a student receives a failing or lowered grade is reasonable for the majority of the students in a class, it may not be for some individuals with disabilities. Some students may require bed rest or hospitalization during a semester, and others may be unable to use normal transportation routes in inclement weather.
- giving information in your class syllabi regarding what services are available on campus for those students who are disabled. Furthermore, it would be a good idea to list the campus disability issues coordinator and ask that students with disabilities make contact with that individual. Here is a sample statement: "If you have a disability that may require assistance or accommodation, or you have questions related to any accommodations for testing, notetakers, readers, etc., please speak with me as soon as possible. Students may also contact the office of disabled services (telephone number) with questions about such services."

One of your responsibilities is to see that students covered under ADA are provided the appropriate accommodations in accordance with the Americans with Disabilities Act. Faculty members need to know what the law requires of them. Ignorance of the law does not excuse them. Having worked with a large number of faculty members over the years, I have found some faculty members to be inflexible and unwilling to make special accommodations to assist disabled students until I have convinced them they are required by law to make certain arrangements. I suggest you set aside one faculty meeting each

TABLE 13.1 Appropriate Language When Referring to Those with Disabilities

Avoid	Preferred Usage
handicapped	A person with a disability
A blind person	A person who is blind
A deaf person	A person who is deaf
Mute	A person without speech
Retard, feebleminded	A person with mental retardation
Birth defect	A congenital disability
Confined to a wheelchair	A person who uses a wheelchair
Crazy, insane	Mental/emotional disability

year to review that portion of ADA that pertains to classroom teaching. This would be a good time to discuss appropriate ways of communicating with certain disabled students. For example, when speaking to a person in a wheelchair, we should speak to the person at eye level. When dealing with a hearing-impaired student, ask in writing what method of communication works best. Speak clearly and look directly at the person, not at an interpreter. Also, always speak directly to a visually impaired person and not to any companion. If the person lip-reads, speak in a normal, unexaggerated manner, and use short sentences. You are likely to be asked to repeat yourself. Be patient. Good lighting is important, and you should make sure that there are no physical barriers between you and the person with whom you are speaking.

Just as there are ways of communicating, we should become sensitive to the appropriate language to use when referring to those with disabilities. Table 13.1 provides some examples of appropriate language. Likewise, Table 13.2 shows some words we should avoid using because of their negative connotations.

TABLE 13.2 Words to Avoid

Abnormal	Defective	Lame	Stricken
Afflicted	Deformed	Maimed	Sufferer
Confined	Imbecile	Palsied	Victim
Crippled	Invalid	Retard	Withered

We quickly recognize those students and faculty who are physically disabled, but it is much harder for us to identify those who have learning disabilities. Moreover, we tend to have less sympathy and understanding for those with learning disabilities, believing that many are just using this as an excuse. What do we mean by learning disabled? Who are they? Stupka and Eddy (1995, p. 6) offer the following definitions:

- A permanent disorder that affects the way in which individuals with normal or above-average intelligence take in, retain, and express information. Like a fuzzy TV picture, incoming or outgoing information may become scrambled as it travels between the eye, ear, or skin, and the brain.
- Commonly recognized in learning disabled adults as problems in one or more of the following areas:

  reading comprehension
  spelling
  written expression
  math computation
  problem solving

  Less frequent are problems in organizational skills, time management, and social skills. Many learning disabled adults may also have language-based and/or perceptual problems.
- Often inconsistent. It may present problems on Mondays, but not on Tuesdays. It may cause problems throughout grade school but disappear during high school and resurface again in college. It may manifest itself in one specific academic area, such as math.
- Frustrating. Persons with learning disabilities often deal not only with functional limitations, but also with the frustration of having to prove that their invisible disabilities may be as handicapping as paraplegia.
- A learning difference. A learning difference is not a form of mental retardation or emotional disorder.

Disabled students can grow and learn, and with your help they have a chance of becoming productive citizens who feel good about themselves. Once you have seen them go on to jobs where they are valued employees, you and your faculty—like the disabled student—will feel good about the role you played in providing ADA-covered students with a chance to get a quality education.

REFERENCES

ADA compliance guide. (1993). Washington, DC: Thompson Publishing Group, Inc.

Duston, R. L., Russell, K. S., & Kerr, L. E. (1992). *ADA compliance manual for higher education: A guide to Title I.* Washington, DC: Schmeltzer, Aptaker, & Shepard, P.C.

Runyan, M. K., & Smith, J. F., Jr. (1991, September/December). Identifying and accommodating learning disabled law school students. *Journal of Legal Education,* 43, 3 & 4.

Staff. (1991, July 26). Rules and regulations. *Federal Register,* 56, 144.

Stupka, E., & Eddy, B. (1995, December). Learning disabled student strategies. *Recruitment & Retention in Higher Education,* 9 (12), 6.

14

Total Quality Management in Higher Education

Once students have tasted the job of learning in an educational institution which runs according to quality management principles, they will not accept something inferior.

—Myron Tribus

In higher education circles, many educators have taken the concepts of total quality management seriously, while other have scoffed at it, claiming it's a fad that works well for companies like Ford Motors but is not well suited to academe.

While many chairpersons have already looked into total quality management and have formed an opinion, many probably have not. This chapter will give a brief overview of total quality management and attempt to illustrate its usefulness.

W. Edwards Deming is generally considered to be the father of total quality management (TQM). He failed to find a receptive audience when he first began discussing his ideas in this country after World War II. The Japanese invited him to their country to see if his ideas had any applicability to their industrial rebuilding, and they were very enthusiastic about what he had to say. They adopted TQM concepts, and some assert it was the beginning of their spectacular rise as one of the world's dominant manufacturers. They got a big start on American manufacturers in implementing TQM, and Americans are still playing catch-up to the Japanese in several industrial areas. Many people think first of the automobile industry when they think of Japanese production quality, but it doesn't stop there. They advanced rapidly in electronics as well with TQM concepts.

DEMING'S 14 POINTS ON TOTAL QUALITY MANAGEMENT

Deming outlined his beliefs by listing 14 points for managing quality and productivity (Deming, 1986). While Deming focused chiefly on the manufacturing sector, many believe his ideas apply to education as well.

1) Create constancy of purpose for improvement of product and service, with the aim of becoming competitive and staying in business, and to provide jobs.
2) Adopt the new philosophy. We are in a new economic age. Western management must awaken to the challenge, learn its responsibilities, and take on leadership for change.
3) Cease dependence on inspection to achieve quality. Eliminate the need for inspection on a mass basis by building quality into the product in the first place.
4) End the practice of awarding business on the basis of price alone. Move toward a single supplier for any one item on the basis of a long-term relationship of loyalty and trust. Minimize total cost by working with a single supplier.
5) Improve constantly and forever every process for planning, production, and service; to improve quality and productivity; and thus constantly to decrease costs.
6) Institute training on the job.
7) Adopt and institute leadership. The aim of supervision should be to help people and machines and gadgets do a better job. Supervision of management is in need of an overhaul, as is supervision of production workers.
8) Drive out fear, so that everyone can work effectively for the company.
9) Break down barriers between departments. People in research, design, sales, and production must work as a team to foresee problems of production and others that may be encountered with the product or service.
10) Eliminate slogans, exhortations, and targets for the workforce that ask for zero defects or new levels of productivity. Such exhortations only create adversarial relationships, since the bulk of the causes of low

quality and productivity belong to the system and thus lie beyond the power of the workforce.

11) a. Eliminate work standards (quotas) on the factory floor. Substitute leadership.
    b. Eliminate management by objectives. Eliminate management by numbers, and numerical goals. Substitute leadership.
12) a. Remove barriers that rob the hourly worker of his or her right to pride in workmanship. The responsibility of supervisors must be changed from sheer numbers to quality.
    b. Remove barriers that rob people in management and engineering of their right to pride in workmanship. This means abolishing the annual or merit rating and management by objective.
13) Institute a vigorous program of education and self-improvement.
14) Put everybody in the company to work to accomplish the transformation. The transformation is everybody's job.

How are these points applicable to education? Is it possible to use Deming's ideas in higher education—in and out of the classroom? Let's examine these questions.

First, I think we all concede that in virtually all endeavors—higher education included—there is always room for improvement. Thus, if we can use some of Deming's ideas to improve what we do, we certainly should embrace them. Many who have adopted TQM concepts say they would not turn back to previous practices. As Myron Tribus (1992) said, "I must close with a warning. Once people have learned to walk, they will not return to crawling. Once students have tasted the job of learning in an educational institution which runs according to quality management principles, they will not accept something inferior."

We must think of TQM as a set of guiding principles rather than rigid rules. It is first and foremost a compass used by people continuously striving to follow the path leading to success.

APPLYING DEMING'S 14 POINTS TO HIGHER EDUCATION

The following analysis is an adapted version of information that appeared in Cornesky's *The Quality Professor* (1993), which shows Deming's 14 points applied to higher education.

Point 1: Create a Constancy of Purpose

Many departments have poorly defined, confusing objectives. Their mission statements are obscurely written or generally meaningless. The task for your department is to produce a mission statement that clearly defines its objectives. The statement and departmental objectives should be reviewed regularly.

Point 2: Adopt the New Philosophy

After agreement on a mission statement and departmental objectives has been reached, all must accept and support them. Commit yourself to quality. Make it central.

Point 3: Cease Dependence on Inspection

I think this is particularly valuable for higher education. If we build quality into our educational processes, then we can depend less and less on inspection. Frankly, if we inspect at the "end of the line," it's too late anyway. If we discover at the end of a term that some students have not learned or improved their skills, then it's too late to attempt adjustments.

Point 4: End the Practice of Awarding Business on the Basis of Price Alone

Those who work for state colleges or universities surely must have perked up when seeing Deming's admonition about price-based decisions—that is what state governments generally require of most spending units. The results of this practice are often destructive. Obviously, we see how this is done in the classroom as well when we depend on the simple methods of teaching and testing.

Point 5: Improve Constantly and Forever

A department—no matter how strong—can be improved, and you must constantly seek ways to strengthen its weaknesses. You and your faculty need to seek ways to identify weaknesses and work together to find solutions. TQM embraces the idea of continuous quality improvement.

Point 6: Institute Training on the Job

Faculty members generally have had no experience with TQM. They will need training, as will students when TQM is introduced into the classroom. You will need to provide faculty and students with information about TQM if you choose to implement it and reap its benefits.

Point 7: Adopt and Institute Leadership

This should be an exciting point for those already in leadership roles. It will be necessary to look carefully at existing leadership practices to see if they're functioning productively. Moreover, other faculty members and students will have opportunities to step forward to develop and use their leadership skills. You can empower both faculty and students to become responsible for development and learning.

Point 8: Drive Out Fear

It is essential that you provide leadership that eliminates fear from the department and the classroom so that the faculty members and students can work and grow effectively. No one who fears for his or her job can be expected to take constructive risks, and without risks, innovations are difficult to achieve.

Point 9: Break Down Barriers Between Departments

If you've been a chairperson very long, you know that working associations with other departments on your campus are all too rare. Departments that actively work with other departments to identify problems, implement change, and improve quality are exceptions to usual practices. A new kind of thinking is required by the principles of TQM. We must act as if there are no departmental barriers to examine our institution to build and maintain quality.

Point 10: Eliminate Slogans and Exhortations

This is an area that I would dispute, because I believe that slogans can be effective tools for focusing on who we are and what we are about in higher education, though no one believes that a slogan or exhortation by itself will produce quality. Still, used in conjunction with other efforts, they may have their place.

Point 11: Eliminate Quotas and Numerical Goals and Substitute Leadership

Faculty members resent being evaluated only on the basis of how much they have published. They expect—rightfully, Deming would say—that quotas and numerical goals hinder quality more than any single working condition. We must be careful when pinning stars on faculty members who publish the most. We must introduce other factors—including collegiality—into evaluations.

Point 12: Remove Barriers that Rob Workers of Their Right to Pride

Faculty members should be given an opportunity to accomplish things in and out of the classroom that show they have talent. They need chances to develop pride. Praise should be forthcoming, for example, when a faculty member chairs a committee where much is accomplished. Let the faculty member know—both publicly and privately—that he or she has served well.

Point 13: Institute a Vigorous Program of Education and Self-Improvement

The chairperson who understands the concept of TQM will be aware of the need for continuing faculty growth and development. You must find a way to pay travel expenses for those who want to attend conferences and workshops. The "quality chairperson" will aggressively promote faculty development programs, released time, and other incentives.

Point 14: Involve Everyone in the Transformation to Quality

Students, staff, and faculty need to participate if TQM is to work. Ask each group what needs to be done in the department to bring about improvement. Faculty members need to plan ways to implement TQM in the classroom, just as you need to see its value for the department.

CROSBY'S 14 POINTS FOR QUALITY IMPROVEMENT

Philip Crosby was another pioneer in the field of total quality management. He also developed 14 points on total quality management (Crosby, 1984), which differ somewhat from Deming's.

1) Commitment from management
2) Quality improvement team
3) Measurement
4) Cost of quality
5) Quality awareness
6) Corrective action
7) Zero defects planning
8) Employee education
9) Zero defects day
10) Goal-setting
11) Error-cause removal
12) Recognition
13) Quality councils
14) Do it over again

Crosby's points for quality improvement also can be applied creatively to the academic sector, and we should take the best that TQM has to offer to assist in the strengthening of our department and its programs.

We should take advantage of TQM just as we use learning outcome assessments and other tools to identify and explore weaknesses. We owe that to our students. Indeed, if we learn nothing more than how we should be dealing with customers—and if we accept students as our customers—then we will find the idea of TQM worthwhile.

REFERENCES

Bogue, E. G., & Saunders, R. L. (1992). *The evidence for quality.* San Francisco, CA: Jossey-Bass.

Chaffee, E. E., & Sherr, L. A. (1992). *Transforming postsecondary education.* ASHE-ERIC Higher Education Report No. 3. Washington, DC: The George Washington University, School of Education and Human Development.

Cornesky, R. (1993). *The quality professor.* Madison, WI: Atwood.

Crosby, P. B. (1984). *Quality without tears.* New York, NY: McGraw-Hill.

Deming, W. E. (1986). *Out of the crisis.* Cambridge, MA: MIT Center for Advanced Engineering Study.

Seymour, D. T. (1992). *On Q: Causing quality in higher education.* New York, NY: ACE/Macmillan.

Tribus, M. (1992). *TQM in education.* Unpublished manuscript.

Yudof, M. G., & Busch-Vishniac, I. J. (1996, November/December). Total quality: Myth or management in universities? *Change,* 28 (6), 19–27.

Fundraising for the Department

Alumni interviews show overwhelmingly that the faculty is the key determinant in motivating alumni to provide financial support to their colleges.

If you are able to raise private funds to support the mission of your department, the quality of instruction can be enhanced greatly. Likewise, your reputation as an administrator will be viewed more favorably. Despite these incentives, few chairpersons engage in ongoing efforts to raise private funds. There are reasons for this, of course. First, almost none of us have any formal training in fundraising. We don't know how to go about it, and we feel uncomfortable asking for money. Second, it is a time-consuming effort, and we find ourselves putting it off to attack more pressing matters, especially those for which we are better trained or suited.

SOME BASIC CONCEPTS

Educators can be more successful fundraisers, especially if they keep in mind several basic concepts.

Show how giving money to your department is a good investment.

Many of us have come to believe that the best way to raise money is simply to demonstrate that we have a great need for it. That doesn't work anymore. Most of those who give money are tired of hearing organizations simply plead poverty. Instead, they want to know what your department can do to meet the needs of others. Donors want to invest their money, not merely give it away. They expect a return on their investment. You need to show how a gift will be invested and what returns it will produce.

Get to know potential donors.

You are not likely to be successful when potential donors know next to nothing about you and your department. Listen carefully to what they say and find out what they want—then make your approach accordingly.

Develop a strategic plan.

Design a plan for the department's future. What does future enrollment look like? If growth is expected, how will you handle it? If the number of students is expected to decline, what action will follow? How will curriculum offerings change in the years ahead? What new equipment will be needed? These and other questions need to be carefully thought through and spelled out so that you can share the information with those you are asking to support your program. If you can provide a quick summary of a plan as well as detailed information about what it will take to fulfill your vision, raising private funds will be easier.

Remember that academic enterprise and fundraising are linked.

The quality of classroom instruction is a factor in alumni giving. Weak programs are not likely to get much support, and strong alumni giving encourages private donations.

Alumni interviews show overwhelmingly that the faculty is the key determinant in motivating alumni to provide financial support to their colleges. When we earned our first degree, many of us left with the feeling that we owed a debt to the college. It was the closeness with faculty that fostered such a feeling. Indeed, many of us still keep in contact with former teachers and former students.

Here's a personal illustration of how others think about quality before giving. I became chairman of a weak, troubled department several years ago, and I was expected to turn it around. I remember very well meeting with a community leader who said he would help the department financially if I would improve the quality of instruction, raise standards for students, and get rid of some weak faculty members. I planned to do all these things anyway. I had to.

The community leader was true to his word. A few years later he came to me and asked how he could help. In the end, he endowed a distinguished chair. Interestingly, other giving also picked up. Our student scholarship fund grew exponentially over a five-year period.

Ask your alumni for support.

Before doing so, however, be sure to establish some kind of ongoing communication with your alumni. Your pleas for financial support will be largely ignored if you go to your alumni without first having some kind of regular communication with them. You will be surprised how interested and responsive many will be once you inform them about department activities and provide them with information on how they might invest in the department.

The easiest way to develop communication is to publish a regular alumni newsletter. A better way of developing a personal dialogue is to form a departmental alumni association. Your campus alumni director should be able to help with this. To get started, identify some local alumni who were active as students and who have maintained contacts with faculty members. Ask them to serve on a committee to get an alumni association started.

In the department I just made reference to, we established an alumni association, and its members were active and supportive and helped us to raise funds for the department. Indeed, through their own activities the association was able to raise between $15,000 and $20,000 each year. The effort that went into founding the association was richly rewarded.

Build bridges with the outside community.

It helps you get to know potential donors—individuals, foundations, and corporations. It means telling the outside community your vision for the department. It means becoming known in the community. It means attracting the attention of alumni and others who can make a difference in your department by supporting it financially.

This requires interpersonal skills. It helps, I think, to be excited about your department and to know virtually everything about it. Know your faculty and students.

Sponsor special fundraising events.

The nature of your program may dictate in part the kind of special fundraising events you can sponsor. "Roasting" one of your distinguished alumni has fundraising possibilities. Years ago a department I chaired worked with our alumni association to sponsor a roast. We were fortunate to have among our alumni an entertainer whom we asked to serve as master of ceremonies. He agreed. Thus, we had Soupy Sales at the top of our ticket, which gave us a huge boost when it came to promoting the event and selling tickets. We sold corporate table and individual tickets and raised $20,000 that we put into student scholarships.

Set aside time for fundraising.

One of the biggest obstacles you will face is that you don't seem to have time for fundraising. Most chairpersons I know—particularly those with large and complex departments—seem to have more to do than they can get done even without fundraising, which takes time. The best approach: Delegate, then support the persons or team you've named to the job.

One thing that can be discouraging, especially for the fundraising beginner, is that even if you devote a lot of time to fundraising, your efforts will not necessarily be successful. Even professional fundraisers have learned to accept rejection as a part of the process.

Get training in fundraising.

Another big obstacle is that most chairpersons are not trained as fundraisers: They don't know where to start, they are embarrassed to "beg," and they are quickly hurt by rejection. If you've not had any training, you could begin by reading some books on the subject, getting advice from development officers at your school, and attending some workshops on fundraising. Any training you get generally will pay off.

Listen to your faculty to get names of prospective givers.

Most departments have some faculty members who have been around a long time and who are well-connected in the community. They know who has money and who is likely to give. They know the individuals who have some ties to your department or those who could become friendly. Get them to help devise a strategy for cultivating these connections.

Obviously, there are others that you should seek out to help identify prospective donors. Take advantage of anyone who is willing to help.

Evaluate a gift carefully before accepting it.

You don't want to appear to be ungrateful, of course, but you need to know the terms of any gift. Will it be costly to administer? Could its "strings" cause problems?

Some years ago, one of my predecessors as department chairperson accepted a fairly small gift to be used for student scholarships. After I had become chairperson, we got a large oil painting of the person honored by the gift, and were asked by the family to display it in the department. We happily complied. Then we started getting family complaints because we were not getting widespread publicity whenever we awarded the scholarships. (The scholarships had not been large ones at the time of the gift, and because of inflation they now were insignificant when compared with most of the scholarships we awarded.) We tried to explain to the family that we were grateful, and we did the best we could to get publicity. Our explanation was unsatisfactory, and the family removed the gift and gave it to another department on campus. It was one of those gifts that probably should never have been accepted. The donors should have been steered to the development office.

Consider the appropriateness of a gift.

Would you, for example, accept money to endow a chair in the name of someone with a particularly troubling reputation? The person giving the money probably is going to expect publicity. You know, of course, that the publicity will come at great expense if the person is widely mistrusted or disliked.

Use the gift in the way it was intended.

You have a special responsibility to keep your word to those who are generous and kind enough to give to your department. If the money is earmarked for faculty development, you have an obligation to use it solely for that purpose. Whoever follows you as chairperson must know that promises were made and that they must be kept. You will need to keep good records of the gift and its terms.

Use your public relations office to help with the publicity whenever you get a gift.

Unless the donor wishes to be anonymous, he or she will expect some kind of announcement to be made about the gift. Obviously, the bigger the gift, the more publicity is expected. Your university's public relations staff will know what to do to get publicity that will please the donor.

Always thank the donor, no matter the size of the contribution.

A well-composed letter of thanks is sufficient in many instances. A plaque or a certificate can clearly demonstrate appreciation. Whatever you do, it is important that you let the donor know how much you appreciate his or her generosity.

Coordinate your fundraising activities with your dean and the development office.

It is essential that those charged with the primary task of raising funds at your university—the development office personnel—know and approve of what you are doing. Unless all fundraising is well-coordinated, it can become chaotic and unsuccessful. If the development office personnel, for example, are working closely with a potential donor on a large gift, they will not want you approaching that person for the time being. Moreover, it may be that if your dean and development office know what your plans are, they can give you some assistance.

Develop a case statement that summarizes the fundraising program to be implemented.

Here you need to spell out and document your needs. Tell who will benefit, how the gift can be made, and what the benefits of giving are. Explain in some detail why a potential donor should give to your department rather than to others in need. Tell why your department exists, and describe your mission statement.

In times of fiscal restraint, when budgets are becoming tighter and tighter, you are likely to be expected to turn to the private sector for partial support. As already noted, fundraising takes skill, time, and persistence, and not everyone can do it. If you are fortunate to have some success, probably you will be back another day to try for still more funds. Your department will be well served by your efforts.

Developing Outcome Assessment Programs

Assessment can be an important tool to assist the department in becoming stronger and more effective.

Institutions of higher education in America have been closely scrutinized by all different sorts of publics in recent years, and many have aggressively questioned their effectiveness. As a result, more politicians and governing bodies are demanding evidence of excellence and accountability. Thus, the increased interest in assessment.

Most departments have had some kind of assessment program in place for years, though it may be informal. This chapter describes ways to develop formal outcome assessment programs.

If an outcome assessment program is to succeed, strong leadership and support are required. You must be positive and supportive in order to convince faculty that assessment is not a threat and to get them involved in the process. Assessment has many academically beneficial results, and the time and effort spent to develop and administer the program will not be wasted.

Effective communication is as critical to the success of outcome assessment programs, as leadership is. Make certain that all faculty know the meaning, purpose, and uses of assessment. Be prepared to answer faculty questions about the need for assessment. Of course, in some instances such questions are moot because outcome assessment programs are required by the governing board. Beyond that, however, you need to point out that assessment is an important tool that will assist the department's effectiveness in producing the desired educational outcomes of its graduates.

DEVELOPING DESIRED EDUCATIONAL OUTCOMES

One of the first steps in developing an assessment program is to specify desired educational outcomes. They include the knowledge, skills, values, attitudes, and behaviors that graduates are expected to possess as a result of having earned a degree. These should be determined by the faculty.

In many instances, these goals are already outlined elsewhere—in your catalog or in promotional material. If you've been through accreditation, you are likely to have some statement on file to help you get started.

After identifying educational outcomes, you must then select assessment methods. For the purposes of illustration, let's identify several educational outcome targets and then select assessment methods for each. Let's assume your department is Business Administration.

The American Assembly of Collegiate Schools of Business (AACSB) has broad curriculum-related outcomes as a part of its accreditation standards. The Atlanta Board of Regents (1992) published a manual that included this statement regarding educational outcomes:

> Students graduating from the School of Business Administration will be prepared for imaginative and responsible citizenship and leadership roles in business and society—domestic and worldwide. All business graduates will demonstrate competency in a common body of knowledge including the following areas:
>
> 1) A background of the concepts, processes, and institutions in the production and marketing of goods and/or services and the financing of the business enterprise or other forms of organization
> 2) A background of the economic and legal environment as it pertains to profit and/or nonprofit organizations along with ethical considerations and social and political influences as they affect organizations
> 3) A basic understanding of the concepts and applications of accounting, quantitative methods, and management information systems including computer applications
> 4) A study of organization theory, behavior, and interpersonal (oral and written) communications

5) A study of administrative processes under conditions of uncertainty including integrated analysis and policy determination at the overall management level
6) Students must also demonstrate competence within their specific major area of study

DEVELOPING AND ADMINISTERING ASSESSMENT METHODS

Measuring learning outcomes can be done in many ways. You may want to see what other schools in your area are doing. Likewise, you may want to explore what standardized tests are available to assist with the measurement, provided you are thinking about using tests.

Here are some general assessment methods you will want to consider:

Capstone course. This method is used quite widely. Essentially it covers the range of major area subject matter. Coursework, tests, and projects are designed to elicit demonstrations of student proficiency in business knowledge and skills. It provides a good opportunity for assessing student competence attained through major area coursework.

Entrance and exit examinations. By administering both of these examinations, a determination of so-called "value added" can be made. Entrance examinations are obviously not intended to measure achievement at your institution, but they are essential for establishing the baseline of academic competency from which your accomplishments can be judged.

Survey of employers. One valuable way of assessing what students got out of the business administration program is to survey those who have employed your students. Faculty members should analyze the results to determine strengths and weaknesses of the program.

Portfolio review. Students can be required to assemble portfolios that contain examples of their work—papers they've written, projects completed, etc. Students should be told of this requirement at the beginning of their studies, and they should be reminded from time to time of the necessity of keeping their work and preparing a portfolio. Some schools collect portfolios and file them in the name of each student major in the program. Student portfolios have gained increasing acceptance as a means of evaluating both general knowledge and learning in the major field of study.

Survey of students. Graduates of your program should be surveyed on a fairly regular basis—perhaps every five years—to determine their satisfaction with their studies in your department. Also, you can ask them to evaluate the strengths and weaknesses of the program itself. Figure 15.1 is an example of such a survey that you may want to use once every five years. The purpose of such a survey is to determine how graduates feel they are using their training and how each course has contributed to the overall education of those who have earned degrees from the department.

Exit interviews. Many schools rely on exit interviews to assess programs. Graduating students are asked a series of questions regarding the overall quality of education provided.

Licensure examinations. Various disciplines have used licensure examinations for some time, and they are among the best end-of-program assessment procedures.

Do not rely on just one of these methods. Multiple methods should be used to assess each learning outcome. Regardless of the methods, they must provide ways to diagnose program weaknesses and strengths. That way faculty members can determine specific ways to improve the program's quality.

I encourage you to seek some advice from someone on campus who is a specialist in testing and measurement. You must make certain that your evaluation methods are valid and reliable.

Faculty members should be assigned assessment responsibilities. Have one faculty member take responsibility for each assessment method, and remind them that they must maintain the confidentiality of student data.

In explaining what assessment can do for the department, it is good to remind faculty members that you will be able to adopt better and more specific program outcomes, gain support from the administration for their program initiatives, and learn about their collective teaching effectiveness. Once faculty members see that these benefits are achievable, they will likely take more interest in working to refine and improve the program.

Faculty members need to know that there are other ways of assessing learning outcomes. A good faculty discussion should produce ideas beyond

FIGURE 16.1 Alumni Survey

Please help us determine how well the courses and activities of the department are meeting their objectives. Complete the survey and return it in the enclosed postage-paid envelope. Your assistance will be very much appreciated. Thank you.

Name:____

Address:____

Occupation:____

Year of graduation from City University:__________

EVALUATION OF COURSES OFFERED BY THE DEPARTMENT

Rank each of the following courses according to their value to you. For example, if you took Ancient History and found it to be the course most helpful to you, give it a ranking of 1. If you found the History of Medicine to be the least helpful of the 10 history courses you took at City University, rank it 10.

____The Great Civilizations to 1300

____The World & the Rise of the West

____History of Medicine

____English History to 1642

____Ancient History

____War in Modern Times

____Women in the United States

____Latin America: Independence to the Present

____India & Southeast Asia: Modern

____History of Black America Since 1885

____Modern Europe Since 1815

____American History to 1877

____American Colonial History

____American Labor History

____China & the Western World, 1500–1900

____Methodology

____ The Twentieth Century World

____ History of Modern Science

____ The American Military Experience

____ English History since 1642

____ European History, Medieval

____ The Rise & Fall of Nazi Germany

____ Latin America: Discovery of Independence

____American Social, Cultural, & Intellectual History, 1607 to Present

____History of Black America to 1885

____European History, 1492–1815

____ Religion in America

____ American History Since 1877

____ American Legal History

____ American Business History

____ China and the 20th Century

____ American Social, Cultural, & Intellectual History, 1865 to Present

(continue listing all courses)

Rate the quality of each of the following in your academic program of study.
1 = Poor, 4 = Excellent.

	Poor	Fair	Good	Excellent
1. Overall quality of faculty	1	2	3	4
2. Availability of my adviser	1	2	3	4
3. Willingness of my adviser to help	1	2	3	4
4. Fairness of grading in my courses	1	2	3	4
5. Quality of instruction in my courses	1	2	3	4
6. Opportunities for interaction with faculty	1	2	3	4
7. Intellectual climate of the department	1	2	3	4

If you participated in any of the activities listed below, please evaluate them by circling the appropriate number.

History Honorary:	No Value	1	2	3	4	5	Outstanding
National History Day:	No Value	1	2	3	4	5	Outstanding
Moffat Lectures:	No Value	1	2	3	4	5	Outstanding

In the space below, please provide a frank evaluation of the value you attach to the education you received in the Department of History.

We appreciate the time you took to complete this questionnaire, and we hope you will return it without delay. Thank you.

those mentioned in this chapter. The benefit of having faculty members talk about different approaches to measurement methods should be evident: If they develop their own approaches as a group, more are likely to buy into the concept and view the program as their own.

Assessment is not a panacea. It won't solve many of your problems, but it has tremendous value in its own right. If it assists in strengthening the department, everyone wins and all will feel a sense of accomplishment.

Finally, while many departments have not yet put together assessment programs, the time will come soon when most—if not all—will have mandates to do so. As resources become tighter, legislators and governing bodies will insist on more accountability. The strong department that can objectively demonstrate its strengths is likely to be at the top of the list of those departments receiving funds.

REFERENCES

Atlanta Board of Regents. (1992). *A resource manual for the University System of Georgia.* Atlanta, GA: Board of Regents, Office of Research and Planning.

Communicating

We all need to be reminded from time to time that communication is a two-way process.

Your effectiveness as a chairperson will be judged in part on how well you communicate. Faculty members want leaders who will impart information regarding all matters that affect them. They want leaders who can communicate their needs to university officials and other publics. Indeed, most position announcements for chairpersons list among the desired qualifications the ability to communicate effectively.

What does it mean to be an effective communicator? It means many things, but foremost in the context of administrative leadership, it means providing various publics with information about your department. Effective communication with your faculty means providing comprehensive information on the operation of the department. It means telling how departmental funds are allocated and spent, and being open and candid about decisions and actions. It also means communicating about policy changes, and providing anything else needed to facilitate the carrying out of individual responsibilities.

In addition, you also have responsibility for communicating with students of your department, alumni, and the general public.

COMMUNICATING WITH FACULTY

Faculty Meetings

Schedule faculty meetings on a regular basis, at least one a month. Special meetings can be called as needed. Prepare and distribute in advance a formal agenda so that faculty members know what to expect. Also let them know how to get items on the agenda. Faculty members complain about attending too many meetings, but they will be less likely to complain about a departmental faculty meeting if agenda items merit discussion and time is not wasted.

It is your job to chair the faculty meeting. Follow these basic guidelines:

1) Make certain the meeting starts on time.
2) Allocate appropriate time for the discussion of all items.
3) Bring the discussion to a halt when all sides of an issue have been discussed adequately.
4) Make certain that issues that can be resolved are.
5) Show appropriate leadership by suggesting how certain issues can be handled.
6) Bring the meeting to a close when all business has been transacted.
7) Provide the faculty with written, minimal meeting procedures that guarantee each person's right to speak on all deliberative issues and allow for orderly, timely decision-making.

Memoranda

You will need to communicate some matters to the faculty between faculty meetings. A short memo can accomplish this if a written message is important. While I dislike contributing to the never-ending stack of bureaucratic memoranda, from time-to-time putting things in writing is a necessity. If you don't write, you will find that some faculty members will claim they did not know about a deadline or an assignment. All important matters of agreement between one person and another should be written. Written communication reduces the chances of misunderstanding.

Email

Email is an effective way to communicate with faculty and other administrators. It also can be used to communicate with alumni and fellow professionals around the country. It has many advantages that are particularly easy to recognize: communicating instantaneously at a relatively low cost and freeing up clerical personnel for duties other than typing, for example. It does, however, have drawbacks unless certain guidelines are followed.

Limit the number of email messages to nearby colleagues. If we are not careful how we use email, it can greatly reduce the contact we have with our colleagues, and professional interaction is healthy for lots of reasons—for faculty and for the department. There is a tendency to shoot off a quick email to a nearby colleague in order to save time, when a face-to-face meeting or telephone call might be more appropriate. Words—no matter how colorful or how well crafted—are often quite sterile when they appear on a screen or a written page, especially when compared to the same spoken words. The nonverbal language we introduce in face-to-face meetings helps us communicate and brings us in contact with our colleagues. Body language and voice intonation can add much to what we are trying to communicate.

Email messages ought not to be used for reprimands. It would be terribly insensitive to send an email reprimanding a faculty or staff member. If you are unhappy with the performance of any individual you supervise, you owe it to that person to meet face-to-face to discuss the matter. Indeed, sensitive information of any kind should be delivered face-to-face.

Hard copies are essential for certain kinds of communication. I use letterhead stationery when writing letters of thanks or congratulations to faculty and staff. They are more personal, and copies go in their personnel files. Likewise, I have taken to writing more short personal notes to try to make up for the impersonal email communications. As hard as we might try, an email message is not terribly personal.

I am personally taken with the Internet and how we can use it to improve communication, but it is not a panacea to effective communication. It is a tool to help us, but it won't solve all of our problems. If your campus is not wired or if all your faculty are not on-line, this means of communication cannot be fully exploited.

Face-to-Face Meetings

Face-to-face meetings with faculty members are needed occasionally. Indeed, they can help build positive relationships and are generally the most effective method of communication. Set aside time to spend with individual faculty members even if there is no important business to discuss.

While face-to-face meetings often do not result in concrete progress toward achieving goals, their importance should not be underestimated. They can do much to improve faculty morale and give faculty members a sense that you care about them as individuals.

Voice Mail Messages

Telephone systems at many universities provide a convenient way to pass information to your faculty. Systems such as "Audix" have the advantages of cutting paperwork and getting information to faculty members instantly. Keep a file copy of your Audix messages so that you have a record for future reference.

These systems enable you to send messages to one person or several hundred, and they can be sent immediately or at a specified time. Also, you can relay to others any messages you receive.

Formal Publications

Some departments publish formal newsletters two to three times each semester. With technology now available, producing professional-looking newsletters is a fairly easy task. Newsletters should be distributed to campus leaders as well as to members of the faculty. (See the appendix for sources of newsletters.)

Harold C. Shaver, director of the W. Page Pitt School of Journalism and Mass Communications at Marshall University, publishes the *Monday Morning Memo* each week for the faculty and staff in his department. It is an efficient way of providing information. I've stolen his idea and developed an email version of his *Monday Morning Memo* that goes to all our faculty in the College of Mass Communication at Middle Tennessee State University. I've received positive feedback, including a comment from one faculty member who said that it was a unifying force for the college. I don't know whether or not that's true, but it does provide a convenient way for me to get out lots of information to our faculty.

We all need to be reminded from time to time that communication is a two-way process. It is just as important to hear what faculty members say and think as it is to inform them. Faculty members need opportunities to respond about departmental and personal matters. They can provide valuable input, and they resent not having opportunities to give their ideas on policy matters. I have heard more complaints about too few department faculty meetings than about too many.

Communicating with Alumni

An alumni newsletter is a valuable way to keep alumni informed about department activities. Moreover, it is a good way to let them know what their former classmates are doing. One of the most popular sections of any alumni newsletter is news about the alumni accomplishments. The appendix lists sources of departmental alumni newsletters.

Letters also can be sent to alumni. They can go out to all alumni of your department, or selective mailings can be made. There are times when a newsletter will not be as personal as desired. A call for donations to a scholarship fund, for example, is likely to get more response if individual letters are sent out.

There also are times when communication with alumni needs to be even more personal. A telephone call or a private meeting may be necessary at certain times.

Communicating with Students

Pamphlets, brochures, catalogs, calendars, and fliers are all used to get information to students. One word of caution: Written documents provide terms of a contract unless a disclaimer in each piece warns that there is no contract implied in the publication.

When you need to get information to students on short notice, posted fliers plus announcements by faculty members in classes is probably the most effective method.

If you publish student information that pertains to graduation requirements or policies affecting scheduling of courses, make certain that the same information is provided to all faculty members who have the responsibility for student advising.

Bulletin boards that are maintained with care can do much to provide students with information. Bulletin boards need attention, however. Those that are multilayered and are full of outdated announcements are for all practical purposes useless.

Communicating with the General Public

Find out on a regularly basis what newsworthy events or activities your faculty and students are involved in, and provide that information to your office of university relations so that news releases can be prepared. Appointing a faculty or staff member to be responsible for gathering information and getting it to the office of university relations is worth considering.

Here are some other steps you can take to improve efforts to reach the general public through the news media:

- Encourage your faculty to think and look for potential news stories within the department.
- Encourage your faculty to think about the human elements of story ideas.
- Give your university relations office a list of trade publications that are potential news outlets for activities of your department.
- Get to know those who work in the university relations office, and have one of its professionals attend a faculty meeting to discuss ways that his or her office can help get stories placed.
- Encourage your faculty to accommodate the needs of the university relations office staff and news reporters and to be available to provide assistance when asked.

Working with the News Media

Some people in higher education seem to be naturals at working with the news media, while others find it stressful and altogether unsatisfying and unrewarding. With a little study and effort, however, most of us can learn how to work effectively with news media personnel whom we encounter. Learning how reporters and editors work will help you do a better job. Even understanding some very basic principles of news writing and news gathering can help you to become more successful in getting your message to the general public. Several years ago, for example, a chairperson said to me, "I don't understand what's happening, but every time I write a story and give it to the newspaper, the most important part of the story is missing when it's printed." During the course of our conversation, it became clear that he was burying what he thought was the most important part of the story deep into whatever he wrote. I suggested he put the most important elements of the story at the very beginning. His response was, "Gee, I hadn't thought of that." News reporters and news editors always have that on their minds.

Think visually. Editors like to use good, strong pictures with stories if pictures are available. You can help them do their job by suggesting picture ideas or making pictures available if you have them.

Don't duck reporters. Although you would prefer that only good news from your department gets into the news, it is not always realistic to expect that. You need to be available to answer a reporter's questions, even if you don't like the questions. Be honest and forthright.

Do not allow yourself to be caught off guard. If we respond to questions when we are caught off guard, we risk giving unthoughtful—or heaven help us, stupid—answers that can be embarrassing to us personally and to our department. If a reporter calls to talk to you, ask what he or she wants to talk about and then tell him or her that you will call right back. This will give you time to decide how you might answer questions on the topic. You may even want to write out some answers before you return the reporter's call. Whatever you do, don't fail to return the call.

Be concise with any answers to questions. Don't say anything that you would not want to see in print or hear on radio or television. Even though I have had experience as a reporter myself, I learned the hard way that "off the record" is not respected by all reporters. I remember being disappointed when I viewed a television story for which I was interviewed because the real point I wanted to make was left on the cutting room floor.

I had been invited to give the keynote speech at a conference that had lots of public appeal, and when I was interviewed by local television I was too full of myself for my own good. As a young, inexperienced academic, I assumed that the television station would run the whole five or six minutes of the interview. It doesn't happen that way, of course, and the one point I would have like aired was edited out. I should have spoken only to that point.

You probably know that reporters are not likely to let you see the story they write before it is printed. Don't even ask. However, that doesn't mean that you have to give up all control after you've been interviewed for a story. If I don't know the reporter, I am very cautious, and I am likely to say things like, "I am not sure that I am making myself clear. Would you mind reading that back to me?"

Here are additional practical suggestions for dealing with reporters:

- Make sure to get the name of the reporter and his or her publication or broadcast station.
- Don't hesitate to refer the reporter to someone else if you are asked questions that are out of your area of expertise.
- Be cautious about answering hypothetical questions.
- Watch out for silence. A good reporter knows that most of us are uncomfortable with silence, and he or she can sometimes get people to talk about things they don't want to by asking a question and then keeping silent.

- Be cautious about being drawn into controversy. You will need to be alert to reporters' questions designed to get a comment from you regarding some ongoing campus feud.

Communicating with Your Dean

It is important that you keep your dean informed about important departmental matters. Obviously, you can use all the forms of communication that you use to communicate with your faculty. In addition, it is important to provide progress reports to your dean from time to time—at the end of the academic year, for example. John McDaniel, Dean of the College of Liberal Arts at Middle Tennessee State University, puts together a progress report for his provost and others (see appendix). It is a good summary of what all of the faculty members in his college have accomplished during the academic year.

If you publish a departmental newsletter, make certain that your dean and other university administrators are on the mailing list. Above all else, it is important that you sit down with your dean from time to time to discuss what's happening in your department, and to let him or her know your concerns.

The Role of Communication in Improving Morale

Studies of faculty morale show that many faculty members lack confidence in the leadership of the institution, and that can cause a major morale issue. The same studies show, however, that faculty members have the most confidence in their chairpersons. "These findings suggest that faculty feel more trust for those they know better and presumably communicate with more frequently. This finding may serve to alert senior administrators to the need for increased communication and interaction with all members of the campus community" (Johnsrud, 1996, p. 118). Increasing the level and quality of communication is a forceful vehicle for improving faculty morale. Another finding on the study of faculty morale that is important for department chairpersons to know about is that "Relations existing between the chair and faculty members and within the department as a whole are crucial to the morale of faculty" (Johnsrud, 1996, p. 120).

> One of the primary roles of the department chair should be to build and nurture a positive collegial climate in the department for all faculty. To accomplish this objective, the selection of chairs should be

> monitored carefully and ongoing training instituted. Training should include attention to issues of professional work climate, professional development and academic support, evaluation, sexual harassment, and affirmative action. Department chairs should also be trained to recognize and confront inappropriate conduct. Chairs are in key positions to recognize and eliminate discrimination at the department level (Johnsrud, 1996, p. 120).

Certainly, you need to have strong communication skills to be an effective chairperson, and improving interpersonal, supervisory, and public communication skills is a lifelong undertaking. Thus, the successful chairperson participates regularly in communication workshops designed to improve his or her interpersonal, supervisory, and presentational communication skills. Rewards follow those who do.

Effective communication is essential for all who hold leadership positions. Good leaders find ways to reach their students, faculty, alumni, and the general public. They use many tools to get their message out, and they listen to what others have to say. They view communicating as a dynamic process that is universally important.

REFERENCES

Johnsrud, L. K. (1996). *Maintaining morale: A guide to assessing the morale of mid-level administrators and faculty.* Washington, DC: College and University Personnel Association.

Managing Change

Futurists believe that we must act decisively and transformatively to create Information Age universities.

Change can be a seductive, exhilarating activity for those who like it, but it can produce a great deal of anxiety for those who don't. It can threaten their security and should be avoided at all costs. As Machiavelli said, "There is nothing more difficult to take in hand, more perilous to conduct or uncertain in its success, than to lead in the introduction of a new order of things."

REASONS FOR RESISTING CHANGE

Why do people resist change? Gibson and Hodgetts (1991, p. 333) list the following reasons:

A vested interest in the status quo. Many employees feel that they have it made under the existing system. They have carved out their own little empires and shielded themselves from problems they do not want to confront. A change in the status quo affects their safe haven.

Fear of the unknown. Most people are uncomfortable when they lack specific information about people and processes that affect them. Most want to be in control of their own destinies; the unknown is intolerable.

Fear of increased responsibility. Many employees are already working ten hours a day and taking work home with them in the evening. They may resist or even undermine organizational change because they are convinced that change will mean additional responsibility and more work.

Low propensity for risk. Most people are willing to assume a small amount of risk but unwilling to take on a great deal. When changes are introduced, many resist because they feel the risk associated with them is too great.

Economic losses. Some employees perceive change as threatening to their jobs or the jobs of colleagues. Unions are especially alert to this kind of change. These fears are not totally unjustified, as some technological advancements have indeed brought about workforce reductions.

Resistance to technology. Technology has caused much employee concern in recent times, and employee anxiety will likely accelerate during the coming years. Faced with new high-tech methods and processes, employees are apt to feel unable to keep up.

Habit. Once something becomes second nature, it is often sanctified as the "right way to do things." Habits are hard to break.

Tradition. Tradition is closely linked to habit. However, although habits are personal, tradition is often passed along from one individual to another, and in organizational settings it is synonymous with corporate culture. It is the way that everyone in the firm has always done things, and it is expected that employees should continue to follow these guidelines. Many people feel honor bound to do so. In this case, change is resisted because it strikes at the heart of the organization's perceived values. When you can, avoid making change that will upset tradition. Making changes where traditions are involved requires sensitivity. Let me illustrate:

I joined a faculty as department chair, succeeding a gentleman who had held the position for 44 years. He was a legend who was worshipped by many friends and acquaintances. His renown actually didn't bother me in the least, but one young faculty member thought that having this gentleman's picture displayed prominently in our offices was a put-down to me. He thereupon took it on himself to rearrange things; one night he moved the picture to a room across the hall without getting anyone's approval.

When I arrived the next morning, all hell had broken loose. Secretaries and former faculty members were crying and angry. They were arguing bitterly with the man who had moved the picture. I ordered the picture returned to its original place and had a frank talk with the faculty member; I explained that it was not up to him to make such changes and that I was in no way offended by honors given the founder of our department.

Of course, there are times when tradition must be thrown out in favor of a new way of doing something, but we cannot ignore people's reactions to the loss of a tradition. Bolman and Deal (1991) write about what they call the rites of mourning. "From a symbolic perspective, transition rituals must accompany significant organizational change. In the military, for example, the change of command ceremony is formally scripted. A wake is held for the outgoing commander, and the torch is passed publicly to the new commander in full ceremony. After a period of time the old commander's face or name is displayed in a picture or plaque on the wall of the unit" (Bolman & Deal, 1991, p. 391).

The point of these transition rituals is that it gives employees an opportunity to bid farewell to the past so that they can get on with the future.

THE CHANGES AHEAD

Alvin and Heidi Tofler (1994) discuss the matter of massive change facing humankind in the coming decades. They also point out resistance to the change. "A new civilization is emerging in our lives, and blind men everywhere are trying to suppress it. This new civilization brings with it new family styles, changed ways of working, loving, and living, a new economy, new political conflicts, and beyond all this an altered consciousness as well" (Tofler, 1994, p. 19).

The Toflers, who also gave us *Future Shock,* describe the changes facing humanity as "the deepest social upheaval and creative restructuring of all time" (Tofler, 1994, p. 9).

Munitz (1995, p. 9) says that "Radical changes are occurring that will alter fundamentally the nature of the university as we have known it for nearly a century."

If indeed we are facing the kinds of changes that many futurists predict, then those of us in higher education face turbulent times. Our workplace will undergo remarkable changes. Among the changes we can already see developing are:

- The use of technology for teaching is increasing.
- Distance learning is becoming more common.

- Formal education occupies a greater amount of time in our lives. People engage in formal education well beyond the years it takes to earn a couple of degrees.
- Traditional methods of teaching, particularly the lecture method, are waning. More and more teaching is being done on computers.
- There is increased emphasis on active learning experiences for students.
- Many faculty members give classroom assignments that are to be submitted electronically.
- International activity is increasing at most colleges and universities.
- There will likely be a net loss of full-time faculty and an increase in the number of part-time teaching appointments.
- More students hold jobs during the school year. The most recent figures show that at least 40% of current students hold jobs while attending school.
- Colleges and universities continually face financial problems.

While these changes are significant, they pale when compared with the changes that higher education will face in the coming years. The challenges for those of us in higher education are staggering as we move farther into the Information Age. What has worked for us in the past will not necessarily prove helpful for us in the future. Moreover, most futurists believe that we will be dealing with increasing numbers of students. They believe that if individuals are going to remain in the workforce, they will need to earn the equivalent of 30 credit hours every seven years. About one-seventh of the workforce, which is estimated to be about 141 million by the year 2000, will need to be enrolled full time. This could equal over 20 million FTE learners from the workforce. "Using our existing education model, these learners would require an additional 672 campuses with an enrollment of 30,000 students each" (Dolence & Norris, 1995, p. 7).

Futurists believe that we must act decisively and transformatively to create Information Age universities. As Dolence and Norris (1995, p. 87) point out, "Campus leadership must find ways to stimulate discussion, debate, and dialogue on the need for a transformative vision." They also state that department chairpersons will be among the most important leaders who "have the insight and vision to lead and stimulate a far-reaching campus dialogue on the emerging Information Age university. These leaders will serve as systems architects, teachers, and challengers of the status quo. Campuses with this sort of leadership will flourish" (Dolence & Norris, 1995, p. 87). Finally, they point out that our choice is clear: "Accept the risks of pursuing the transformation of higher education to an Information Age model, or the certainty of stagnation and decline as Industrial Age colleges and universities fall farther and farther from favor" (Dolence & Norris, 1995, p. 94).

If universities are going to survive and prosper in these times, then risk-taking must be a controlling factor in university management. Gilliland (1997, p. 32) points out, "Private sector experience suggests that the human resources practices that promote success in an environment of rapid change, complexity, and unpredictability support at least three values: flexibility, access to information by people at all levels, and risk-taking."

It seems clear that if departments—or colleges and universities, for that matter—are to survive, they must change. Furthermore, it will not be the kind of change we've experienced in the past. Instead, it must be dramatic, and the academic department will be the fulcrum of change. The decisions and actions you take in the coming years will make a difference in how well your department is positioned to foster transformation. The decisions will likely determine whether your department will be able to take advantage of transformation activities five and ten years in the future.

Here are some things you can do to move your department forward:

- Begin using the Internet for undergraduate education.
- Provide faculty members with released time to study changes that are taking place. You must raise everyone's knowledge base.
- Encourage strategic thinking.
- Accept the idea that in these times a missed opportunity can be as lethal as a mistake.
- Accept the idea that the current educational model is insufficient to meet the needs of learners in the coming millennium.
- Exercise true leadership in shaping the debate and helping the campus build a new set of shared values regarding learning in the Information Age.
- Encourage and support innovation in learning.

As a chairperson you must do all you can to counsel and inform those who resist change. In today's environment there is no choice but to change, and it helps if you understand the causes underlying a faculty member's resistance to it. Alan E. Guskin, Chancellor of the Antioch University System, says universities now face the most significant challenge in 40 years, that of coping with the effects of high operating expenses combined with high tuition and/or taxes. He says that we must make "radical changes in how we organize our administrative structures and educate students" (Guskin, 1994, p. 33). Tinkering around the edges will not do the job, Guskin says. "Significant restructuring is in order, which should include changing the curriculum, calendar, assessment procedures, and cutting of up to 33% in administrative services and the size of the faculty" (Guskin, 1994, p. 33).

It seems clear that in the coming decades we will be teaching much differently. Undoubtedly we will be taking advantage of new technology. Guskin makes the point that we will be working with greater numbers of students but will teach less. "Students will spend more time learning by themselves and with their peers and much more time engaged with powerful, interactive technologies. . . . [They'll spend less actual time] but more creative, intensive, and focused time with faculty members" (Guskin, 1994, p. 33). This will enhance student learning, he predicts.

We need to remember that change is not a linear process. In her book, *Transforming Higher Education,* Madeleine F. Green observes: "It [change] stops and starts, goes sideways, shifts emphasis, and loses intensity and momentum. Not only is its path uneven, but the role of leadership is not necessarily clear at the time" (Green, 1997).

I have worked with faculty members who thrive on producing change, and such people undoubtedly will embrace new ideas without rancor. Still, as publishing consultant Sandroff points out, "Almost everyone feels afraid when they're asked to change. It's what you do with the fear that counts" (Sandroff, 1993, p. 54). Those who deal positively with this fear are constantly on the lookout for something they believe needs changing; they are energized by being a part of initiating change.

I also have worked with faculty members who will go to extreme lengths to get out of change's way. Once years ago, a colleague went out and got drunk on hearing that the chairperson had taken another job. None of us saw her for days. She couldn't accept the idea that there was going to be a change.

Faculty members react to change differently, but with practice, they can get better at it. Gerald Kraines, President of Levinson Institute, recommends that managers hone their change skills in the following areas:

Information. Managers often are immune from the stress of change and so are frequently preoccupied and neglect to share facts with subordinates. But even when the message people hear is painful to them, they're more comforted by facts than by general reassurances. If you don't know what's going to happen or have been told some things are confidential, tell people that.

Identification. Part of the reason that people join an organization in the first place is the wish to attach to something larger and more powerful than themselves. Major change can make it feel risky to trust or identify too much with the company, so people will often pull back and identify with their individual leaders.

Values. Values help steady people under stress and lead them to feel good about themselves. When an organization changes, people wonder if its values will change too. They need leaders who can explain the unchanging values that the organization and work unit stand for and also why certain other values need to change.

Mourning. Since all change is a loss and must be mourned, leaders who show their sadness allow subordinates to show theirs. This will help relieve feelings that could undermine future aggressive efforts (Kraines, 1992, p. 3).

You will face resistance nearly every time you try to make a change, no matter how insignificant it is. Unfortunately, this resistance generally is not minimized even when plans are carefully thought out and presented. But the department that resists change risks its future; maintaining the status quo in higher education is not an option.

Not only is change inevitable, it often is massive. If we recognize and accept the proposition that we must change, then we have an opportunity to manage it. Faculty members must understand that change is society's only constant.

STRATEGIES FOR DEALING WITH FACULTY RESISTANCE TO CHANGE

Ease-in Changes

Select plans that require the least drastic change in order to solve a problem. A physician doesn't perform major surgery to alleviate a mild headache. Likewise, before we set out to change something we ought to determine what, why, and how it should be changed. If minor changes will produce the desired results, then we ought to make only minor alterations.

Make the change temporary. Announce that the proposed change is being presented on a trial basis, and that it will become permanent only if it succeeds.

Consider the Timing

There are times when hiring a new person to implement change is easier than gaining cooperation from those who are opposed to any kind of change. Obviously this is not always possible, so you may have to postpone change until a foot-dragging faculty member retires.

I've actually had the experience of waiting for a certain person to retire. In that instance, most faculty members in a department wanted to move their program to another department. Virtually everyone agreed it would be a smart move. However, one long-time, influential faculty member opposed the move and began lobbying other faculty members and calling in past favors to convince her colleagues to join her in resisting the move. As it turned out, she was retiring at the end of the academic year. I simply put the matter on the shelf until she had retired, and then we made the move with no opposition. And as it turned out, it was a change that benefited virtually all involved. Certainly, everyone was happy with it.

Plan Carefully

Before implementing any kind of change, plan carefully to avoid possible chaos and minimize disruption. When change is not carefully planned, it can produce upheaval, which in turn causes stress. Because adapting to change of any kind requires psychic energy and is therefore tiring, it is important to reduce other draining variables that are caused by poor planning.

Communicate

As mentioned throughout this book, good communication is key to the success of a department chairperson. When change is the subject, it takes on even greater importance. Part of your plan for change should be your communication strategy.

Choose your words carefully when announcing change. It perhaps seems a bit obtuse, but sometimes we can get support for change by not talking about it as change. We can talk about faculty development, self-renewal, etc., all of which are code words for change. As Robert Eaker, Dean of the College of Education at Middle Tennessee State University, says (with tongue in cheek): "I am all in favor of improvement; it's just the change I'm against."

Let the faculty know what's happening. Regular communication prior to the introduction of the change helps alleviate anxiety. Moreover, you need to continue communicating during and after the change. Faculty members want to be informed, and their imaginations sometimes run wild when they don't hear from you. This is especially true of those who oppose change.

In his book, *Managing Transitions,* Bridges underscores the importance of regular communication. "To make a new beginning, people need The Four P's: the purpose, a picture, the plan, and a part to play. For any particular individual, one or sometimes two of these P's will predominate. . . . So it is important to remember to cover all four of these bases when you talk about the new beginning you want to help people make" (Bridges, 1991, p. 52).

Present options. Rather than announcing that specific changes will be implemented, it is often effective to tell faculty members that changes must be made and then to list optional plans that would correct a certain problem. They can then help choose which option would be best.

Be open and honest. The faculty members should know exactly what the change will mean. Explain it and then urge them to be equally forthright with you.

Explain the consequences of not changing something. If the curriculum is outdated and competing schools have updated theirs, most faculty members will see the need for making changes. If enrollment drops off significantly, the reasons for this must be examined and changes devised. If faculty members know that funding will fall off sharply because the department is producing fewer student credit hours, they usually understand that change is in order, if told about the problem.

Anticipate Opposition

There are people who simply cannot be convinced that any kind of change should be made. They will do whatever they can to sabotage efforts, especially when the change affects them. You must recognize this and learn to work around such individuals. One way is to get enough support to make the change and then institute it, which means those who are balking will have to accept it. Of course, don't expect this to be done willingly. You may have to have a straightforward talk with faculty members who defy change. And by all means, talk it over; don't avoid discussions simply because they might be unpleasant.

Meet individually with those who are likely to oppose change. Find out what their fears and concerns are. Sometimes fears are imagined and come about because of lack of information. Meeting and explaining what the change involves and the necessity for it may help to alleviate concerns. A faculty member's first reaction to change is to contemplate how it will affect him or her in terms of salary, work assignment, or promotion. You should let faculty members know that their jobs or the status of their jobs are not in jeopardy (when, of course, that's true).

Try convincing recalcitrant faculty members that they're movers and shakers. I've occasionally gone to faculty members whom I knew to be fearful of change and persuaded them that they were the movers and shakers of the department who could convince others that changes were needed. I would meet individually with them and say something like, "John, I know good ideas excite you just as they do me. I think we need to make some departmental changes to accommodate some ideas. Let me explain." I then proceeded to lay out plans and concluded by saying, "John, can you help me convince our colleagues that we must make this change? I really need your help."

You would be surprised how often this works.

Send resistant faculty members to workshops or conferences. Sometimes those who oppose change can be brought around if they learn something about the program to be implemented. Suppose, for example, that you know you are going to be expected to develop and administer an outcomes assessment program. If you know your faculty well enough, you will know who may be opposed to the program.

Look around to see if there are any workshops or conferences on the topic. If there are, send one or more department members to the conference. Obviously, if funds are limited, you would be well advised to spend money on the one who is likely to be the most vocally opposed to the change.

After the conference, have the faculty member(s) tell what they learned about assessment programs. Have them talk about how to get them started, how to identify learning outcomes, and how to develop methods for measuring them.

Treat the faculty member's concern with dignity. If you put down or ridicule the faculty member because of his or her concerns, you will deepen the resistance. Try to understand how and why resisting faculty members feel as they do.

Use peer pressure. Occasionally, obstinate faculty members can be pressured by their peers into accepting change. This is especially true when they have close friends in the department who favor the change. If that is the case, it is wise to talk to those who support the change and ask that they talk to those who are likely to be against it.

Use outside consultants to recommend change. I have on occasion invited outside consultants to campus to help convince the faculty that certain changes were needed. In each case, I knew the consultant and knew what he or she would recommend. The consultants had exceptional credentials and the resistant faculty members found that they couldn't get very far arguing with experts. With their arguments shredded, they acquiesced.

Demonstrate Leadership

Introducing and implementing change requires the strongest leadership skills. It is not a task for the weak of heart, but the rewards of active leadership are tremendous.

Be decisive, and create an atmosphere of entrepreneurship. In his book, *Lincoln on Leadership,* Phillips writes, "Genuine leaders, such as Abraham Lincoln, are not only instruments of change, they are catalysts *for* change" (Phillips, 1992, p. 137). He points out that Lincoln quickly took charge and "effected the change needed by being extraordinarily decisive and creating an atmosphere of entrepreneurship that fostered innovative techniques. In doing so, he not only got things moving, he also gained commitment from a wide array of individuals who were excited at the prospects of seeing their ideas implemented. He adopted a 'more than one way to skin a cat' attitude and would not be consumed with methodology. . . . Lincoln's obsessive quest for results tended to create a climate for risk taking and innovation. Inevitably there were failures, but Lincoln had great tolerance for failure because he knew that if his generals were not making mistakes they were not moving" (Phillips, 1992, p. 137).

In his annual message to Congress in 1862, Lincoln said, "Still the question recurs 'can we do better?' The dogmas of the quiet past are inadequate to the stormy present. The occasion is piled high with difficulty, and we must rise with the occasion. As our case is new, *so we must think anew and act anew.*"

A study of other great world leaders would undoubtedly reveal that they were, or are, both instruments *of* change and catalysts *for* change.

Get faculty members involved. Create a task force to study and recommend a course of action. If most members of the task force are the kind of faculty members who support change, they normally prevail even when others oppose a recommended change. Faculty members who are involved in studying the need for change generally will lend their support to seeing that the change works. They have a stake in the new program or activity.

Apply a range of leadership strategies. In his book, *Leadership,* James MacGregor Burns points out that "a number of strategies have been developed to overcome resistance to change: coercive strategies, normative strategies (achieving compliance by invoking values that have been internalized); utilitarian strategies (control over allocation and deprivation of rewards and punishment), empirical-rational strategies (rational justification for change), power-coercive strategies (application of moral, economic, and political resources to achieve change), and reeducative strategies (exerting influence through feeling and thought)" (Burns, 1978, p. 417).

Burns goes on to point out that a common thread running through all the strategies is their difficulty, which is something we've already emphasized. You must bring about change, no matter how difficult the job becomes.

Bolman and Deal present an example of the need for the rites of mourning in the case of a group of physicians in a large medical center who changed from a privately held to a publicly held practice. They explain the problem of morale associated with the change. For nearly a year after the change, nurses and staff noted a significant change in the physicians. Their morale deteriorated, their behavior became more erratic, and they seemed to be impossible to work with. At a management retreat, a senior orthopedic surgeon responded to the wholesale criticisms of physicians. Through a voice choked with tears, he said, "None of you have any idea what we are going through." His remarks brought the real issue to the attention of everyone—especially the physicians themselves.

A retreat was arranged for all 200 physicians. The key event of the two days was a dinner featuring skits, songs, and poetry. Many of the physicians who were most upset about the change were featured in the program. The interplay of sadness and satire recognized the transition, and let the physicians express their loss and move on as employees, rather than owners, of their practice" (Bolman & Deal, 1991, p. 392).

We must remind ourselves from time to time that not all change is good. Certainly deterioration can be a mark of change. We must court the kind of change that will enrich and strengthen our programs.

Sadly, in some instances catastrophes are required to produce change. Some companies have gone bankrupt before being convinced that changes were necessary. Likewise, explosive forces are often required to bring about substantial changes in individual beliefs, attitudes, customs, or procedures once they have become hardened (Gardner, 1981). You must provide the leadership that produces change before it's too late.

Persuading others to support change will be a continuing challenge. It will require your most persuasive talents—and a good store of patience. Despite the problems that come with making changes, as a leader you must accept this challenge. Use the brightest faculty members you have to assist you in planning for change. See what other universities are doing and how any related change has worked for them.

On the positive side, change often brings about a new vitality; it often energizes even the foot-dragging faculty members. You will feel good when you see once-reluctant professors speaking proudly about what we are now doing. Let them feel good; don't say "I told you so." Then when you must make further changes, you can remind them of past successes.

Lay the Proper Foundation

A final word on effecting and managing change. Take the time to lay the proper foundation for change, and while you should not procrastinate about making changes, you should also take steps to ensure that certain conditions prevail. Higgerson (1992, p. 19) cites the following conditions as conducive to change:

- The department mission is understood and accepted.
- The department has mutually accepted goals.
- The department goals are perceived as being compatible with the goals of individual faculty.
- Members of the department have mutual respect for each other.
- Department issues are discussed in an atmosphere of open communication.
- Differences of opinion are aired constructively.
- Good morale exists among the faculty, staff, and students.

Higgerson (1992, p. 18) also cites conditions that will impede change:

- The department has no sense of community or identity.
- Faculty possess a high degree of self-orientation.
- Little or no trust exists among colleagues.
- Communication regarding department issues is closed.
- Differences are aired destructively.
- Low morale exists among faculty, staff, and students.

Change can create a mood of excitement in the department. It can give new life to a lifeless one. Moreover, with the right kind of leadership, change can set a department on a new course toward excellence. Students for years to come will be the beneficiaries.

REFERENCES

Bensimon, E. M., Neumann, A., & Birnbaum, R. (1989). *Making sense of administrative leadership.* Washington, DC: The George Washington University.

Bolman, L. G., & Deal, T. E. (1991). *Reframing organizations.* San Francisco, CA: Jossey-Bass.

Bridges, W. (1991). *Managing transitions.* Reading, MA: Addison-Wesley.

Burns, J. M. (1978). *Leadership.* New York, NY: Harper & Row.

Dolence, M. G., & Norris, D. M. (1995). *Transforming higher education.* Ann Arbor, MI: Society for College and University Planning.

Gardner, J. W. (1981). *Self-renewal.* New York, NY: W. W. Norton.

Gibson, J. W., & Hodgetts, R. M. (1991). *Organization communication.* New York, NY: HarperCollins.

Gilliland, M.W. (1997, May/June). Organizational change and tenure. *Change,* 29 (3).

Green, M. (1997). *Transforming higher education: Views from leaders around the world.* Phoenix, AZ: ACE/Oryx.

Guskin, A. E. (1994, July/August). Reducing student costs and enhancing student learning. *Change,* 26 (4).

Guskin, A. E. (1994, September/October). Reducing student costs and enhancing student learning. *Change,* 26 (5).

Higgerson, M. L. (1992, Fall). Department chair as change agent. *The Department Chair: A Newsletter for Academic Administrators,* 3 (2).

Kraines, G. (1992, April 6). Coping with change. *Administrator,* 11 (7), 3.

Lipton, E. (1996, September 22). New vs. old dominion: Some cling to a VMI way that others say is past. *The Washington Post,* A9.

Machiavelli, N. (1968). *The prince.* Amsterdam: Teatrum Orbis Terrarum.

Munitz, B. (1995, Fall). Wanted: New leadership for higher education. *Planning for Higher Education,* 24, 9.

Phillips, D. T. (1992). *Lincoln on leadership: Executive strategies for tough times.* New York, NY: Warner.

Sandroff, R. (1993, July). The psychology of change. *Working Woman,* 8 (7), 52-56.

Tofler, A., & Tofler, H. (1994). *Creating a new civilization.* Atlanta, GA: Turner.

19

Time-Saving Tips for Effective Chairpersons

If you are asked to do something that does not contribute to your goals, you need to learn how to decline.

To be effective, you must be well organized and use your time wisely. Although I have read books and been to conferences and workshops designed to help me save time and to become better organized, only a few of the ideas I picked up could be incorporated into my way of doing things. Finally, I sat down and tried to determine what I could do, considering my own personality, to use time more wisely. A number of things occurred to me, and I now use them effectively enough to feel comfortable passing them on to you. If they don't work for you, you might come up with your own list—as I did. Moreover, you will discover as I did that computers and other time-saving devices won't change your bad habits, but they can add efficiency to your normal routine.

Make a "To Do" list every day, and follow it.

Perhaps your memory is better than mine, but I find myself forgetting to do something unless it's written down. And when I put something on my "To Do" list, it gets done. "To Do" list pads are available, but I've found that I can easily prepare my own. In times past I have made up sheets and duplicated them, while at other times I am satisfied with merely typing "Things To Do" at the top of a page and then listing those things that I need to get done.

Establish goals.

If you set both short- and long-term goals, you almost always will have something to do. After your desk is cleared and you've finished with the projects on your "To Do" list, you can set out to fulfill your goals. Establishing goals will help give your life direction.

Handle all paper as few times as possible.

Once is ideal. Until I adopted this as a part of my behavior, I tended to keep stacks of paper that I went through several times a day. I bet I handled some pieces of paper 20 times or more. I have found that when I open mail, I immediately take care of those that require very little of me. I put into an "Action" folder those messages that are going to require more time to handle.

Hemphill (1997, p. 26) has developed a paper management system that I find workable. She says that every piece of paper can be managed effectively by putting the piece of paper or the information on it ". . . into one of seven places: 1) 'To sort' tray, 2) Wastebasket, 3) Calendar, 4) 'To do' list, 5) Rolodex/phone book, 6) Action file, 7) Reference file."

Keep a log of how you use your time.

Do you ever wonder where all your time goes? By logging how you use your time, you can see where it has gone and how you've wasted it. By studying how you use your time over a period of a few weeks, you can find ways to better manage it. Table 19.1 shows an example of a work log you could use.

TABLE 19.1 Work Log

Date	Name	Task	Interruptions	Phone Calls	Due	Completed

Keep your desk organized.

Most of those who work in the field of time management recommend that we keep our desks organized to help us save and manage time.

Delegate responsibility.

In the beginning I found it difficult to delegate responsibility. For some reason I felt that I had to do everything. I suspect it was my own insecurity that caused me to be that way, but I had to learn to give work to others.

I had not been on my current job very long when I learned that I was spending 20 to 30 minutes a day on an activity that could be delegated, so I transferred responsibility for it to a colleague. He appreciated my trust in him; I valued the extra time it gave me each day. Make yourself turn some chores loose. Give up some of the minor projects even if you can't bring yourself to let loose of others. You will soon find that you have associates who can be trusted to do things well and on time.

Train your support staff to help you save time.

A very simple example of this is to insist that those answering the telephone for you get callers' telephone numbers so that you can call them back. It is not unusual for me to have a half dozen or more calls to return when I have been out of the office for an hour. If I have to look up every number before returning the calls, I am wasting my time.

I am sure there are many other such examples. Your support staff should understand that time is important, and they should do all they can to help you save it.

Buy and use time-saving devices.

There are many new tools that help us use time more effectively. The computer is one. The pocket tape recorder is another. I carry one in my book bag, which I use to take papers back and forth from home to office. When I am in the car I talk into the tape recorder—to remind myself of something that needs to be done, preserve ideas, or dictate a memorandum.

Although some of these devices are quite sophisticated, most are user friendly. For example, the *Memo Manager* is a digital voice recorder with a four-page graphic LCD screen that visually displays every message for easy retrieval. And then, of course, many light but powerful laptop computers are available. You must match your personality and work habits with the devices, however; otherwise they become nothing more than expensive gadgets that take up space.

I have just begun using *Day-Timer Organizer 2.0* on my computer. It has a lot of time-saving features. For example, when making telephone calls, you can dial from your on-screen address book. It features a "To Do" list, calendars, a note section, a way to keep track of your expenses, and other assorted desk organizers.

Develop a tickler system.

Devise some way of systematically reminding yourself of something that you need to do.

My system is very simple. It requires 31 index guides (one for each day of the month), an index file box, and some cards.

Using this card system is simple. If you have a project that must be completed by January 15, for example, fill out an index card with that information on it and place the card behind the index guide number 15. Each day you or your secretary will need to check the card behind the index guide for that day. With good input, there is no reason for you to ever miss a deadline.

Use pocket or desk organizers.

A number of my colleagues use organizers such as *Day-Timer, Day Runner, At-A-Glance,* or *Filofax.* Though I have tried them, none has proved particularly useful for me. On the other hand, I know many who swear by them and would never be without one.

Use available software programs.

There are many of these on the market and they are constantly changing. For example, *Now Up-to-Date* is a personal organizer that maintains your schedule, reminds you of upcoming events, manages your to-do list, and keeps associates up-to-date. It has on-screen reminders that warn you in advance of important appointments or deadlines.

Other software programs are available that have nothing to do with planning and organizing but may still save you time. For example, if you must evaluate faculty and/or staff people on a regular basis, Employee Appraiser assists effectively.

My favorite software program that helps me with keeping organized is *First Things First*. It has a screen where I enter tasks, projects, or appointments, and a picture of a desk file holder with a red flashing arrow appears on my computer screen whenever I need to be reminded that I must take care of something. Moreover, *First Things First* allows me to prioritize the items I enter by assigning them a priority number from one to four, with Priority 1 being the most important. Then, there are several ways that I can select for being reminded. For example, if I wish to be reminded in advance—say a week or ten days before a deadline—I can enter that, and if an entry is something that recurs, the reminder will also recur. Investigate which programs are available that may be useful for your needs.

Learn to be straightforward with others.

At first glance, this reminder may seem inappropriate for this chapter, but I feel that it is apt. Playing games with others is time consuming.

I used to work with an administrator who would always resist any request, but then would always give in. One had to argue with him for 15 minutes when making any proposal. It was a game with him—but it was my time that was being wasted. (Of course he also was wasting his time, but it would have been a waste of time for me to worry about that!)

Learn to say no.

If you are asked to do something that does not contribute to your goals, you need to learn how to decline. Chairpersons have many demands on their time. If they are going to be effective leaders, they must learn to say no when asked to take on assignments or attend events. We must learn to be very protective of whatever time we have. Giving time to others is noble but can rob us of time we need to do our jobs.

Learn speed reading.

If you are a slow reader, you know how handicapped you are. One of the most helpful courses I ever took as an undergraduate student was a speed reading and vocabulary development course. Because I read quite fast I can get through a lot of paperwork in relatively short order. If you have the opportunity to enroll in a speed reading course, do it; it will not be a waste of your money or time.

Do more than one thing at a time when you can.

Commuting time can be used productively if you tape record memoranda or listen to educational or self-improvement tapes. I often have lunch at my desk, and I read while I eat. It's relaxing and refreshing.

Get rid of unnecessary interruptions.

Whenever you have interruptions, ask yourself "Was that interruption necessary?" Then find what you can do to get rid of those that are unnecessary.

This leads to the question about whether or not you should have an "open door" policy. If you do, you will certainly have interruptions, and they can be time consuming. Frankly, I like having one, and I am willing to spend extra hours on the job to pay for it. However, when I have lots of deadlines to meet, I often close my door. Faculty members and others have learned that most of the time they can see me, but that on occasion I just don't have time unless they need to see me about something especially important. In that case, they get on my calendar.

Determine what activities are a good use of your time.

We should allow ourselves time to do certain things without feeling guilty (see discussion of stress management in Chapter 26). For example, is time spent with faculty, staff, or students a waste of time? Is playing racquetball a waste of time? Only you can answer those questions. I believe that spending time with faculty, staff, or students and playing racquetball are both good uses of my time. If you agree, then you know that to accommodate these activities, you must be willing to put in longer days if necessary. Prioritize your work, which will allow you to focus more efficiently on what you must get done.

Don't try to be a perfectionist.

Learn to let go. It is so easy to want to go over and over our work so that there will be no mistakes that we waste time we could be devoting to other important activities. The notion that everything must be perfect slows you down.

Get out of your office.

It pays to take a break and to get away now and then from the stack of work on your desk. Take a walk across campus, visit with faculty members, or find other ways to relax. You often can come back to your work with more vitality.

I don't scoff at books on how to save time and be better organized, and I am all in favor of supporting those who want to attend conferences or workshops on the topic. However, I urge you also to inventory your life and work habits and develop your own techniques for saving time and becoming better organized. Try some of the tips I've provided. They may prove useful.

REFERENCES

Hemphill, B. (1997). *Taming the paper tiger.* Washington, DC: Kiplinger.

20

Handling Promotion and Tenure Issues

Accurate annual evaluations make the promotion and tenure process less painful.

Few things cause more anxiety for faculty members than the matters of promotion and tenure. And why not? Their careers are often at stake. You play a big role in deciding which faculty members in your department are promoted and granted tenure. You will undoubtedly fret a lot over the decisions you have to make—especially when those being considered are borderline cases. Tough calls cause sleepless nights, gray hair, and the urge to go fishing.

Although promotion and tenure are often lumped together, as they are in this chapter, they are totally separate and different, though the criteria are very often intertwined. Promotion in rank is a recognition of achievements as well as the considered potential of the person being recommended. Tenure, on the other hand, is a personnel status in an academic organizational unit or program of the university. Its primary benefit is that the academic or fiscal year appointments of full-time faculty members who have been awarded tenure are continued until relinquishment of that status (subject to adequate cause, for financial exigency, or for curricular reasons).

Promotion typically carries a salary increase with it, while tenure does not. Whereas the criteria for both are often not vastly different, committee members need to assess a candidate differently. We typically think of promotion in terms of the candidate's accomplishments to date. On the other hand, tenure is more likely to be viewed in terms of the candidate's long-term potential and promise. Tenure offers job protection that does not come with promotion. Tenure gives substantive meaning to academic freedom and applies to teaching, research, and creative activity.

What can you do to relieve faculty anxiety about these matters and to ease your fretfulness? The first suggestion is that you have departmental guidelines dealing with both promotion and tenure. The guidelines should be as specific as possible (see appendix for sample guidelines) to help faculty members know what is expected of them. Make the measurement of criteria as objective and quantifiable as possible. Still, even the best promotion and tenure guidelines will require judgment calls on your part.

There is something you must remember as you develop promotion and tenure guidelines: They must meet or exceed the policies of the university. For example, if university criteria for promotion to the rank of full professor say that a terminal degree is required, you cannot say that anything less is sufficient. On the other hand, you can be more demanding. If, for example, university criteria do not call for a terminal degree, your department might decide that a terminal degree is required. You also should determine, before developing your guidelines, who on campus must approve them. Generally, your dean and vice president for academic affairs must sign off on promotion and tenure guidelines, and some schools require approval by a faculty senate.

Promotion and tenure guidelines also will reduce untenured faculty members' anxieties, which I think is the more important reason for having them. Faculty members have the right to know from Day One exactly—to the degree that it is possible—what is expected of them. Make it a point to hand out promotion and tenure guidelines at the new faculty orientation.

At a university where I once taught, one department has guidelines that are unusually specific and quantifiable. New faculty members are able to look at them, assign themselves points for certain activities, add them up, and know where they stand. During evaluation sessions with the chairperson, untenured faculty members or those seeking promotion are told how many points they have and where that puts them in relation to what is needed. They are told, for example, "If you continue to make this kind of progress, you will have no trouble with tenure," or "If you don't improve your progress, you can't be recommended for tenure." The chairperson can point to specific weaknesses if necessary.

There are advantages to such a system. It is relatively easy to see how faculty members score, and they either come up to a certain score or they don't. Those who score above a certain level are recommended for tenure; those who don't, aren't. The disadvantages are that most faculty members believe that points can't be assigned to everything. Moreover, many disagree on how many points ought to be assigned to different kinds of activities. Unless there is general agreement regarding the point values, faculty members will not endorse the guidelines.

Accurate annual evaluations make the promotion and tenure process less painful. If you've been honest and objective in your yearly evaluation, the decision comes easily. If you have honestly given high marks on teaching, research, and public service, you are likely to recommend tenure when the time comes. On the other hand, I have worked with chairpersons who gave faculty members strong evaluations, but then recommended that tenure be denied. How does that make sense? It doesn't, and you might have to explain your answer in court.

Recommending tenure is a heavy responsibility: You are affecting the fate of a fellow human being and determining whether a faculty member will soon be unemployed. You also are deciding whether you want that person on your faculty for the next 30 years or so. You must weigh all the materials submitted with the application against the performance criteria. You must fairly assess the faculty member's teaching, scholarly activity, public service, and any other specified criteria.

Many years ago at the first meeting I had as chairperson to make a decision on tenure for one of our faculty, the discussion began when one professor said, "I am in favor of granting tenure to Ken. He's such a nice guy." I pleaded with the faculty not to make the decision based on niceness. We can find nice people in the park, but do we want them on our faculty? We must stick to the stated performance criteria.

In the end we did not recommend tenure for Ken. He had weak teaching skills, and he had made no research progress. When the discussion got down to serious business, we couldn't find any reason to recommend tenure. It didn't make any of us feel good to have to make the decision, but we made it nonetheless, and I am convinced we did the right thing.

HELPING FACULTY WITH PROMOTION AND TENURE

If we are indeed responsible for hiring faculty members, what do we owe them? The following are examples of some things we can do to assist faculty members earn tenure and get promoted.

Provide untenured faculty members with a mentor. We can help new teachers adjust to academe by providing each with a mentor. It is important to see that each new faculty member has the tools and guidance to do well and proceed toward tenure and promotion. After all, the cost of hiring a faculty member is significant, and replacement would be costly as well.

Too often we say to new teachers, "You are responsible for teaching these classes. Here are some old syllabi, and there is your classroom." What we leave unsaid, of course, is "you're on your own now."

A good mentor will talk to the new teacher about teaching. He or she will discuss the culture of the institution and the department. The mentor can be there when the new faculty member needs support.

You must ensure that the process works and be willing to change mentors if rapport is not established.

Schedule periodic meetings with all new faculty members. It's a good idea to meet periodically with them to see how they are doing and to let them know you have an interest in them. When there is more than one new faculty member, you might meet with them as a group. Give new department members an opportunity to tell you of problems they're experiencing and offer to help them.

Recommend new faculty members for committee assignments. Serving on committees helps new faculty members get to know their colleagues and begin building their record of service. A note of caution: Be careful not to overextend faculty, especially new faculty members who are not likely to have a lot of extra time.

Give the names of new faculty members to those looking for speakers. I often get calls requesting speakers for civic groups, workshops, conferences, etc. Just as I recommend new faculty members to serve on committees, I try to involve them as speakers on campus or before public groups.

Sponsor brown bag lunches or workshops on improving teaching and/or research techniques. Informal sessions at which a panel presents ideas on teaching or discusses some aspect of research are useful for new faculty members. They—and veteran faculty members, for that matter—can get useful guidance from such professional development sessions.

You can sponsor these weekly or monthly, depending on how large the department is. Sessions can vary. For example, at one session on teaching you may want to deal with test construction and at another one, ways to contend with problems of student attendance, etc. For sessions on research, you might ask active researchers to talk about their work or to present research techniques.

Some seminars on teaching that we sponsored focus on preparing effective exams, cooperative learning strategies, role playing, and the characteristics of an "effective teacher." Obviously there are many suitable topics.

Develop a visitation program for all untenured faculty.
The program might provide for classroom visitors to come to a class twice during the semester on an unannounced basis. Visitors are asked to stay for the entire class period and meet later with the teacher to provide feedback and advice. Each classroom visitor is expected to complete a form and share it with the person visited. Both parties sign the form, indicating that they have discussed the visit. Copies of the form are then given to the department chairperson and made available to those who evaluate faculty members for promotion and/or tenure. Figure 20.1 is an example of a visitation form.

The classroom visitation program provides a simple way of identifying faculty members who may be struggling with their teaching. Moreover, it is a way for all untenured faculty members to know what experienced faculty members think of their teaching methods. This program also is especially useful with part-time faculty members.

Sponsor a special program for all faculty members applying for tenure and/or promotion. A program to spell out specifically what faculty members should include in their portfolios is particularly helpful. Obviously, it must be scheduled before most faculty members actually start working on their portfolios. These sessions also could be used to review performance criteria and their application.

In recent years portfolios have grown to unreasonable size. I've seen them so large that they are submitted in several boxes. Those standing for tenure and/or promotion need to be reminded—and reassured—that certain materials are neither wanted nor needed.

Encourage untenured faculty members to be involved professionally. Talk with new faculty members about the importance of belonging to professional organizations, attending meetings, and volunteering for committees or special

FIGURE 20.1 Faculty Classroom Evaluation Form

Instructor____________________________________ Course No. ______
Evaluator____________________________________ Date: __________

Class format/Class objectives:

Organization/Class management:

General impressions:

Suggestions:

Signature of evaluator: ____________________________ Date: ________
Signature of faculty evaluated: ________________________ Date: ________

Original: Faculty evaluated Copy: Evaluator Copy: File

NOTE: A faculty member's signature does not necessarily constitute an agreement with the contents of the classroom evaluation. Furthermore, the evaluator's signature indicates that the faculty member was not informed as to the exact date or class period for the evaluation.

Form developed by: Dr. Jan Quarles, Chairperson, Department of Journalism, Middle Tennessee State University.

projects. Most professional organizations I am acquainted with have plenty of work that needs to be done, and they welcome volunteers.

Encourage untenured faculty members to apply for research grants. Faculty members often overlook research grant possibilities. Point out all notices and encourage application, especially from those without tenure.

Make funds available for faculty members to attend conferences and encourage them to submit papers. Faculty members should not be expected to pay their own way to conferences. Young faculty members generally do not have the money. Encouraging them to prepare and submit papers to give at conferences makes funding their trip easier.

Some universities that are especially aggressive at recruiting have start-up funds they set aside for new faculty members. They can be used to help do research, attend conferences, etc. Whatever you do to assist faculty members in these matters will generally help you in evaluating and making promotion and tenure decisions.

Regularly provide untenured faculty members with a checklist that outlines progress, or lack thereof, in meeting the tenure expectations. While this procedure can be time-consuming and agonizing at times, you owe it to those you hire in tenure-track lines and to the department. Despite the clear need for interim progress reports, I can't count the times I've seen this neglected. On several occasions I have had talks with chairpersons concerning their strong belief that a faculty member was not performing at the expected level, only to find evaluations by the complaining chairperson in the faculty member's personnel file that suggested just the opposite.

On numerous occasions I have discovered that tenure-seeking faculty members had been given vague, or even contradictory, performance instructions. This can happen if you as chairperson do not reconcile instructions that can come out of what is given by the department's peer review committee and you. What's a faculty member to do if peer review committee members say, for example, that the person's publishing record is sufficient, when you've made it clear to the same faculty member that you expect considerably more?

It is critical to the welfare of all those expecting to earn tenure and to be promoted that they have a clear understanding of what is expected, and it is not enough to provide this orally. A clear, concise, written set of expectations should be provided to all faculty members who will be standing for tenure and promotion.

THE PROMOTION AND TENURE PORTFOLIO

Untenured assistant professors are anxious about their chances for earning tenure and being promoted. They are often uncertain about what they should include in their portfolios, and they are not made to feel any better when they see boxes of materials that others have submitted. Unless faculty members are given guidelines for compiling a portfolio, the only thing they will have to go on are the examples and suggestions of others. Moreover, to help their chances with either promotion or tenure, they will likely err on the side of including too much rather than not enough. The consequences of this are that promotion and tenure review committee members will get far more information than they need and far more than they have time to read.

What should a faculty member include in his or her promotion and/or tenure portfolio? To begin with, faculty members standing for tenure or going up for promotion should see what the criteria are. They should then begin compiling data to prove that they meet or exceed the minimum criteria. The following list of items provides a starting place for assembling a portfolio to submit for promotion and/or tenure:

1) A current curriculum vitae
2) Documentation to support teaching effectiveness
   a. student evaluations
   b. peer evaluations
   c. teaching portfolios
   d. unsolicited letters from students, alumni
   e. students' scores on standardized tests, before and after a course has been taken, if possible
   f. evidence of help given colleagues on teaching improvement
   g. new courses developed
   h. participation in teaching workshops and seminars
   i. any efforts of instructional innovations and evaluating their effectiveness
   j. any honors or teaching awards
   k. written comments from those who teach a course for which a particular course is a prerequisite
   l. alumni ratings or other graduate feedback
   m. invitations to teach for outside agencies
3) Documentation to support research effectiveness (copies of books, articles, papers, etc. should be available in the office of the faculty member going up for tenure and/or promotion and should be made available if committee members request them):
   a. letters from other scholars commenting on research
   b. letters documenting help provided to colleagues
   c. book contracts for works in progress

   d. letter accepting an article for publication
   e. letter indicating acceptance of a paper
4) Documentation of public service
   a. unsolicited letters lauding committee work, problem solving achievements, etc.
   b. statement summarizing work with a professional organization

DEALING WITH FACULTY MEMBERS WHO HAVE BEEN DENIED TENURE

When tenure is denied, special problems may develop. At most colleges and universities, faculty members who are denied tenure after serving three or more years are permitted to return for a year after notification of denial. Some, of course, will elect not to return if they are able to find another job. On the other hand, many stay for the extra year—and this can present unusual problems. The individual may resent those who were responsible for denial, and faculty relations therefore can be strained. Some people become so hurt and angry that they give as little effort as possible to the job.

As chairperson, you must try to deal with the problem. Explain to the person that he or she should use the final year to do the very best job possible. Explain that you are likely to be contacted as a reference by others as he or she looks for another job, and that you will honestly report on current efforts. Talk about using the experience to grow—that is, to learn from mistakes.

To avoid such a tense situation it is wise in some cases to terminate the unpromising faculty member before the third year begins. To do this means giving special attention to the performance of new faculty members. The visitation and mentoring programs will help and also will turn up emerging problems. Giving extra time to monitoring the performance of new and untenured faculty people is time well spent.

Minimizing Legal Risks

Benjamin Baez and John A. Centra (1995, p. 149) make several recommendations to minimize legal risks.

- Institutions should eliminate or minimize any practices that are not specifically addressed in their written policies.

- All units in an institution should be governed by a single reappointment, promotion, and tenure policy, although units will have different standards.
- Faculty members preparing for their reviews should receive as much information as possible about the process.
- A faculty member should receive information about any performance problems far enough in advance of a review to be able to improve.
- Institutions should be aware of the key legal, political, and social interests associated with affirmative action.

WHAT PERCENTAGE OF YOUR FACULTY SHOULD BE TENURED?

This becomes a particularly critical question in times of change. If drastic program changes are needed, and your faculty is nearly 100% tenured, your options are limited. On the other hand, you will have flexibility if a good percentage of your faculty is not tenured.

One remedy is to keep some of your positions open by designating them temporary. Although it seems insensitive to terminate some untenured faculty members for programmatic reasons, you may have to do that or lose even more.

As a dean, I faced the problem of five people possibly seeking tenure in a department of 12 faculty members. It was in a year when we were searching for a department chairperson, and all five of the potential tenure applicants would be going up in their fifth year instead of waiting until the sixth. In order to retain as much flexibility for the new chairperson as possible, I met with those considering going up for tenure and asked them to wait until the following year to apply. I explained that I would, of course, have made a tenure decision if they had been in their final year, but because they were not being hurt, I hoped they would understand my position.

This brings up the question of the wisdom for going up for tenure early, if your university permits that. I advise against it, especially at those institutions where it is up or out, no matter when a faculty member applies. In general, faculty members who take extra time to beef up their credentials make a wise decision.

Another way of dealing with a possible glut of tenured professors is for universities to establish tenure quotas. For example, a university may decide that no more than 80% of the total faculty in a given department may be awarded tenure. Thus, when the number of tenured faculty reaches the maximum (in this case, 80%) allowed percentage, then "tenure density" has occurred. Courts have supported the right of institutions to determine what criteria—including tenure density—are to be used in tenure decisions.

RESEARCH VERSUS CREATIVE ACTIVITY

Most universities specify that faculty members must be engaged in scholarship, defined as research and/or creative activity. Most of us have little difficulty coming to grips with what is meant by research but are uncertain about what creative activity means. It is important that we define both clearly, especially in those academic units where faculty members are engaged in both.

The policy statement shown in Table 20.1 should provide useful insight into the meaning of creative activity (in this case for a mass communication program).

Diamond (1994, p. 17) lists six specific conditions that exist under which most disciplines would consider the activity scholarly or professional. The six conditions are:

1) The activity requires a high level of discipline-related expertise.
2) The activity breaks new ground, is innovative.
3) The activity can be replicated or elaborated.
4) The work and its results can be documented.
5) The work and its results can be peer-reviewed.
6) The activity has significance or impact.

EVALUATING ON-LINE SCHOLARLY ACTIVITIES

The matter of how much weight to give to on-line scholarly activities for purposes of promotion and tenure is a contentious issue that is not likely to go away. Guernsey (1997) notes that while candidates for promotion stock their portfolios with Internet-related accomplishments, many evaluations committees are skeptical. "Behind the closed doors, committee members are asking questions that betray equal parts confusion and suspicion. Should a candidate's Internet project count? Is it teaching, scholarship, or service? Does editing an electronic journal require the same kind of rigor as editing a print journal? Who is refereeing all this stuff, anyway" (Guernsey, 1997, p. A21)?

These questions will likely be more easily dealt with by those disciplines that already accept nontraditional research and publication and creative scholarly activity as valuable. However, in the years to come, the traditional disciplines will have to deal with these questions, and the chairpersons of these departments would be well advised to develop policies dealing with online scholarship. As a point for beginning discussion, the list developed by Diamond could prove useful.

WHO MAKES PROMOTION AND TENURE DECISIONS?

At public universities, a governing board generally will make the final decision on who is promoted and tenured. On campus, the final recommendation is that of the president of the university. Most decisions on promotion and tenure start at the departmental level. There faculty members standing for either promotion or tenure are reviewed by a committee made up of their peers. The peer review committee will make a recommendation either to the department chair or to the dean or both. Regardless, you as the chairperson will make a recommendation to your dean. He or she in turn will make a recommendation to the vice president for academic affairs. Depending on the university, there may be a university-wide committee that also offers a recommendation to the vice president for academic affairs. Either way, the vice president for academic affairs will make a recommendation to the president who in turns makes his or her recommendation to members of the governing board.

POST-TENURE REVIEW

An increasing number of universities are developing policies and procedures for reviewing tenured faculty members. They recognize the changing circumstances of the modern university. They typically outline specific conditions that directly impinge on the need for post-tenure review. Most mention the budget situation facing public universities. As we know, most universities have faced periods of lean budgets, which has meant no increases in faculty size. Thus, any quality improvement or rise in reputation has had to come out of

TABLE 20.1 Creative Activity

1) *Definition.* "Creative Activity" consists of the creation, production, exhibition, performance, or publication of original work. Such activity is characterized by the development of original ideas and information through the practice of the forms of mass communication. The product of creative activity may be communicated as professional presentations in print media, electronic media, or emerging technologies. Appropriate formats may include photographs, film, video recordings, audio recordings, graphic designs, digital imaging, and nonacademic publications.

2) *Examples.* Creative activities to be considered include, but are not limited to:

   A. articles, reviews, and commentaries in professional periodicals, newspapers, and magazines that meet standards of high quality in the practice of mass communication; also, graphics and visual materials, including radio and television tapes, that are original presentations to professional or public audiences and that meet standards of high quality in the professional practice of mass communication

   B. development and management of mass communication seminars and workshops and related audiovisual and printed materials for professionals that advance knowledge and understanding of professional practice and improve professional performance

   C. books, industrial videos, and printed materials that meet standards for quality in mass communication, that advance knowledge and understanding of professional practice, and that improve professional performance

   D. internships, consultancies, manuscript reviews, and other forms of practical experience that allow faculty members to perform in a creative and professional way

   E. publication of analyses and critical reviews on professional subjects, and published in professional publications

F. publication of articles, reviews, and commentaries on other subjects in newspapers and other popular media, if they demonstrate high standards of professional practice.

G. meritorious work of a demanding nature in professional positions with the media during summers or leave time, or with approval of the dean, part-time during a regular term. Such work should demonstrably enhance the faculty member's teaching.

H. publication of textbooks or other books in mass communication if the books break new ground and successfully advance concepts, ideas, and approaches that transcend ordinary instruction manuals

I. professional achievement in the graphics-visual arts area and in other professional fields represented by mass communication faculties. The work should be original and should advance the state of the art of the profession.

3) *Evaluation criteria.* The faculty member's creative activities are expected to include work that clearly is major, as opposed to minor. Characteristics by which major work is distinguished from minor work include:

A. the scope of the audience (such as regional or national as opposed to local)

B. the nature of the audience (including respected academic or professional peers)

C. significance of the topic (an idea or finding that serves important academic, professional, or public interest)

D. the rigor of the standards met by the work (recognized by prominent academic or professional groups)

E. the stature of the reviewers of the work (educators or practitioners who are widely respected for their accomplishments)

F. the breadth, depth, and originality of the creative effort

G. the impact of the work in improving educational or professional practice or elevating the general understanding of freedom of expression and the ethical responsibilities of the mass media

constant faculty size, rather than by the addition of faculty positions, the method most commonly relied upon previously to build departments.

The Florida Board of Regents recently voted to require tenured professors in the state university system to undergo regular performance evaluations. One regent said the post-tenure reviews would make it easier to fire tenured professors who are "driving through their careers on autopilot" but would also reward outstanding professors. According to a spokesman, professors who receive poor reviews could be subject to disciplinary action, including dismissal.

Since January 1, 1994, faculty members are not required to retire except when the university can prove sufficient dereliction or neglect of duties to support dismissal. This has made a significant change in the way some departments operate: Instead of simply waiting for an unproductive faculty member to retire and then hiring a young, energetic go-getter, unproductive faculty members may now linger on for a decade or longer beyond what would otherwise have been mandatory retirement.

The other condition that causes some universities to develop post-tenure review has to do with universities being faced with intense and growing external demands for accountability. Post-tenure review has been a response to the need for changing academic practices.

The underlying philosophy that drives a university's post-tenure review process will depend in part on whether it is intended to be summative or formative. Those that are meant to be summative are used to make personnel decisions, whereas those that are formative suggest a review process that is developmental in nature. "While the philosophy of most post-tenure review policies drafted today is formative, almost all have summative aspects" (Licata & Morreale 1997, p. 5).

Chairpersons, as primary participants in the post-tenure review process, need to understand its purpose as well as its process. While the general purpose of post-tenure review policies can be labeled summative, formative, or some combination of both, the specific purpose of any such policy should be spelled out in the university's policy. From Licata and Morreale (1997) we see Georgia State University's purpose for its post-tenure review policy:

> The main purpose of post-tenure review at GSU is formative, but it has a summative element. The formative evaluation is a five-year comprehensive review of all tenured faculty. . . . The summative aspect of the policy comes about mainly through a variable workload policy. The faculty member's workload in teaching, research, and service is

adjusted based on the evaluation and faculty development document (p. 50).

Licata and Morreale (1997) provide profiles of nine institutions "as case studies of how the concept of post-tenure review was actually developed, implemented, and articulated within differing parameters of institutional mission and campus culture" (p. 43). In their profiles, they assess problems with procedures and lessons learned. From looking at lessons learned and studying other post-tenure review plans, it seems fair to make the following general comments about post-tenure review:

- It can be a very time-consuming process with lots of paperwork.
- Its effectiveness rests heavily on how well chairpersons do their job of evaluating; they must be able to carry out the process in a conscientious and evenhanded way. Many chairpersons will need help to learn how to construct effective evaluations.
- Developing an effective post-tenure review policy takes a lot of time, and it is important that all voices are brought to the table for discussion early in the process of development. Administrators who attempt to create a post-tenure review policy and procedure on their own will likely fail.
- For any post-tenure review system to be effective, constant vigilance is required. University policies are likely to need regular refinement and improvement.
- Post-tenure review procedures can produce faculty resistance and cynicism.
- Post-tenure review has in many instances proved itself to be worth the cost of time and effort because it boosts morale for the productive faculty member.
- Unless properly constructed, post-tenure review can have a stigma attached.
- Post-tenure review can be a force for continuous faculty development and validation.

At some universities, all faculty members come up for review on some sort of cycle. At others, faculty members are identified to be reviewed. The review process is generally conducted by the department chair and a select committee. After the review, a report is completed. If substantial and chronic deficiencies are identified, a professional development plan is drawn up. This is an agreement indicating how specific deficiencies in a faculty member's performance shall be remedied. Generally such plans are formulated by the department chairperson and the dean with assistance of and in consultation with the faculty member. The plan will identify the specific deficiencies; define specific goals or outcomes that are needed to remedy the deficiencies; outline the activities that are to be undertaken to achieve the needed outcomes; set timelines for accomplishing the activities and achieving the outcomes; indicate the criteria for annual progress reviews; and identify the source of any funding if required.

While motives for instituting post-tenure review are certainly mixed, a growing number of American colleges and universities are initiating policies. According to Licata and Morreale (1997, p. 2), "attempts to estimate their extent reveal a marked pattern of growth." They cite one study showing that 61% of respondents had a post-tenure review policy in place and another 9% had one under development.

STATUS OF TENURE

Legislators and taxpayers all across the country are questioning the need for tenure. Many argue that with First Amendment protections, tenure is no longer needed. Some openly predict that tenure as we know it is out. Whether that is true or not, the concept of tenure is being scrutinized, which is coming about largely because of political reality. "Professors sense that, at the very least, they had better discuss tenure, to keep outsiders, like state lawmakers, from taking matters into their own hands" (Leatherman, 1996, p. A12). Indeed, some states are experimenting with faculty appointments where no tenure will ever be awarded. Florida opened a new university that will be staffed by faculty members who cannot earn tenure. Also, the board of regents of the University of Texas system voted to require that the performance of tenured professors be reviewed every five years. The policy allows tenured faculty members to be dismissed if their performance is found to be poor. The president of Metropolitan State College of Denver appointed a committee to examine ways to evaluate tenured professors and make sure they are still doing a good job.

It seems fair to conclude that tenure is on shaky ground and that many forces are at work to destroy it, and an increasing number of younger faculty do not support traditional tenure to the degree that older faculty do. Power (1997, p. A52) points out in a 1996 survey conducted by the Higher Education

Research Institute of the University of California at Los Angeles, that 44% of faculty members under the age of 45 said they believed tenure was an outmoded concept, whereas only 30% of faculty members over the age of 55 agreed.

Gilliland (1997) makes a strong argument that tenure is an important element in helping universities cope with changes they must face. She says, "[O]rganizations that succeed in an environment of change and unpredictability promote flexibility, information access and dialogue, and risk-taking" (Gilliland, 1997, p. 33). She observes also that tenure is a system that promotes risk taking and therefore should be retained, though she calls for significant modifications that would affect how chairpersons perform their jobs.

Members of promotion and tenure review committees often are anxious about the responsibility of making decisions that can have powerful impacts on people's lives. Thus, academic leaders need to meet from time to time with committee members to address some of their concerns and to remind them that their task is critical to the well-being of the department—and to the university as a whole. It is probably fair to say that few decisions faculty members make in their job will be more important than those having to do with tenure and promotion.

While difficult personnel decisions are never easy to make, they are less painful if you've done all you can to make the process orderly and support those who apply. Also, promotion and tenure decisions are made much easier if you've already faced making tough decisions by failing to reappoint those not deserving of tenure and/or promotion. I can't count the number of times I've seen chairpersons take the easy way out when it came to making reappointments only to regret it when they've had to face up to tenure and/or promotion. If you have fairly evaluated faculty performance and recommended for reappointment only strong faculty members, your promotion and tenure decisions should not be all that difficult.

REFERENCES

Baez, B., & Centra, J. L. (1995). *Tenure, promotion, and reappointment: Legal and administrative implications.* ASHE-ERIC Higher Education Report No. 1. Washington, DC: The George Washington University.

Diamond, R. (1994). *Serving on promotion and tenure committees.* Bolton, MA: Anker.

Gilliland, M. W. (1997, May/June). Organizational change and tenure. *Change,* 31–33.

Guernsey, L. (1997, June 6). Scholars who work with technology fear they suffer in tenure reviews. *The Chronicle of Higher Education,* A21.

Leatherman, C. (1996, October 25). More faculty members question value of tenure. *The Chronicle of Higher Education,* A12.

Licata, C., & Morreale, J. C. (1997). *Post-tenure review policies, practices, precautions* (AAHE's New Pathways project inquiry # 12). Washington, DC: American Association for Higher Education.

Power, B. (1997, June 20). The danger inherent in abusing academic freedom. *The Chronicle of Higher Education,* A52.

Strategies for Faculty Development

An exchange program can be particularly exhilarating, and faculty members involved in them can feel challenged in new ways.

Faculty members, whether young or old, need support for faculty development. Teachers always need to continue learning, and that need is more pressing now than ever before. As chairperson, you will need to find ways that will motivate your faculty to grow and develop. It is not an easy task.

If you have no formal faculty development program, let me suggest that you start one. To begin with, meet with each faculty member to determine what his or her principal desires are with respect to professional development. Try to assess the frustrations each faces along with the satisfactions. These meetings should help provide some direction to the kind of faculty development activities the department could sponsor.

SOME FACULTY DEVELOPMENT ACTIVITIES

In an earlier chapter I talked about holding brown-bag lunches to discuss teaching. This is a good faculty development activity to start with. Properly planned, these lunches provide an opportunity for faculty members to improve their teaching skills. Veteran teachers who are recognized for their teaching skills can be called on to cover any number of topics of interest on teaching.

In addition, the following activities will foster faculty development. Each plays a role in a comprehensive development program.

Encourage sabbatical leaves for faculty members. Most colleges and universities have some kind of leave program that permits selected teachers to take off a semester or year for self-renewal. Generally, faculty members apply by completing a form in which they spell out what they plan to accomplish during their leave. Most universities require that faculty members have been employed for several years—most often seven, which is how we came to use the word sabbatical. (According to Mosaic law, the land and vineyards were to remain fallow and debtors were to be released every seven years.)

Initiate faculty exchange programs. An exchange program can be particularly exhilarating, and faculty members involved in them can feel challenged in new ways. Faculty exchanges take many different forms. Often they follow formal exchange agreements between universities. Faculty members then arrange with comparable educators at other universities to teach each other's classes. In some instances, the faculty members even exchange homes for the period.

Exchange programs often involve industry or government. A faculty member with a law degree might join a firm for a time and one of the firm's lawyers would teach in his or her place. While technically not an exchange, simply visiting another campus to see how others teach or handle research can be a rejuvenating experience.

Schedule class visits. One way to grow and develop is to learn from our colleagues. Suggest to faculty members that they sit in on their colleagues' classes. They may learn new techniques, and they may pick up some ideas to try in their own classes.

Apply for released time. Some colleges and/or departments permit selected faculty people to have released time from their classes to do research, develop new classes, or otherwise become involved in useful projects. They usually are expected to apply for released time by proposing what they would do with the time. Often faculty members are expected to give a report at the end of the term to show what they accomplished.

Explore university growth opportunities. Faculty members will sometimes take classes to learn something new that they feel will help them be better teachers. Classes in research, computer use, foreign languages, psychology, or education can provide chances to grow and learn.

Many universities also offer workshops and seminars that can help faculty members grow. Recently I received an announcement about one such seminar on our campus—"Computer Conferencing: Alternative to Lectures." It purports to teach how to convert lecture-based courses to computer-conferenced courses, creating new flexibility for students and faculty.

Many universities offer summer research grants that enable faculty members to spend their summer doing research rather than teaching. The grants provide funds to make this possible.

Many departments bring in guest speakers. They can teach or inspire us. Either way, they help us grow or want to grow.

Enrolling in continuing education courses offers still another opportunity for self-renewal. I took such a course not long ago on how to use a special computer software program, and I found it especially useful and enjoyable.

Take on special assignments. Occasionally universities offer opportunities to work in an administrative office. For example, at the university where I am now employed, the provost's office selects faculty members to work as interns. Several deans provide faculty internships as well; these permit faculty members to take on administrative projects.

Apply for faculty development grants. Many universities offer faculty development grants. They require that faculty members complete an application, and submit a short report upon completion of the project.

Experiment with new teaching technologies. If your faculty teach their classes primarily by lecturing, they might try using another technique. Urge them to try discussions or the case-method approach. Have them introduce some audio and videotapes. Better yet, they can make their own videotapes to show in their classes.

Develop a new specialty area. It is truly invigorating to teach new courses. If faculty have been teaching the same ones for a number of years, they might have lost some of their edge. Delving into a new course can be refreshing. Certainly it forces faculty members to dig into the literature and come up with new ideas.

Team teach with a colleague. Just as taking on a new course can be invigorating, team teaching a course with a colleague can also be stimulating.

Faculty members can learn from a colleague, and the added pressure of preparing so that they won't be embarrassed in front of their colleagues likewise is a vitalizing experience.

Tape record your teaching. A good way for faculty members to begin a program of self-improvement is to tape record their teaching. They probably will find things that need to be improved, and working to improve them can be rewarding. They may even want their colleagues to critique their taped sessions.

Develop a peer evaluation system. Talk to your colleagues who are interested in improving their teaching to see if any are interested in a peer evaluation program. Those involved would sit in on each other's classes, review syllabi, and critique each other's lecture notes.

Attend regional and national conferences. Most of us return from conferences with new ideas and renewed vigor. Certainly opportunities for learning and growth are available if faculty members seek them out. Try to fund travel for those who attend conferences. Generally there is not enough money for all faculty members to attend all the conferences they would like, so this means developing a system for equitable distribution of the travel funds you have.

Here are some other faculty development activities initiated at universities around the United States (Tierney, 1994).

Faculty orientation program. The University of Oklahoma has developed a semester-long faculty orientation program that includes weekly seminar-style meetings, and faculty participation has been high. During the 14-week program, a range of topics are covered: special teaching techniques, course design, evaluation of one's teaching, health and counseling services, time management, and tenure-review process.

Mentors. The University of North Dakota has adopted a scholars' mentoring program where new faculty get a chance to work and network with some of the top faculty at the institution. One aspect of the program involves reading and then discussing Ernest Boyer's *Scholarship Reconsidered* (Boyer, 1990), where the goal is to get new faculty to develop their own understanding of what it means to be a scholar.

Western Carolina University has adopted a mentoring program designed to serve not only new faculty but senior faculty as well. New faculty benefit by learning more about their institutions, while senior faculty benefit through the new roles and responsibilities they assume as mentors.

Faculty guides. The University of North Carolina at Chapel Hill has developed a guide to campus resources geared for the "perplexed UNC teacher." The guide offers suggestions on subjects ranging from developing teaching skills to dealing with personal problems. UNC also has developed a guide to help faculty better supervise and train teaching assistants. Emphasized are issues related to defining the relationship between faculty and TAs, providing support and feedback for TAs, and finding good teacher training resources.

Faculty workshops. The University of Wisconsin system offers an annual Faculty College where faculty spend four days participating in teaching-related workshops on topics such as active learning, the ethics of teaching, critical thinking, and collaborative learning.

The Great Lakes Colleges Association for the past 17 years has offered an annual Course Design and Teaching Workshop. The program targets not only beginning faculty who seek assistance, but also senior faculty who hope to revitalize their teaching performance.

Special interest groups. Augsburg College in Minneapolis has organized a gay/lesbian study group for its faculty as well as a mentoring program connecting new faculty to faculty sponsors who provide guidance to their less-experienced colleagues.

Teaching resources. Stanford University has prepared an extensive handbook on teaching which includes a bibliography of works about college teaching. The university also has an extensive videotape library where topics relate to course conceptualization and development, discussion leading, lecturing, and student-teacher interactions.

Management teams. In the spirit of Total Quality Management, the University of Colorado at Denver has implemented Student Management Teams designed to bring students and professors together to work on academic matters. The program emphasis is on how reflection and discovery can improve teaching and learning.

MOTIVATING FACULTY MEMBERS TO GROW

Many chairpersons choose to ignore faculty development. They usually argue that it is not their responsibility to see that faculty members continue to upgrade their skills and knowledge. On the other hand, some believe deeply that to move the department forward, they have no choice but to encourage faculty members to participate in faculty development activities. Assuming you are a chairperson of the latter sort, how do you motivate faculty members to see the importance of continuing to learn and grow?

First, let faculty members know that you expect them to be actively involved in development activities. You need to set a good example by taking advantage of opportunities that come your way. Appoint a committee of faculty members to organize and coordinate seminars on improving teaching. Have those faculty members who are active researchers do seminar sessions.

You also should appoint a planning committee and charge it with developing a strategic planning document. When it's finished, present it to the faculty and get their reaction. Get faculty members to buy into the plan and begin implementing it. Generally such an effort will require some new thinking and learning.

Unfortunately, there are some faculty members who balk at learning new things or participating in any faculty development activity. You must try to persuade them that it is in their best interest to become involved, and that they owe it to the department, to the institution, and to their students. One success in this area makes all of the persuading worthwhile.

REFERENCES

Boyer, E. L. (1990). *Scholarship reconsidered: Priorities of the professoriate.* Princeton, NJ: The Carnegie Foundation for the Advancement of Teaching.

Tierney, W. G., & Rhoads, R. A. (1994). *Faculty socialization as cultural process: A mirror of institutional commitment.* ASHE-ERIC Higher Education Report No. 93-6, 81–82. Washington, DC: The George Washington University.

22

Dealing with Curriculum Matters

If you aspire to be anything other than a caretaker, you will recognize the need for regularly examining the course offerings in your department.

Unless we update courses regularly and develop new courses, our departments will quickly become outdated, some faculty members will become restless, and students will find other places to study. The rate of change in course offerings in the past was nothing like what we can expect for the future. With new knowledge developing so much more swiftly, we must make changes in our curriculum on a fairly regular basis. As chairperson, you have the responsibility of initiating periodic review of the curriculum, which may involve updating or changing courses, ensuring that the curriculum works to support the goals of the department, and working with faculty to resolve any problems that are likely to develop over territorial issues.

While the chairperson does not normally initiate or design curriculum changes, he or she should ask important questions about the curriculum and gather information that pertains to its relevance. Is it in need of updating, and if so, in what ways? What curricular changes can be made to make the curriculum more relevant? These and other important questions should be asked regularly by the chairperson. You may want to ask the curriculum committee to look at the entire curriculum and prepare a study that answers some of questions, such as whether it is in need of updating and whether it is relevant. Most of the time the curriculum committee only evaluates new course proposals and has no reason to look at the entire curriculum unless asked.

If you aspire to be anything other than a caretaker, you will recognize the need for regularly examining the course offerings in your department. There are usually some faculty members in the department who recognize the need for updating the curriculum and who will push you to add new courses or change existing ones.

WAYS TO EVALUATE THE CURRICULUM

There are a number of approaches that can be used to evaluate the curriculum, and any or all of those that follow can be effective in determining the state of your department's current curriculum.

Conduct course audits.

One of the best techniques is course audits. They enable your faculty to carefully examine each course and to justify its existence. You should examine all courses in the department to see if they have a justifiable reason for being. After a course has been taught for years—especially when it has been taught by a number of different faculty members—it often evolves into a different course. Think about it. One faculty member is particularly attached to certain ideas and will emphasize them in the class, whereas another faculty member gives those ideas short shrift and emphasizes instead ideas that appeal to him or her. Over time, faculty members add new assignments, discard old ones, change the emphasis of the course as indicated above, and the course is quite different from what it was when it was first offered. Perhaps it's even different from what it was intended to be. We all know that as a course passes from one instructor to another it often becomes a very different breed; any resemblance between it and its original description is purely coincidental. I believe we do a disservice to our students when we tell them one thing in the catalog about a course and then teach something else.

Minor modifications are desirable and should be encouraged; however, when changes alter the basic objectives of the course or make it into something that does not resemble the course description, an examination is in order. Here are suggestions on how to conduct course audits.

Procedure for course audits. Faculty members should be told the purpose of course audits, and they should be provided a schedule showing when their course will be audited. The purpose of the course audits is to provide faculty with an opportunity to explain the contents of a course, how it is taught, what students are expected to learn, how they are tested, and what their assignments are. It allows others to determine whether the course is doing what it was designed to do and what the course's educational value is. The following outlines the steps to be taken in conducting the audits.

1) Faculty members should submit course outlines for each course to be audited.
2) Faculty members should obtain and submit outlines of similar courses taught at recognized (and agreed-upon) universities.
3) A meeting will be scheduled at which faculty members will present their courses before the chairperson and two other faculty members. (Course outlines should be reviewed in advance by those who will hear the presentations.)
4) The purpose of the presentation is to allow faculty members to explain:
   A. The objectives of the course
   B. How the objectives are being realized
   C. What kind of assignments are made to students
   D. How grades are determined
   E. What textbooks are used as well as how they are used
   F. Any unusual teaching techniques employed
   G. The grade distribution for the last three times the course has been taught
   H. What special assignments are given to graduate students if the course is double-numbered
   I. What variance exists from the original course description
5) Faculty members should be challenged to defend their teaching methods, assignments, and grading.
6) Those hearing the presentation should take notes and prepare evaluations. These will be summarized by the chairperson and then given to the faculty member whose course is being audited.
7) If substantial changes are recommended, another meeting between the faculty member and those making the recommendations should be set up to discuss the evaluations.
8) The faculty member whose course is being audited should prepare a report indicating what, if any, changes he or she intends to make.

It is not likely that all courses in the department can be audited during a single academic term. Indeed, it is probably best to plan on completing audits for all course offerings over a two- or three-year period. While they take time, the audits are worthwhile if properly done. They cause faculty members to analyze and reevaluate their teaching—and the effectiveness of the courses themselves.

Another approach for evaluating a college course is one developed by Robert Diamond. (See the appendix for questions developed by Diamond to consider in evaluating a college course.)

You should regularly examine other university catalogs to see what other schools offer. Likewise, you should talk to other chairpersons at conferences about what courses they offer. Ask especially if they are offering anything new. Also, if you chair a professional program, you need to keep current with what is happening in the work world so that your students are learning what they need to in order to succeed professionally. One effective way to do this is to arrange for focus group sessions with professionals. My colleagues and I have conducted these sessions over lunch and found them to be particularly useful. Attending professional meetings and meeting in a professional's work environment also helps to find out what professionals are looking for when they hire our graduates.

Sponsor a retreat to talk about the curriculum.

A successful retreat requires a considerable amount of time planning. First you need to decide on what kind of time you need for the retreat. Is it possible to take care of the matters in a half day, a full day, or a weekend? For curriculum matters, a full day is likely sufficient. Other important considerations include:

1) Where will the retreat be and what will it cost? These often are interrelated. Typically we think of retreats as being off campus, but there is no reason why you cannot have one on campus, unless there is no space available. My preference is for having them off campus, but this usually means having to pay to rent space. Occasionally, you will have corporate friends who will allow you to use a conference or board room. Obviously, if you have the money in your budget to rent space, your options are increased.
2) What are other costs and who will pay them? Some arrangements will need to be made for lunch and for coffee and soft drinks during for midmorning and midafternoon breaks. If the departments do not have funds for food and refreshments, faculty will have to be asked to share the costs, and most will not mind doing this. This determination needs

to be made in advance and faculty members consulted if they are expected to pay.

3) What should the agenda be? A formal agenda needs to be prepared. Obviously you cannot just go into the retreat and announce simply that curriculum is the agenda and anything goes. Instead, you should plan to approach the subject more formally. Here is a sample agenda that might work:
    A. Discussion of disposition of courses that have not been taught in last five years. Why are they not being taught? Should we continue to keep them on the books? Why or why not?
    B. Do we have courses whose titles are no longer adequate or accurate? Are there suggested changes in any course titles to be considered?
    C. Do we have course descriptions that are no longer adequate or accurate? Are there suggested changes in any course descriptions to be considered? Should we assign a faculty member(s) to rewrite course descriptions?
    D. Are there new courses we should consider?
    E. For those courses that have prerequisites, do we need to reconsider whether the stated prerequisites are appropriate? Should any changes be made or considered?
    F. Is the core curriculum adequate and appropriate?
    G. Are the nonmajor requirements adequate and appropriate?
    H. Do we have courses in which students do not seem to be getting out of them what they should?
    I. Are our assessment activities adequate for measuring effectiveness of our curriculum?
    J. What are we doing to ensure content consistency for courses where multiple sections are regularly offered?
    K. Are we currently using the best textbooks available in all our courses?

Obviously you could change the questions into statements if you prefer, and there are several other important matters that you might add to this agenda.

4) Who is going to serve as moderator?
5) Do we need to make copies of any materials to pass out during the retreat?

6) Should we assign someone to take notes and write a report?

As you can see, a number of decisions must be made and planning must be done if the retreat is to be successful.

Meet in small groups.

There are times when meeting in small groups to discuss curriculum matters makes more sense than doing it in a retreat of all faculty. We know that there are times when small groups can be more productive than large ones for any number of reasons. If that is the case with your faculty, this may be the better approach for you. Certainly if you have a large faculty, you may wish to begin by having small group meetings and then taking ideas that come out of them to the larger group for a final decision.

Develop minicourses.

Minicourses offer a way to try out a course idea and to see if it has the potential for being offered as a regular course. If the course works, you have the opportunity to turn it into a regular course. Minicourses, as I define them, are courses that do not run the entire length of the term. For example, in a 15-week semester you might offer three minicourses of five weeks each. One of the real values of this concept is that they allow you to offer courses for one hour of credit—and certain courses should not receive any more credit than that, especially until they are fully developed.

Special topics courses at some universities permit you to achieve some of the same results. Either a minicourse or a special topics course can generally be added without going through the bureaucratic maze required for adding a new course. Faculty members—and even students—often come up with solid ideas for these kinds of courses. Once several years ago in analyzing survey data from our alumni, we discovered that many of our graduates were telling us that we needed a course in graphic design. We tried it out as a special topics course before taking it before the department, college, and university committees to get it approved as a regular course. This allowed us to begin offering the course immediately and to work through the problems of teaching and refining the course before asking for it to be approved as a regular part of our curriculum. The biggest advantage was that we were able to serve students immediately rather than having to wait a year or two before the course was in place.

We have to be responsive to student needs. Universities cannot afford to be as slow as they have been in responding to curricular changes, and yet we are not currently geared up to doing this. One suggestion is to have the assistant vice president for academic affairs serve as a curriculum ombudsperson. His or her duties would be to examine course proposals and allow them to be introduced pending some kind of up or down vote by a university curriculum committee. It would be higher education's answer to fast-tracking.

Invite reviews.

A review of the curriculum by someone who is not in the department can be helpful as it provides a fresh, objective perspective. Reviews can be conducted by a number of different individuals.

By outsiders. You can invite notable educators in your field, or if yours is a professional department, professionals, to examine your course offerings. I think it is generally a good policy to have others look at what we are doing; often we are too close to make objective judgments about our programs. One of the values of accreditation is that outsiders examine your department on a regular basis. Even if you don't have an accreditation body, you can achieve—at least in part—essentially the same thing by having others do a thorough examination of your curriculum.

If you ask outsiders to examine your curriculum, you need to provide them with specific instructions so that you and they agree on what you are asking be done. Here is an example of what you might ask for:

1) Do you see any gaps in our course offerings? In other words, are there legitimate areas that we are not currently addressing?
2) Do you see too much overlapping of what we offer?
3) Do the prerequisites seem appropriate?
4) Are the course descriptions adequate? Do you believe they provide enough information about what is covered in the courses?
5) Do you believe our core is sufficient? If not, what should be changed?
6) Do you believe our nonmajor requirements support the kind of education we are attempting to provide? Would you recommend any changes?

By your planning committee. The planning committee is concerned about the future, and few things could be more pertinent to the future than the courses we offer, which should have something to say about how well we prepare our students for the future. The committee should do a systematic study of what similar departments at other universities across the country are doing and what recent alumni think about course offerings. Also, we should consult those who hire our students to find out if they believe our students are adequately educated.

INTRODUCING NEW COURSES AND CHANGING EXISTING ONES

Universities have policies and procedures for adding and/or changing courses. The forms that must be filled out are all quite similar from one university to another.

The first step after completing the appropriate forms is to take the proposed course addition or change before the department's curriculum committee. Usually after it has signed off on the proposal, the next step is to take it on up the line for approval. Generally, this means that it goes before a college curriculum committee, university curriculum committee, and the vice president for academic affairs. Generally, your college dean will sign off on it before it goes to the university curriculum committee. though this varies from campus to campus.

Some things committee members and you must think about seriously before giving approval to new courses are:

- Who do we have to teach the course?
- Do we have the necessary resources to teach the course? For example, if you need special equipment, is it available, or do we have funds to purchase it?
- Will proposing the course create problems with any other department on campus? If so, can we solve it by getting permission from the affected department(s)? Just because a problem may be created is not good reason for not onsidering adding a course. On the other hand, we must develop a strategy for solving the problem to everyone's satisfaction.
- Does the course duplicate anything we are already doing?
- Do the library holdings support such a course? If not, can they be purchased?
- How will the course fit into our curriculum? Will it be required? Will there be prerequisites?

- How will adding the course affect enrollment?
- Are there special space considerations?
- How many students would we anticipate taking it each term?
- Will we need to offer more than one section of the course?
- How often should the course be offered?
- How does offering the course fit into our overall mission?
- What, if any, laboratory equipment and/or facilities are required to teach the course?
- What is the course's educational value?

If your department is going to be on the cutting edge, you must introduce and change courses fairly regularly—especially in certain fields where knowledge is fluid and mined so rapidly. We need faculty members who can recognize the need for changing and adding courses. We need teachers who are willing to take on new teaching assignments.

Faculty members should be provided some incentives for designing new courses and making the preparations for teaching them. I believe giving released time and providing some travel funds is at times required. Also, this extra effort should be taken into consideration when you are evaluating faculty members or giving merit salary increases.

ELIMINATING COURSES

Determining when to eliminate a course seems at first thought to be a relatively simple matter. It's not. Some universities allow departments to place courses they no longer teach into an inactive bank so that they can be called back up should the department decide at a later date to offer the course. Others insist that courses that have not been offered for a set period of time (three or five years, for example) must be dropped from the catalog and the course scrapped. Then, should the department wish to teach the course at a later date, it must submit a proposal for a new course.

Personally, I do not favor keeping untaught courses in the catalog. It is misleading to potential students who look at your catalog to help make a decision about attending your university and majoring in your department.

Here are some questions to guide your thinking when confronting issues surrounding the elimination of a course:

- Is the course offered regularly? If not, when was the last time it was offered?
- What were the enrollments during the past half dozen times it was offered?
- Do we have faculty qualified to teach the course? Interested in teaching it?
- What is the educational value of the course?
- How does offering the course affect the enrollment in other classes?
- What factors favor keeping the course?
- What factors favor eliminating the course?
- Is this a course taught at most other universities?

ASSIGNING COURSES

Who should teach what courses?

Making teaching assignments is simple in some respects and difficult in others. For example, if you have a course that only one person is qualified to teach, then your decision is obvious. What gets complicated is assigning to one faculty member the course that everyone in the department wants to teach. You look for the best teacher of the course, and you probably develop some kind of rotation plan out of fairness to all involved.

Then there are questions about who teaches when. Some faculty members don't mind evening courses, others don't mind early morning courses, and so the story goes. Often you have to assign some faculty members to times they dislike. Once again, a rotation plan can help to solve this problem.

I believe that setting the schedule should be participatory. I did this by making up a draft schedule and then asking each faculty member to examine it and discuss it with me if they wished to offer suggestions for change. Then, if I could accommodate all requests, I made them. When I couldn't, I explained why.

It is important to be fair to all faculty members, but it is even more important to be fair to students. If you have faculty members who for some reason cannot teach courses with large enrollments, it is a tremendous disservice to both students and faculty to assign them. Trying to match the right faculty member to the right course (by size, content, level, etc.) is never easy, especially in departments that are large.

Should I hire part-time faculty members?

The answer is yes if you can find qualified persons, and if you have the funds. This is a real problem for some department chairpersons. In certain specialized areas it is next to impossible to find qualified individuals from off campus, especially if you are in a small, isolated community.

Hiring part-time faculty members is a way to save money for the university; we usually pay them so little it's embarrassing. Too many universities resort to this practice simply because of the economy, and students end up the losers.

One problem that you as chairperson will soon discover if you hire part-time faculty is that, because of other off-campus commitments, they may come in just before class and leave right after it is over, which means that advising and assisting students fall on full-time faculty members. When you hire a large number of part-time faculty, this can create many problems for full-time faculty who already feel overworked.

Each chairperson must decide the pros and cons of hiring part-time faculty, because the situations vary so much from one school and community to another. What might work for one department chairperson is not a good solution for another.

If you do hire part-time faculty members, remember that you have a responsibility to them. You must look after their welfare just as you do that of your full-time faculty, and you must realize that they will have a different set of concerns. You need to assist by providing each with a mentor, and you should visit their classes from time to time. You ought to consider the possibility of putting on a special training program for them. In it you could address common teaching problems and discuss university and department policy that would be helpful. Also, you should examine their syllabi and look carefully at their student evaluations so that you can get a feel for how they are doing, and where they might need help.

Should our department teach interdisciplinary courses?

By all means examine this possibility. Well-conceived and well-taught interdisciplinary courses offer a lot to students. Moreover, they can be enjoyable and challenging to teach. Talk to some of your colleagues at conventions to see what, if any, courses they teach as interdisciplinary.

Whether it is trying to get faculty members to teach interdisciplinary courses or trying to get them to teach a course they've not taught before, you will find that one of the most difficult matters dealing with the curriculum is making any kind of change. As we know, many faculty members resist change, and resistance to change in curriculum is particularly strong. Some faculty members will fight to the very end to keep from making any changes, even in the face of convincing evidence that change is needed. All of your persuasive powers will be called upon as you attempt to make changes in your curriculum. The welfare of your department is in many ways tied to your curriculum, and you must do everything you can to see that your curriculum is current and meets the needs of your students.

Another matter that presents a challenge is when a decision is made to get rid of a sequence where there is generally healthy enrollment. An example of this comes to mind from a talk I had with a colleague whose faculty decided to get rid of a filmmaking sequence. They had decided that it was too costly, and their placement of students was less than satisfactory. Despite that, when the decision was announced, the students were upset, and no amount of explanation seemed to satisfy them. They wrote letters to government officials and made life generally miserable for the chairperson for a long period of time. If you have to face something of this magnitude, I suggest you develop a well-conceived plan for dealing with all kinds questions that are likely to come your way.

Dealing with matters of the curriculum can be aggravating and time consuming. Moreover, you will find that it is often difficult to make many big changes. Most faculty members feel comfortable making small changes—they will tinker around the edges and present this as overhauling the curriculum. All of your persuasive skills will be called upon if you are to do what you should in those matters dealing with the curriculum, but if you are the kind of chairperson who invites change, you will find these tasks exciting and fulfilling.

Creating Positive Relations with Your Dean

More than anything else, your dean does not like to be taken by surprise—he or she does not take kindly to being blindsided.

You and your dean generally want the same thing: a positive working relationship. Your dean wants your department to run smoothly, stay within budget, and provide students a good, solid education. Moreover, your dean wants and expects you to provide the kind of leadership that will enable your faculty to work in harmony.

Most deans do not want to micromanage your department—they don't have time for that. Your dean expects you to take charge, to be the leader, to be a strong advocate for your faculty and department, and to be collegial as well.

Here are some ideas that can help you work effectively with your dean.

- ***Keep your dean informed.*** Your dean needs to know what's going on. More than anything else, your dean does not like to be taken by surprise—he or she does not take kindly to being blindsided. Sometimes it is the little things that make a difference in how the dean regards your leadership. If you must be out of town, let your dean know, and let him or her know how to get in touch with you in the event something comes up on which you will need to consulted.

- ***Keep the lines of communication open.*** Your dean should know your goals and objectives, and you should send a copy of whatever plans you develop. Let your dean know of any potential problems. Likewise, if faculty members in your department do something that merits congratulations or commendations, let your dean know so that he or she can extend congratulations.

- ***Take responsibility for your decisions.*** Not every decision you make will produce the desired results. Just as you are willing to accept praise for good decisions, you must be willing to admit when you are wrong. You don't like to hear excuses from faculty members in your department, and your dean does not want to hear excuses from you. Good deans know that if you are going to be creative and innovative, you are going to make mistakes from time to time.

- ***Meet deadlines.*** When deans establish deadlines there are reasons; often the information you submit must in turn go into the dean's report to the vice president for academic affairs. If you are late, it may well cause your dean to be late.

- ***Stay within your budget.*** As mentioned earlier, deans expect their chairpersons to keep good track of their funds and not to overspend. Most deans will keep a small amount of money in reserve for emergencies, but they don't like to use the funds for those who are poor managers. If you have trouble, get some help from the financial affairs office and set up a system for tracking in your budget.

- ***Know university policy—and follow it.*** One of the first things you should do upon being appointed is to study the university's policy manual carefully and become familiar with the policies. Generally your secretary will know university policies thoroughly, but what if your secretary retires or takes another job?

- ***Try solving departmental problems yourself before going to your dean.*** The dean wants to help with problems when asked, but will not appreciate your running in every time a problem comes up. Do what you can to deal with the problem. If finally you cannot get it solved, then go to your dean.

- ***Be open with your faculty and share information with them.*** Over the years I've been puzzled that many faculty members never seemed to get information that I asked chairpersons to share with them. Occasionally I have found chairpersons who were so insecure that they hid information as a way of controlling their faculty. Information is often power.

I am a strong proponent of sharing all budget information with chairpersons, and I expect them to share budget information with their faculties. I have not always been able to convince some chairpersons that they should do this. Yet the strong, secure chairpersons have always complied.

• ***Be a strong advocate for your faculty and department, but be collegial.*** Deans expect you to be an advocate, but they do not want you to be so narrow in your advocacy that you are willing to hurt other departments in the process.

I do believe that you must be a strong departmental advocate, of course. The exceptional chairperson will know exactly when to stop—just before stepping over the line of hurting other departments. Chairpersons can present vigorous, robust arguments in support of positions they take that may be different from the one their dean takes. They should be able to push hard to persuade the dean to accept their view. However, once the matter has been resolved, it is wrong for a chairperson to go back to his faculty and lobby to get his or her way with the dean.

• ***Be honest and forthright.*** Just as you should be honest and forthright with faculty in your department, you must likewise be honest and forthright with your dean.

• ***Try to understand your dean and his or her role.*** The dean's job is not the same as yours. He or she must deal with several different departments. Most deans do all they can to be fair to all departments. There are times, I am certain, when it doesn't appear that the dean is being fair to you. When that happens, discuss the matter and try to see things from the dean's point of view. Just as you must at times make decisions that are not popular with all of your faculty, the dean will have to make some decisions that not all chairpersons like.

• ***Don't talk behind your dean's back.*** This is related to the paragraph above. Don't "bad mouth" your dean. You would be surprised how fast news travels and how many times the dean learns what you have said. Professionalism requires that we not talk behind another's back. Moreover, this brings up the matter of trust. Your dean must be able to trust you. If he or she cannot, you probably will not remain in your position very long. And, of course, when it gets back to your dean that you are talking behind his or her back, your dean's trust in you will be shattered.

• ***Consult with your dean before you make difficult, far-reaching decisions.*** When you must make decisions that some of your teachers are going to be unhappy about, it is a good idea to let your dean know what you're doing. When decisions are going to make a difference in the lives of a lot of faculty, staff, or students, you owe a full explanation to your dean.

• ***Don't make problems for your dean.*** Your dean has enough problems without your creating any more. Often you can avoid creating problems simply by keeping the dean informed. Let your dean know, for example, if you have a faculty member who is experiencing problems; then try to deal with those problems yourself. Your dean will step in to settle things when your problems get too big, but it's wisest not let them get that big.

• ***Sit down for a candid talk with your dean from time to time.*** These chats can be therapeutic. Chairpersons have a tough job, and there are times when a pep talk or reassurance helps. At other times a good discussion on educational philosophy is helpful. These discussions help us to keep our focus.

• ***Convey to your faculty a sense of partnership with your dean.*** What you say to your faculty about college policy, and how you say it, often can reveal much about your relationship with your dean. If you have the opportunity to present your side of an issue, you should support whatever decision is finally reached on it. Don't routinely tell your faculty that you argued for a position but the dean overruled you; if you do this often, your faculty will come to have no confidence in the college's leadership. Instead, indicate that there was a lot of discussion surrounding the issue and the decision was not arbitrary.

• ***Work to become an effective spokesperson for your department.*** Your dean—and the faculty members in your department—expect you to be an effective spokesperson. This means you must have in your head a lot of information about the department—the essence of its mission statement, its goals and objectives, enrollment, etc. Use every opportunity you can to fairly promote the department and its faculty, staff, and students.

A suggestion: Keep a list of potential news stories. Encourage your faculty to share expertise when the media seek a local perspective about a news event. If, for example, you have an expert on Iran in your department, you should introduce him or her to local media to provide views about that part of the world.

One thing you might consider is publishing a booklet to introduce your faculty to the news media. Give background on each member of your faculty and provide information relative to his or her expertise. (Check this with your university relations department, of course.)

Your dean shares in the responsibility to create positive working relations. Deans should provide support for and encourage development of chairpersons. Deans should serve as teachers and mentors to chairpersons. They should consider the following strategies (Green & McDade, 1991):

- Sponsor an orientation program for all new chairpersons.
- Provide help for chairpersons to stay active in their field.
- Conduct periodic workshops for chairpersons.
- Provide funds to help chairpersons meet their professional development needs.
- Discuss expectations for each chairperson.
- Help chairpersons develop workable goals.
- Take advantage of self-assessment, professional development plans, and evaluations to help chairs in their development.
- Help new chairpersons—especially those who are new to the campus—understand the culture of the institution and the department.

Having a positive working relationship with your dean and with other administrators across campus is good for your department and is worth working for. Regular talks can develop better understanding.

If your performance evaluations suggest that you are lacking some interpersonal skills, review the points in this chapter to see if there are areas where you could improve. Also, it would probably be to your benefit to talk with your dean to ask what you might do to improve your interpersonal skills. Of course, if you ask that question, you must not resent any criticism. Take it as you should and see what you can do to correct any problems.

An effective relationship is not just to your advantage; it's to your dean's advantage also.

REFERENCES

Green, M. F., & McDade, S. A. (1991). *Investing in higher education: A handbook of leadership development.* New York, NY: ACE/Macmillan.

Surviving the Technology Revolution

A new civilization is emerging in our lives, and blind men everywhere are trying to suppress it.

—Alvin and Heidi Toffler

If you are anything at all like most university administrators bracing to meet the challenges of the coming millennium, your head is in a spin. And while frustration may at times rule your working life, excitement about what lies ahead makes life not only bearable, but at times exhilarating. Despite the wide-ranging emotions that you must deal with, there are complex issues related to the use of technology in education with which you must come to terms. In this chapter we will explore these issues so that you can explain to faculty members what to expect, thereby easing the anxiety some may feel about technology and its impact on higher education.

HOW WILL I KEEP PACE WITH TECHNOLOGY?

Most universities cannot keep current with new technological developments, though there are some that somehow manage to remain well ahead of others. While universities will not likely keep pace with technological developments, they will nonetheless be forced to make changes to accommodate to the emerging information age. Brown and Duguid (1996, p. 11) point out, “It’s probably less helpful to say simply that higher education will change because of changing technologies than to say the emerging computational infrastructure will be crucially important in shaping an already changing system.”

Most of those looking at the future of education agree it will move from synchronous to asynchronous. Television as it primarily exists today is synchronous; i.e., viewers must come to it at set times and places. For example, if we wish to view tonight's news broadcast, we must find a television set and tune in at specified times unless we want to tape it to watch later. First-run movies are synchronous in that we must go to certain movie theaters when they are showing. Movies that we rent from our favorite video store are asynchronous, which means we can decide time and place to view them.

As we take advantage of what the so-called information superhighway has to offer, we are likely to be using computers to deliver education to students asynchronously. Students enrolled, for example, in an intermediate statistics course will be able to log onto the World Wide Net and locate the course. They will then be able to "talk" to their instructor. They may do this at 2 a.m. in the quietness of their dorm rooms where they will be able to ask questions of their statistics teacher. One student might say that he doesn't understand the relation among various conditional probabilities and that he wants more information on Bayes' theorem. Other students in the class will be able to get individual help with their problems. The so-called virtual professor will make the delivery of education asynchronously possible so that teaching and learning are more than just watching a video.

WILL TECHNOLOGY DEHUMANIZE EDUCATION?

There is no question that technology will change the way teachers teach and students learn. But will it dehumanize the process? Most believe that it will not. Indeed, those who have commented on education of the future generally see technology as a force for humanizing formal education. Many have commented on how teaching will change: They believe that teachers will give many fewer lectures, using many other approaches, such as coaching, providing more interaction between themselves and their students. If this happens, education will be more humanized in the years ahead.

Gates (1995, p. 185) writes that "Just as information technology now allows Levi Strauss & Co. to offer jeans that are both mass-produced and custom-fitted, information technology will bring mass customization to learning." He goes on to say that "multimedia documents and easy-to-use authoring tools will enable teachers to 'mass customize' a curriculum."

WILL TECHNOLOGY SOLVE OUR PROBLEMS?

Information technologies could help solve some of higher education's most pressing problems. First, information technologies offer economies of scale. The incremental cost of usage per student is likely to be low, though the front-end investment is sometimes large. Because of this, it will be years before universities will begin to realize significant cost savings.

Second, students will tend to be more engaged, and retention should be less of a problem than it is today. If we accept the idea—as many who have made projections about education in the future have—that technology will humanize formal education, then we can see how students will come to have warmer feelings about education. With students as active participants in more of a one-on-one education, they should be more engaged.

Third, we will not have to continue adding to our physical plants. The advent of long-distance learning and asynchronous learning, among other technological advances, should mean that we don't have to keep building new buildings and paying for their increasing operating costs.

Certainly, technology will help solve or ease some of the problems that universities face, but it won't provide all of the answers.

HOW CAN TECHNOLOGY IMPROVE TEACHING AND LEARNING?

What are some of the principal advantages to using technology in our teaching? There could be many.

Distance learning, by providing learning in the home, will increase the educational opportunities for many students, including those who live some distance away from a campus and specially challenged students. Students and faculty will not have to meet at the same time because the computer will store their communications; thus on-line education will be available at any hour of the day or night, seven days a week. Students anywhere in the world can be a part of a single class; teachers around the world can team-teach a course.

Research suggests that the effective integration of technology in the curriculum stimulates students to attempt more complex tasks and material. Green and Gilbert (1995, p. 13) credit Kozma and Johnston in presenting ideas about the role of information technology as a catalyst for the qualitative enhancement of the learning experience:

From reception to engagement. The dominant model of learning in higher education has the student passively absorbing knowledge disseminated by professors and textbooks. With technology, students are moving away from passive reception of information to active engagement in the construction of knowledge.

From the classroom to the real world. Too often students walk out of a class ill-equipped to apply their new knowledge to real-world situations and contexts. Conversely, too frequently the classroom examines ideas out of the context of gritty real-world considerations. Technology, however, is breaking down the walls between the classroom and the real world.

From text to multiple representations. Linguistic expression, whether text or speech, has a reserved place in the academy. Technology is expanding our ability to express, understand, and use ideas in other symbol systems.

From coverage to mastery. Expanding on their classic instructional use, computers can teach and drill students on a variety of rules and concepts essential to performance in a disciplinary area.

From isolation to interconnection. Technology has helped us move from a view of learning as an individual act done in isolation toward learning as a collaborative activity. And we have [also] moved from the consideration of ideas in isolation to an examination of their meaning in the context of other ideas and events.

From products to processes. With technology, we are moving past a concern with the products of academic work to the processes that create knowledge. Students . . . learn how to use tools that facilitate the process of scholarship.

From mechanics to understanding in the laboratory. The scientific laboratory is one of the most expensive instructional arenas in the academy. It is costly to maintain . . . and to provide supervision to student scientists. It is also limited as a learning experience. So much time is required to replicate classic experiments . . . that there is little time left for students to explore alternative hypotheses as real scientists do" (Kozma & Johnston, 1991, pp. 16–18).

HOW WILL TECHNOLOGY CHANGE STUDENTS AND CLASSROOMS?

In the Information Age, knowledge—data, information, images, symbols, culture, ideology, and values—is the central resource. If universities remain the main collectors and dispensers of knowledge, then they will become increasingly important in the coming years.

Some futurists speculate that the campus of the future will be "virtual," with no need for the physical plant that has been the visible center of academia for so long. Others believe that many students will study on campus just as they do today and that many others will get their education via the Internet.

Seagren and Watwood (1996, p. 1) quote the Virginia Commission on the University of the Twenty-First Century as saying that the university is evolving as follows:

- The university will be a network of resources, not a place.
- Offerings will give students a global, multicultural perspective.
- Widespread use of new technologies will improve the quality of instruction, increase contact between students and faculty, and reduce constraints on time, place, and space.
- Living and learning will be more closely integrated outside the classroom.
- Teaching will be more responsive to individual differences.
- Faculty roles, responsibilities, and rewards will expand and change.
- Colleges and universities will be increasingly interdependent with other educational providers and the private sector (Jones, 1989).

We can see radical changes in higher education developing because of technology. At the Harvard Business School, the hallmark of the revised M.B.A. is the Web-based curriculum. It is used to deliver information to students via their computers. "All of the school's more than 70 classes have their own Web sites, and most have links to multimedia and related sites on the World Wide Web" (Mangan 1996, p. A31).

HOW WILL TECHNOLOGY AFFECT TEACHING AND LEARNING?

Collins (1991, pp. 29–30) has documented eight shifts in teaching/learning in the classroom due to the impact of new technologies.

- A shift from whole-class to small group instruction where teachers may have a more "realistic picture" of what their students know and can do
- A shift from lecture and recitation to coaching
- A shift from working with better students to working with weaker students, as teachers are drawn to the students who need help
- A shift toward more engaged students, as students who find traditional classes boring will see information technologies to be encouraging and supporting their long-term effort, and will thereby be inclined to increase their personal investment in their work
- A shift from a policy of assessment based on test performance to assessment based on products, progress, and effort, once teachers have been introduced to this style of assessment
- A shift from a competitive to a cooperative social structure, as some software requires students to work together to accomplish assignments
- A shift from all students learning the same things to different students learning different things, as students work with different pieces of the problem and bring the pieces together for the overall solution
- A shift from the primacy of verbal thinking to the integration of visual and verbal thinking

Some suggest that the "on-line academy" will further polarize our learning system. They suggest that the more expensive, conventional campus is less likely to disappear than to become the increasingly restricted preserve of those who can afford it, and that net access will be for those who cannot. They go on to suggest that an on-line degree will not command the same respect as its distant campus cousin.

WHAT EFFECT HAS TECHNOLOGY HAD SO FAR?

The United States Congressional Office of Technology Assessment surveyed teachers who are now using computers in their classroom. The respondents indicate that technology has already had a significant impact on teaching and learning:

- 72% expect more from their students in terms of proofing and editing their work.

- 70% spend more time with individual students.
- 65% have become more comfortable with students working independent of teacher instruction.
- 63% are able to present more complex materials to their students.
- 61% are better able to tailor instruction to individual student needs.
- 52% spend less time lecturing in class.
- 43% are more comfortable with small group activities.
- 40% spend less time with the whole class practicing or reviewing material.

WHAT DOES THE DEPARTMENT NEED?

As a chairperson, you will find the issues related to the purchase of technology to be nettlesome, and no matter how much you learn about or how conversant you become with state-of-the art equipment, you will still second-guess yourself. Nonetheless, you need to exercise leadership and not allow yourself to become paralyzed by the array of choices available.

Guidelines for Purchasing Technology

Here are a few practical questions that will assist you in thinking about the purchase of hardware and software.

- How will the equipment be used?
- Is there a plan for how to make effective use of the equipment as a tool to support instruction and learning outcomes?
- Is there a plan for teaching faculty how to use the equipment?
- What is the life expectancy of the equipment?
- Are there add-ons or upgrades that can be purchased?
- Who will be responsible for maintenance of the equipment?
- Would it be wise to purchase a maintenance agreement?

Bates (1995) proposes seven criteria for deciding what technology is the most appropriate for particular applications. These form the acronym ACTIONS:

- Access is the most difficult issue because technology may cost students money. However, the knowledge media are making geography less and less of a discriminator.

- Costs of media vary. Useful data are now available on the variation of unit costs with student numbers.
- Teaching and learning is less of a discriminator than access and costs, simply because people are good at learning from a variety of media.
- Interactivity and user-friendliness are important, but remember that interactivity is a very slippery word. Most so-called interactive technologies aren't very interactive.
- Organizational issues are key. Unfortunately, the forms of technology-based teaching that pose the least threat to current organizational practice also hold the least promise for cutting costs and yielding valuable distinctiveness. That is a crunch issue.
- Novelty is sexy and attracts soft money. Make sure any novel technology will be cost-effective after the soft money runs out.
- Speed is important. Windows of opportunity can suddenly slam shut on your fingers. If you wait for a fully validated technology strategy, you'll never do anything.

Guidelines for "Selling" Technology

Purchasing the hardware and software is just the first step: Now you need to make sure that it is used so that your investment will not be wasted. Here are some strategies you can try:

- Keep your faculty engaged with new technological tools.
- Counsel and educate faculty who are possibly feeling displaced by new technology, especially new technology in the classroom.
- Develop a mentoring system, so that faculty who are already "sold" on the advantages of technology can work with faculty who remain skeptical.
- Develop a system of rewards for early adopters and innovators of new technology, especially new instructional technology.
- Develop a method to determine whether new instructional technology approaches are working in the classroom.
- Enlist the support of departmental staff in implementing new technologies and new instructional technology tools.
- Track any freeing up of time that the use of instructional technology brings and how this additional time is being used.

- Inform department members about positive uses of technology by their colleagues.
- Encourage faculty to share information, expertise, and discoveries about technology.

No matter what we think about change or about new technology, universities will change and emerging technology will be central to how they change. Indeed, American universities face change of historic proportions, and how we accept and benefit from the change will depend in part on department chairpersons and their understanding of our technological world. Universities have a great deal to lose or gain depending on their decisions about technology, and whether they lose or gain may depend on the insights you as a chair bring to the decision-making process. It obviously is in your best interest—and that of the department—to keep on top of technological developments.

REFERENCES

Bates, A. W. (1995). *Technology, open learning, and distance education.* London, England: Routledge.

Brown, J. S., & Duguid, P. (1996, July/August). Universities in the digital age. *Change,* 28 (4), 11.

Collins, A. (1991, September). The role of computer technology in restructuring schools. *Phi Delta Kappan,* 27 (2), 29–30.

Daniel, J. S. (1997, July/August). Why universities need technology strategies. *Change,* 29 (4), 17. [With permission of The Helen Dwight Reid Educational Foundation.]

Gates, W. (1995). *The road ahead.* New York, NY: Viking.

Green, K. C., & Gilbert, S. W. (1995, March/April). Great expectations: Content, communications, productivity, and the role of information technology in higher education. *Change,* 27 (2), 13. [With permission of The Helen Dwight Reid Educational Foundation.]

Jones, J. S. (1989). *Case for change.* Richmond, VA: Commonwealth of Virginia.

Kozma, R. B., & Johnston, J. (1991, January/February). The technological revolution comes to the classroom. *Change,* 23 (1), 10.

Mangan, K. S. (1996, November 15). High-tech tools help transform the way Harvard teaches business. *The Chronicle of Higher Education,* A31.

Seagren, A. T., & Watwood, W. B. (1996, July). *The virtual class: A new paradigm for delivering higher education.* Paper presented at SCUP-31, Redefining Higher Education from Planning to Action, Washington, DC.

Toffler, A., & Toffler, H. (1994). *Creating a new civilization.* Atlanta, GA: Turner.

United States Congressional Office of Technology Assessment. (1995, April). *Teachers and technology: Making the connection.* Washington, DC: United States Congressional Office of Technology Assessment, United States Government Printing Office.

25

Managing Generation X

Generation Xers are used to doing things on their own and resent what they call "in-your-face" management.

Today's department chairpersons need some understanding of faculty members they will be hiring in the years to come: Generation Xers, those born between 1963 and 1981 who many current supervisors believe require a different kind of management. Those who have studied Generation X will tell you that these young people are different and that if you ignore their differences and try to manage them according to your own mindset, you risk constant conflict. This chapter will deal with the characteristics that set Generation Xers apart from faculty members most of us have worked with over the years. It also will outline suggestions for managing those who belong to Generation X.

CHARACTERISTICS OF GENERATION X

The "X" in Generation X is the signature of a group that feels it has no identity, or at least no identity that anyone else cares about. Xers are also known by a variety of other labels: twenty-somethings, thirteeners (because they are the 13th generation since the founding of the republic), the lost generation, slackers, or the lurking generation, which is another dark image that refers to a cohort that grew up in the shadow of the baby boomers.

A part of what defines Xers according to many who have studied them is that they are the first latchkey kids. They grew accustomed to doing things on their own and of being alone. They view things differently from the way baby boomers and those of the silent generation do. Dorsey (1995, p. 1) presents characteristics that Generation X men and women bring to the work environment and their lives:

- Have a negative view of the world
- Are immature
- Feel deprived
- Are always questioning the boss
- Keep their options open
- Are very insecure
- Hunger to be noticed
- Have difficulty talking about themselves in interviews
- Are not trained to give service
- Cannot handle difficult people or situations

STRATEGIES FOR MANAGING GENERATION XERS

Although each faculty member in your department will have individual personality traits and needs, in general Generation Xers may require slightly different management strategies than their older, baby boomer counterparts.

Give regular feedback. Generation Xers crave feedback and external validation. Next to complaining about being bored, Xers complain about not getting any feedback. Use feedback as a way to mentor young faculty members. This generation, unlike some earlier ones, can accept criticism, and they yearn to take tests to find out how they compare with their peers.

Avoid micromanaging. While Generation Xers crave feedback, they are used to doing things on their own—remember, they are the latchkey kids who learned independence at an early age. They resent what they call "in-your-face management," but this is more a sign of independence than of arrogance. Provide clear instructions and set deadlines for tangible results, but give them some latitude to manage their own time and work. Focus on results rather than process.

Minimize red tape. Many twenty-something faculty members will argue that bureaucratic red tape wastes their time and energy and ought to be done away with. They believe that red tape stifles creative juices. As one Xer explained, "I like having responsibility and being in charge of my own destiny. I don't know if I'd like lots of bureaucracy and politics."

Develop an atmosphere that supports innovation. This generation works best when they think of themselves as sole proprietors no matter where they are working, and they perform best when they feel challenged and stimulated intellectually and socially. Provide them with opportunities to excel.Twenty-somethings are looking for a combination of autonomy and encouragement, but they do want to know how they are doing.

Share information. While sharing information is important in any setting, it is especially important where Generation X faculty are working. Many Xers are under the impression that managers purposely keep information from them. Moreover, they are experienced consumers of information, which is something they thrive on. Treat their many questions as opportunities to teach, not as threats.

Be a supporter or a coach. This generation is motivated by what they were deprived of, especially family time. Get to know something about the faculty member's family, career goals, and outside interests. Those who manage Xers say that they want to discuss their romantic problems as well as many other kinds of problems that boomers would never have thought of discussing with their boss. Let the person know that you value him or her as an individual as well as a part of the department.

Take advantage of their talents. Generation Xers have tremendous capacity to process lots of information and most of them have well-developed technological skills.

Avoid talking something to death. Managers who want to "talk things over" drive Xers crazy. This is a talked-out generation. They grew up with parents who always wanted to talk about things. This was also the first generation whose parents sent them in droves to counselors and psychologists. They have become weary of constantly showing their emotions and feelings and prefer action to analysis.

Provide them with variety. They get bored easily, but they thrive on taking up new assignments. Many boomers shy away from teaching "new" courses and prefer to teach the same courses year after year. That won't work with this new generation. They will become bored and insist on teaching different courses.

Dorsey (1995, p. 27) lists 20 things managers should avoid when it comes to managing Generation X employees:

- Don't assume they know anything about the world of work or work ethic.
- Don't try to convert them to your value system.
- Don't make negative generalizations about their generation.
- Don't equate youth and irresponsibility.
- Don't talk about "When I was your age . . ."
- Don't ignore their personal lives.
- Don't show disrespect.
- Don't criticize or correct them in front of others.
- Don't be condescending, patronizing, or phony in any way.
- Don't assume they know the rules or policies.
- Don't create vastly different rules or policies for different people.
- Don't leave responsibilities to chance.
- Don't accept anything less than the correct standard of behavior or service.
- Don't focus on personality or attitude. Instead, describe the specific behavior you want exhibited or changed.
- Don't constantly scrutinize people.
- Don't prevent them from speaking their mind on something important.
- Don't ever assume what motivates one will motivate another.
- Don't give perks or rewards without asking what motivates them.
- Don't have them do the same job all day, every day.
- Don't exclude anyone from an important meeting.

In truth, most of the strategies outlined here would work well with most of our faculty whether they are boomers, Xers, or of the silent generation.

While we must be careful in making generalizations, experienced managers who are now hiring younger workers insist that their new employees are different enough to warrant developing and employing new management strategies. If these strategies are helpful in dealing with Generation Xers, that is good. If they are nothing more than a reminder of good management strategies—no matter with whom you are dealing—that is good too.

REFERENCES

Dorsey, J. (1995, August 31). Generation X: Different work values. *Travel Weekly,* 53 (69), 27.

26

Where Do I Go from Here?

If administration is for you, become the best chairperson possible and work your way up the administrative ladder.

So you've developed good leadership skills, you've learned to raise money and keep track of your budget without overspending, you've been innovative, and you've developed a strong faculty that works in harmony. Where do you go from here? Are you content to continue as chairperson? If so, your colleagues are indeed fortunate. On the other hand, you have options. You can apply for a dean's job, or you could return to full-time teaching. There are pros and cons either way, of course.

When I was a chairperson I could see no reason to become a dean, and while I was encouraged many times to apply, I always said no. I couldn't imagine why anyone would want to be a dean. I said to others—only half jokingly—that I would like to be president of a university, but I didn't want to serve in any of the positions between chairperson and the president.

So why did I change my mind? I was offered one of those rare win-win situations. When the dean of liberal arts position came open, I was asked to become interim dean, and I accepted because I thought if I didn't like it, I could always go back to my job as chairperson. On the other hand, if I liked it I might be able to stay on—or even look elsewhere for a dean's position.

As it turned out, I loved the job of dean, and I applied and got the position. Interestingly enough, circumstances changed, and by the second year I couldn't stand the job and felt that I had made a huge mistake. Fortunately, my mood slump was temporary, and it wasn't long before my interest was revitalized. I have never looked back or been sorry for becoming dean. However, it is not for everyone. There is no real glory in being a dean. Full professors, who can pretty much dictate their teaching schedules, do research, and have summers off if they choose, are academicians who should be glorified.

What it comes down to is a matter of choice. If you enjoy administration as I do, then I hope you will consider going on to become dean, vice president, and president. I put off becoming dean until it was almost too late to move on up, though I was invited to interview for a presidency and turned it down because I had just made a move.

There are many ways to serve humankind in education. Custodial workers do their part just as do faculty members, administrators, and clerical staff. It would be hard to run a university without any of these individuals doing their jobs. If you get the most satisfaction out of teaching, then by all means teach. Become the best teacher you can be. Likewise, if administration is for you, become the best chairperson possible and work your way up the administrative ladder.

A DEPARTMENT CHAIRPERSON'S DOZEN

As chairperson, there are many development opportunities for you. As you no doubt know, there are several books out on the subject that deal with some of the problems you face, and I have established a list of books I believe all chairpersons ought to have on their office shelves. They are listed here as "A Department Chairperson's (Baker's) Dozen."

Bennett, J. B., & Figuli, D. J. (1990). *Enhancing departmental leadership.* Phoenix, AZ: ACE/Oryx.

Bensimon, E. M., Neumann, A., & Birnbaum, R. (1989). *Making sense of administrative leadership: The "L" word in higher education.* Washington, DC: The George Washington University.

Black, D. R. (1997). *Maintaining perspective: A decade of collegiate legal challenges.* Madison, WI: Magna.

Brittingham, B. E., & Pezzullo, T. R. (1990). *The campus green: Fund raising in higher education.* Washington, DC: The George Washington University.

Diamond, R. M. (1994). *Serving on promotion and tenure committees: A faculty guide.* Bolton, MA: Anker.

Eble, K. E. (1978). *The art of administration: A guide for academic administrators.* San Francisco, CA: Jossey-Bass.

Gmelch, W. H., & Miskin, V. D. (1993). *Leadership skills for department chairs.* Bolton, MA: Anker.

Johnsrud, L. K. (1996). *Maintaining morale: A guide to assessing the morale of mid-level administrators and faculty.* Washington, DC: College and University Personnel Association.

Lucas, A. F. (1994). *Strengthening departmental leadership.* San Francisco, CA: Jossey-Bass.

Murphy, M. K. (Ed.). (1992). *Building bridges: Fundraising for deans, faculty, and development officers.* Washington, DC: Council for Advancement and Support of Education.

Seagren, A. T., Creswell, J. W., & Wheeler, D. W. (1993).*The department chair: New roles, responsibilities, and challenges.* Washington, DC: The George Washington University.

Seldin, P., & Associates. (1990). *How administrators can improve teaching.* San Francisco, CA: Jossey-Bass.

Tucker, A. (1992). *Chairing the academic department.* (3rd ed.). Phoenix, AZ: ACE/Oryx.

There are several periodicals that contain ideas and information on becoming a better chairperson. Three that I rely on regularly are *Academic Leader, Change,* and *The Department Chair: A Newsletter for Academic Administrators.* There are also conferences geared primarily for chairpersons: the annual Kansas State Academic Chairpersons Conference, American Council on Education programs, a Miami University seminar for academic chairs, the National Community College Chair Academy conference, and others. Attending conferences such as these should benefit the chairperson who wants to do his or her job better. To grow and improve in our jobs, we should also talk regularly to other administrators to see how they do their jobs and to find what works for them in solving problems all chairpersons face.

DEVELOPMENT OPPORTUNITIES FOR CHAIRPERSONS

If you have had a good experience as a department chair, you are more likely to feel that other administrative positions are possibilities. To enhance the experience you have, it is important to take every opportunity you have for professional growth.

Continuing development for chairpersons will be critical in the years ahead. The massive changes that are likely to occur in higher education in the coming years will affect how chairpersons function. As Gilliland (1997, p. 31) argues, we in universities must confront the fact that:

> [T]he environment in which all organizations, public or private, must succeed is now characterized by accelerating change, complexity, and uncertainty. Universities, like all organizations, thus function in an environment of unpredictability, in contrast to the past, in which changes occurred more incrementally, the interactions among the parts of a problem and organization were tractable, and external economic and political pressures were more predictable.

Gilliland goes on to make the point that as operating procedures change within universities, department chairpersons will have to be trained in the proper procedures. She discusses tenure and how significant modifications are needed to bring about desired outcomes of flexibility, information access, and risk-taking. One of the changes she advocates is that of providing and requiring development programs for department chairpersons on "management and procedural issues, leadership effectiveness, the perceptions of constituencies, and the university-wide perspective on important issues" (Gilliland, 1997, p 33).

A chairs' council can help chairpersons with some of these matters. At one university where I taught, we had an active chairs' council, and its regular meetings gave us opportunities to have programs on issues that concerned us and to let others on campus— particularly upper-level administrators—know how we felt about academic issues. We were able to get our jobs defined, and we were able to get a chair's stipend where there had been none before.

RECOGNIZING AND DEALING WITH STRESS

Whether you decide to move further into academic administration, remain as a chairperson, or return to full-time faculty status, you must find balance in your professional life. Much has been written about the stress associated with being a chairperson. Gmelch (1991) in his study of 800 department chairpersons found the leading stressors to be:

1) time needed for administrative duties
2) confrontations with colleagues
3) pressures to keep current in one's discipline, and
4) job demands interfering with personal time.

Tough decisions and worrisome concerns clearly can cause stress. Additionally, stress studies show that other workplace factors contribute to stress (Fraser, 1992), and knowledgeable chairpersons can help reduce the levels of stress for themselves and their faculty. Thus, the following suggestions for recognizing and dealing with stress can be beneficial for you as well as for your faculty.

Set attainable goals. Fraser reminds us that some individuals—especially Type A personalities—overload their schedules and that the best way to alleviate stress is to set attainable goals.

Avoid procrastination. Stress levels can be reduced if we learn to not put off doing what has to be done (Maturi, 1992). Accomplishing something that must be done produces a certain level of satisfaction that combats stress.

Get plenty of exercise. The greatest stresses I have faced had nothing to do with my position but came from a higher-level administrator intent on dismantling the administrative team he had inherited. Moreover, a significant conflict involving students' First Amendment rights contributed to our differences. At any rate, I think exercise is what saved me from having some serious health problems during that period.

Find a way to relax. Regardless of stress level, we all need rest. In the situation I just described, I couldn't get the rest I needed—I couldn't relax. I was absolutely driven with the idea that the president was not going to defeat me. Therefore, I worked unbelievably long hours—often going to my office before 4 or 5 a.m. and not leaving until 6 or 7 p.m. Moreover, I was usually in my office on Saturdays and Sundays. I did that for more than a year before I finally accepted a dean's position at another university. It took some time, but eventually, with rest and relaxation, exercise, proper diet, and a great new job, I was able to recover.

What I have described above is supported by Fraser's contention that "An employee can intensify his own stress level by being his own worst enemy... [t]hese people are aggressive, hostile and driven; they overload their schedules and they distrust others." As much as I do not like to see myself as Fraser describes an employee, I believe for a brief time in my academic career I had become exactly that employee.

Develop a healthy lifestyle. As already noted, diet, rest, and exercise are important to health. Likewise, avoiding smoking, drinking to excess, and ingesting too much caffeine are wise practices. A healthy person, I am convinced, can deal better with the stress associated with work.

Analyze what is causing your stress. Stress is often self-induced. If you know what's causing it, you may be able to modify your behavior to get rid of the stress, or at least reduce its level. If you can isolate the causes, you may be able to persuade yourself that you are worrying needlessly. In time you may be able to get the stress under control.

See your physician. Stress is obviously a health problem, and your physician may be able to treat it. He or she may be able to give you medication on a temporary basis or suggest adjustments in the way you are living.

Share your frustrations with your spouse or a trusted friend. I think most of us realize we can get rid of some of our frustrations if we just find someone we can share our feelings with. If I have been under a lot of pressure and something is bothering me, I know I feel better if I talk it over with my wife at the end of a day. And by talking it out, not only do I feel better, but occasionally I see a way of dealing with the frustration and getting rid of it.

Plan time for yourself and family for entertainment. Just as you need exercise, you need relaxation. The kind of entertainment you enjoy is a matter of taste. I enjoy reading and get rather cranky whenever I can't find enough time to read for pleasure. In recent years I've found it relaxing to go to movies with my wife (a few years ago, my wife could not drag me to see a movie). I enjoy travel and spending time with my family, and my wife and I enjoy dining out.

Attend a conference. Getting out of town is a sure antidote to problems I am experiencing at work. I leave those problems behind and generally find intellectual stimulation with conference activities.

Examine and evaluate your workload. Are you trying to do too much? Are you properly delegating authority to your faculty and staff? Face up to these questions, and look, too, at other ways to manage your time and workload.

Teach a class. I have found that teaching does wonderful things for the way I feel. It helps me keep my sanity. It is always such a great feeling to leave my office for class. I leave behind the paperwork that is stacking up, the decisions that must be made, and the frustrations that come with the territory of a university administrator.

Get involved in a research project. Getting involved in a research project can provide an excellent escape from the stress of being a chairperson.

Get ready for Mondays. Researchers at the University of Maryland have concluded that Monday is the unhealthiest day of the week. They found that there is a higher incidence of heart attacks and irregular heartbeats. Physicians questioned by the researchers said they believe that the stress of the new work week was the critical factor in these health problems. You can relieve part of the stress by setting aside some time over the weekend to get organized and avoid the Monday rush.

Learn to tame the paper tiger. In the Information Age, we are now dealing with two kinds of information worlds—paper and paperless—either one of which could keep us busy from sunup to sundown. As Hemphill (1997, p. 4) points out, "One fact is absolutely clear: Paper-management skills are essential to survive the information explosion in our society." To which we must add: paperless management skills are equally important.

Frequently when I log on to the university's mainframe to see how many email messages I have demonstrates the point of this discussion. It often shows that I have 200 to 300 new messages. Meanwhile my desk is covered with paper, and just outside my door is a stack of mail I've yet to bring into my office. We've learned that while our computers have enabled us to do much of our work without paper, it has also created larger amounts of paper.

And the larger piles of paper, coupled with information that must be read and responded to on the Internet, makes the job more difficult, which in turn creates more and more stress.

There are undoubtedly other good ideas to help those who suffer from stress. In the end, each person must ask whether he or she is paying too high a price for being a university administrator. We know that not all stress is negative; it can be positive and should not be avoided altogether. It is a natural part of life.

Faculty stress comes from a variety of sources, and knowing what causes faculty stress will help you have a better understanding of faculty. According to the UCLA Higher Education Research Institute, the items listed in Table 26.1 are stress sources for faculty.

TABLE 26.1 Faculty Stress Sources

	Total	Men	Women
Time pressures	83.50%	80.70%	90.50%
Lack of personal time	79.80%	76.20%	88.50%
Teaching load	65.00%	62.10%	72.10%
Managing household responsibilities	63.70%	59.80%	73.30%
Committee work	57.59%	55.80%	61.90%
Colleagues	54.20%	53.00%	57.30%
Students	54.40%	48.20%	55.60%
Research/publishing demands	50.40%	51.40%	47.80%
Faculty meetings	49.60%	48.50%	52.30%
Review/promotion process	45.70%	43.80%	50.50%
Physical health	37.90%	36.00%	42.70%
Children's problems	31.50%	32.50%	29.00%
Subtle discrimination	29.20%	21.60%	47.90%
Child care	28.90%	29.00%	28.60%
Care of elderly parent	26.30%	25.50%	28.40%
Marital friction	23.80%	24.70%	21.50%
Fundraising expectations	20.80%	21.90%	18.00%
Long-distance commuting	16.80%	14.30%	22.80%

Source: UCLA Higher Education Research Institute. Reprinted with permission.

Whether you decide to stay on as chairperson, go back to full-time teaching, or move up the administrative ladder, your job will be more challenging and fulfilling if you work hard to improve your skills. Moreover, knowing that you are contributing positively to a noble cause—that of educating people—is rewarding. All the struggles seem to fade into the background when you hear from a former student who has called to thank you.

REFERENCES

Bennett, J. B., & Figuli, D. J. (1990). *Enhancing departmental leadership.* Phoenix, AZ: ACE/Oryx.

Bensimon, E. M., Neumann, A., & Birnbaum, R. (1989). *Making sense of administrative leadership: The "L" word in higher education.* Washington, DC: The George Washington University.

Black, D. R. (1997). *Maintaining perspective: A decade of collegiate legal challenges.* Madison, WI: Magna.

Brittingham, B. E., & Pezzullo, T. R. (1990). *The campus green: Fund raising in higher education.* Washington, DC: The George Washington University.

Cornish, R., Swindle, B., & Dabval, J. (1994, September 9). Managing stress in the workplace. *The National Public Accountant,* 39 (9), 24.

Diamond, R. M. (1994). *Serving on promotion and tenure committees. A faculty guide.* Bolton, MA: Anker.

Eble, K. E. (1978). *The art of administration: A guide for academic administrators.* San Francisco, CA: Jossey-Bass.

Fraser, J. (1992, April 23). Managing stress for success. *EDN,* 37 (9), 256.

Gilliland, M. W. (1997, May/June). Organizational change and tenure. *Change,* 29 (3), 31–33.

Gmelch, W. H., & Burns, J. S. (1994). Sources of stress for academic department chairpersons. *The Journal of Educational Administration,* 32 (1), 79.

Gmelch, W. H., & Miskin, V. D. (1993). *Leadership skills for department chairs.* Bolton, MA: Anker.

Gmelch, W. H. (1993). *Coping with faculty stress.* Newbury Park, CA: Sage.

Gmelch, W. H. (1991, Fall). The stresses of chairing a department. *The Department Chair,* 2 (2), p. 3.

Hannon, K. (1995, October 30). How to be a peak performer. *US News & World Report,* 119 (17), 97

Heckman, L. (1994, November 15). The working woman's guide to managing stress. *Library Journal,* 119 (19), 75.

Hemphill, B. (1997). *Taming the paper tiger.* Washington, DC: The Kiplinger Washington Editors, Inc.

Higgerson, M. L. (1996). *Communication skills for department chairs.* Bolton, MA: Anker.

Johnsrud, L. K. (1996). *Maintaining morale: A guide to assessing the morale of mid-level administrators and faculty.* Washington, DC: College and University Personnel Association.

Lucas, A. F. (1994). *Strengthening departmental leadership.* San Francisco, CA: Jossey-Bass.

Maturi, R. (1992, July 20). Stress can be beaten. *Industry Week,* 241 (14), 22.

Murphy, M. K. (Ed.). (1992). *Building bridges: Fundraising for deans, faculty, and development officers.* Washington, DC: Council for Advancement and Support of Education.

Seagren, A. T., Creswell, J. W., & Wheeler, D. W. (1993).*The department chair: New roles, responsibilities, and challenges.* Washington, DC: The George Washington University.

Seldin, P., & Associates. (1990). *How administrators can improve teaching.* San Francisco, CA: Jossey-Bass.

Tucker, A. (1992). *Chairing the academic department.* (3rd ed.). Phoenix, AZ: ACE/Oryx.

UCLA Higher Education Research Institute. (1991, Fall). *The Department Chair,* 2 (2), 17.

Periodicals

Academic Leader. Magna Publications, Inc., 2718 Dryden Drive, Madison, WI 53704-3086.

Change. American Association for Higher Education, One Dupont Circle (Suite 360), Washington, DC 20036-1110.

The Department Chair. Anker Publishing Company, Inc., PO Box 249, Bolton, MA 01740-0249.

Appendix

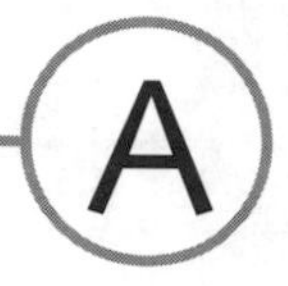

Affirmative Action Program, Proposed Faculty Appointment

1. Department: ______________________________
   School / College: ______________________________
2. Proposed Academic Rank: ______________________________
   Area of Specialization: ______________________________
3. Salary Range: From ______________ To ______________
4. How many total applications (completed) were received? ________
   What efforts were made to inform potential female/minority applicants of the vacancy?
   ____
   ____
   ____
5. How many applicants were interviewed? ______________________________
6. Give sex and race or ethnic composition of search committee.
   ____
   ____
   ____
7. Was the vacancy listed with Central University's Affirmative Action/Human Resource Office: Yes [ ] No [ ]
8. Was a written job announcement prepared? Yes [ ] No [ ]
   a. If yes, please attach a copy.
   b. If no, indicate why not:
   ____
   ____
   ____

9. Provide the name and address of organizations, individuals and publications used to publish the job announcement:

   ____

   ____

   ____

10. Give name, sex, and race, or ethnic origin (Caucasian, Black, American Indian, Asian or Hispanic) of each candidate interviewed. Check, for each candidate, one or more boxes indicating the main criteria by which the selected candidate was determined to possess stronger credentials for the particular position. Provide clarification where appropriate.

CANDIDATES INTERVIEWED

A. Name, sex, race, or ethnic origin of successful candidate:

____

____

1. [ ] Educational achievement.
   Candidate has: [ ] MA/MS [ ] ABD [ ] Ph.D.
2. [ ] Teaching ability. Candidate has______years of teaching experience.
3. [ ] Professional or academic references.
   Did candidate provide references? [ ] Yes [ ] No
4. [ ] Rank and/or salary required
5. [ ] Research or professional specialty
6. [ ] Scholarly research and publications
7. [ ] Other (specify): ______________________________

B. Name, sex, race, or ethnic origin of other interviewed candidate:

____

____

1. [ ] Educational achievement.
   Candidate has: [ ] MA/MS [ ] ABD [ ] Ph.D.
2. [ ] Teaching ability. Candidate has _____ years of teaching experience.
3. [ ] Professional or academic references.
   Did candidate provide references? [ ] Yes [ ] No
4. [ ] Rank and/or salary required

5. [ ] Research or professional specialty
6. [ ] Scholarly research and publications
7. [ ] Other (specify): ____________________

C. Name, sex, race, or ethnic origin of other interviewed candidate:

____

____

1. [ ] Educational achievement.
   Candidate has: [ ] MA/MS [ ] ABD [ ] Ph.D.
2. [ ] Teaching ability. Candidate has______years of teaching experience.
3. [ ] Professional or academic references.
   Did candidate provide references? [ ] Yes [ ] No
4. [ ] Rank and/or salary required
5. [ ] Research or professional specialty
6. [ ] Scholarly research and publications
7. [ ] Other (specify): ____________________

D. Name, sex, race, or ethnic origin of other interviewed candidate:

____

____

1. [ ] Educational achievement.
   Candidate has: [ ] MA/MS [ ] ABD [ ] Ph.D.
2. [ ] Teaching ability. Candidate has______years of teaching experience.
3. [ ] Professional or academic references.
   Did candidate provide references? [ ] Yes [ ] No
4. [ ] Rank and/or salary required
5. [ ] Research or professional specialty
6. [ ] Scholarly research and publications
7. [ ] Other (specify): ____________________

Review and Approval Signatures

____________________ ______ ____________________ ______

Department Chair Date Provost Date

Affirmative Action Recruitment Checklist

School/College/Department: ______________________________

Dean: ______________________________

Position: ______________ [ ] Tenured [ ] Tracking [ ] Nontracking

Dept Chair:________________ Director/Supervisor: ______________

Vita/résumé deadline date: ________________

Date Completed	*Required Activity, Search, Etc.*
________	1. Recruitment Authorization Form is approved and signed by chair, dean, director, and/or vice president
________	2. Received Affirmative Action Packet Data (Request it from Affirmative Action/Human Resources Office if needed)
________	3. Appointment of search committee and name of chair:__________________
________	4. Advertisement of position [ ] Chronicle [ ] Herald Dispatch [ ] Charleston Gazette [ ] Black Issue [ ] Other [ ] Professional journal____________________
________	5. Notice sent to minority schools and/or organizations and female organizations
________	6. Director of Affirmative Action/Human Resources or designee meets with search committee
________	7. Initial screening of candidates
________	8. Search chair contacts director of Affirmative Action/Human Resources or designee before bringing any candidates for interview
________	9. Interview conducted with candidates [ ] Telephone [ ] In person [ ] Video

__________ 10. Search committee determines top candidates and refers to department chair, vice president, or director

__________ 11. Selection of final candidate

__________ 12. Date sent to director of Affirmative Action/ Human Resources or designee for approval

__________ 13. Date sent to vice president/provost/director for approval

LETTERS SENT TO:

__________ Candidates who did not receive interview

__________ Candidates interviewed, not offered job

__________ Candidate offered position

CERTIFICATION STATEMENT

I certify that the recruitment procedures used in soliciting applicants, selecting qualified candidates from among all who applied, and offering of employment have been conducted in accordance with local, state, and federal Equal Opportunity laws. I further certify that the hiring practices and decision uphold the intent and integrity of Central University's Affirmative Action policy.

SPECIFICALLY, I CERTIFY THAT:

1. All candidates who were interviewed and/or considered for the position either met or exceeded minimum qualifications.
2. All candidates were interviewed and considered on the basis of their qualifications for the work to be performed.
3 No employment offer(s) was (were) extended (orally or in writing) to the successful candidate prior to approval by the director of Affirmative Action/Human Resources or designee.
4. Any salary offered at a level higher than that advertised received prior approval from the respective dean, provost, and vice president(s) and/or personnel department prior to the offer.

Department chair's or director's signature:

____

Title: ____________________ Date: ______________

Alumni Survey

1. Name ______________________________
   Street address ________________________
   City, state, zip ________________________
   Telephone (   )________________________
2. Employer____
3. Present position/title ____
4. How many years in present position? _____________
5. Do you consider this position to be in journalism/mass communications?
   [ ] Yes   [ ] No
6. Other positions held in the last 10 years ___________________________
   ____
   ____
   ____
7. Marshall degree(s) earned: [ ] B.A. [ ] M.A. Year(s)____________
   Sequence:
   [ ] Advertising   [ ] Public Relations
   [ ] Broadcast Journalism   [ ] Print Journalism   [ ] Radio/TV
   [ ] Journalism Education   [ ] Other: ____________________
8. Non Marshall degrees earned and emphasis ______________________
9. What aspects of education in the School of Journalism & Mass Communications were most positive and helpful to you professionally?
10. How could your education in the School of Journalism & Mass Communications have been improved (including classes both in and outside the School of Journalism that you wish you had taken)?

11. With 1 being very unhelpful and 5 being very helpful, please evaluate these aspects of your journalism education as they helped you in your career by placing the appropriate number in the space provided. Please leave blank any that do not apply to you.

Very unhelpful 1 2 3 4 5 Very helpful

____	classroom lectures	____	thesis
____	case studies	____	papers/projects
____	exams	____	professional groups
____	academic advising	____	career advising
____	non-journalism classes	____	textbooks
____	computer labs	____	internship(s)
____	outside job(s)	____	team projects
____	other students	____	informal contact with faculty
____	The Parthenon	____	WMUL
____	student agencies	____	guest speakers
____	lab classes (e.g., video editing)		

12. With 1 being unimportant and 5 being very important, please rate the following for their importance in securing your first position by placing the appropriate number in the spaces provided.

Unimportant 1 2 3 4 5 Very important

____	internship	____	class work
____	recommendations from faculty	____	clipbook/audio/video production
____	reputation of SOJMC	____	contacts from faculty/classes
____	outside jobs	____	other: ____________

13. With 1 being unimportant and 5 being very important, please rate the following for their importance in helping you learn about job opportunities by placing the appropriate number in the spaces provided.

Unimportant 1 2 3 4 5 Very important

____	university placement center	____	personal contacts
____	notices posted by faculty	____	other: ____________
____	want ads in professional publications or newspapers		

14. Please pick a number from the scale below to show how much you agree or disagree with each statement that follows and jot your answer in the space to the left of the item.

    1 = disagree strongly
    2 = disagree somewhat
    3 = neutral
    4 = agree somewhat
    5 = agree strongly

    ____ The School of Journalism and Mass Communication prepared me well for the professional world.

    ____ The experiences and perspectives of faculty members reflected an accurate and up-to-date knowledge of the demands of mass communications careers.

    ____ The faculty members adequately represented the diversity of opinion and perspectives present in mass communications fields.

    ____ The School of Journalism and Mass Communications prepared me well to use the technology used in my work.

    ____ I am using skills I acquired during my education at Marshall.

    ____ I would recommend the School of Journalism and Mass Communications to others wishing to pursue mass communications careers.

15. Please use the space below to comment on any of your answers to No. 14.

Course Evaluation: Questions to Consider

No two evaluation designs will be the same, as in each instance the evaluation must be structured to serve the information needs of those involved in the decision-making process. There is, however, a general list of questions that are often used in the evaluation of courses and other programs of instruction. The following list has been designed to assist faculty and administrators who are or will be charged with the task of evaluating a course. While no list could ever be considered complete, these items have been developed from efforts on several campuses that have dealt with the design and implementation of new courses and programs as well as the evaluation of existing courses and curricula. The list is intended to be a functional guide in the design stage of an evaluation. It should serve as a checklist to ensure that all relevant questions have been considered. In using this list, remember that all the questions may not be appropriate in a single project because of limitations in time, staff, and money. It is up to those involved to select and prioritize the specific questions that should be addressed. It is our hope that this list will lead to more responsible decisions regarding which issues will be addressed in the evaluation.

Consider each of the following questions and check those that are appropriate for the specific course you are evaluating.

I. Course Rationale

- [ ] A. What population of students is the course intended to serve?
- [ ] B. What student needs is the course intended to service?
- [ ] C. What institutional, community, or societal needs is the course intended to serve?
- [ ] D. What other defensible needs exist for offering this course?

[ ] E. What other courses serve these same needs?
[ ] F. To what extent does the course overlap with or duplicate these other courses?
[ ] G. On what grounds is the continued existence of this course justified and warranted?

II. Development and Current Status of the Course
[ ] A. When and under what circumstances was the course developed?
[ ] B. How frequently and how regularly has the course been offered?
[ ] C. To what extent has the enrollment increased, decreased, or stabilized from year to year?
[ ] D. What problems have been associated with the course and how have they been resolved?
[ ] E. To what extent is the course intended to be replicable from instructor to instructor or from term to term?
[ ] F. To what degree do the plans or design for the course exist in a written or documented form? In what documents (course approval forms, course outlines or syllabi, memos, etc.) do these plans exist?
[ ] G. How does the current version of the course differ from earlier versions? Why?

III. Credit and Curricular Implications
[ ] A. What credit is awarded for successful completion of the course? On what basis is this credit allocation justified?
[ ] B. In what ways can credit for this course be applied toward fulfillment of graduate and degree requirements?
[ ] C. At what level (lower division, upper division, or graduate) is the course classified? Why? On what basis is this classification justified?
[ ] D. How does the course fit into the overall curriculum of the sponsoring department and college?
[ ] E. In which departments is the course cross-listed? Why? How does it fit into the curriculum of these departments or colleges?
[ ] F. What prerequisite skills or experiences are needed in order to succeed in this course?
[ ] G. What problems are experienced by students who do not have these prerequisites?

IV. Course Objectives

[ ] A. What are the formal, stated objectives of the course?

[ ] B. How feasible and realistic are these objectives in terms of the abilities of the target population and the available time and resources?

[ ] C. How are the stated objectives related to the adult life-role competencies that students will need in everyday life outside of school?

[ ] D. How are the objectives related to the competencies students will need in their subsequent academic careers?

[ ] E. If the course is designed to prepare students for a specific professional or vocational field, how are the objectives related to the competencies they are likely to need in their future careers?

[ ] F. What values are affirmed by the choice of these objectives as goals for this course?

[ ] G. What other purposes, intents, or goals do the faculty, administrators, and other interested audiences have for the course?

[ ] H. What goals and expectations do students have for the course?

[ ] I. To what extent are these additional goals and expectations compatible with the stated course objectives?

V. The Content of the Course

[ ] A. What (1) information, (2) processes, and (3) attitudes and values constitute the subject-matter or content of the course?

[ ] B. How are the various content elements related to the course's objectives?

[ ] 1. Which objectives receive the most coverage or emphasis? Why?

[ ] 2. Which objectives receive only minor coverage? Why?

[ ] C. How is the content sequenced or arranged? Why is this sequence appropriate/inappropriate?

[ ] D. How are the various content elements integrated and unified into a coherent pattern or structure? To what extent does fragmentation or lack of coherence appear to be a problem?

[ ] E. What values and assumptions are implicit in the decisions which have been made regarding content selection and emphasis?

VI. Instructional Strategies

[ ] A. What kinds of learning activities are used?

[ ] 1. What activities are the students expected to engage during class session?

[ ] 2. What assignments or projects are students expected to complete outside of class?

[ ] 3. In what ways are these activities appropriate in light of the course objectives?

[ ] 4. How could these activities be made more effective?

[ ] B. What instructional materials are utilized?

[ ] 1. How and for what purpose are the materials used?

[ ] 2. How accurate and up-to-date are the materials?

[ ] 3. In what ways do the materials need to be improved?

[ ] 4. How could the materials be used more effectively?

[ ] C. What instructional roles or functions are performed by the teacher(s)?

[ ] 1. How could these roles be performed more effectively?

[ ] 2. What important instructional roles are not provided or are performed inadequately? Why?

[ ] D. What premises and assumptions about learning and the nature of the learner underlie the selection of instructional strategies? How and to what extent are these assumptions warranted?

VII. Procedures for Evaluating Students' Achievements

[ ] A. What instruments and procedures are employed as a means of collecting evidence of the student's progress and achievement?

[ ] B. What criteria are used to assess the adequacy of the student's work and/or achievement? On what basis were these criteria selected?

[ ] C. How well do the assessment procedures correspond with the course content and objectives? Which objectives or content areas are not assessed? Why?

[ ] D. To what extent do the assessment procedures appear to be fair and objective?

[ ] E. What evidence is there that the assessment instruments and procedures yield valid and reliable results?

[ ] F. How are the assessment results used? Are the results shared with the students within a reasonable amount of time?

[ ] G. How consistently are the assessment criteria applied from instructor to instructor and from term to term?

[ ] H. What indications are there that the amount of assessment is excessive, about right, or insufficient?

VIII. Organization of the Course

[ ] A. How is the course organized in terms of lectures, labs, studios, discussion sections, field trips, and other types of scheduled class sessions?

[ ] B. How frequently and for how long are the various types of class meetings scheduled? Is the total allocation of time sufficient/insufficient? Why?

[ ] C. If there is more than one instructor, what are the duties and responsibilities of each? What problems result from this division of responsibilities?

[ ] D. What outside-of-class instruction, tutoring, or counseling is provided? By whom? On what basis?

[ ] E. How well is the student work load distributed throughout the course?

[ ] F. To what extent are the necessary facilities, equipment, and materials readily available and in good working condition when needed?

IX. Course Outcomes

[ ] A. What proportion of the enrollees completed the course with credit during the regular term? How does the completion rate vary from instructor to instructor or from term to term?

[ ] B. What proportion of the enrollees withdrew from or discontinued attending the course? Why?

  [ ] 1. To what degree does their discontinuance appear to be related to factors associated with the course?

  [ ] 2. How does the attrition rate vary from instructor to instructor or from term to term?

[ ] C. At the end of the course, what evidence is there that students have achieved the stated objectives?

  [ ] 1. For which objectives was the course most/least successful?

  [ ] 2. For what kinds of students was the course most/least successful?

[ ] D. What effects does the course appear to have had upon students' interest in the subject matter and their desire to continue studying and learning about this subject?

[ ] E. What other effects did the course have upon the students?

  [ ] 1. How were their values, attitudes, priorities, interests, or aspirations changed?

  [ ] 2. How were their study habits or other behavioral patterns modified?

  [ ] 3. How pervasive and/or significant do these effects appear to be?

These guidelines were developed by Robert M. Diamond and Richard R. Sudweeks at the Syracuse University Center for Instructional Development. Reprinted by permission of the authors.

Departmental/College Newsletter Sources

Sample departmental and/or college newsletters may be obtained from the following sources, upon request.

Source	Newsletter
School of Mass Communications University of South Florida 4202 East Fowler Avenue, CIS 1040 Tampa, FL 33620	*The Editor*
Edward R. Murrow School of Communication College of Liberal Arts Washington State University Pullman, WA 99164-2632	*The Murrow Communicator*
College of Journalism & Mass Communications University of South Carolina Columbia, SC 29208	*InterCom*
Department of Chemistry Middle Tennessee State University P. O. Box 68 Murfreesboro, TN 37132	*Chemistry Newsletter*
College of Communications The Pennsylvania State University 208 Carnegie Building University Park, PA 16802	*The Communicator*

Monday Morning Memo / Electronic

INTEROFFICE MEMORANDUM

Date: 13-Nov-1997 04:22 p.m. CST

From: Deryl R. Learning DLEAMING

Dept: Mass Communication Tel No: 898-2564

TO: 68 addressees

Subject: Monday Morning Memo—November 17, 1997

Monday Morning Memo—November 17, 1997—Vol. II, No. 11

Teaching Brown Bag Set.

Dan Pfeifer will conduct two brown bag workshops on syllabus writing. The meetings will be Wednesday, November 19, at noon and Thursday, November 20, at 3:30. Both sessions will be in the dean's conference room. These sessions are part of a series on teaching excellence sponsored by the college's committee to improve teaching. Dan suggested bringing a syllabus with you as this will be an open forum to discuss elements, organization, and other aspects of course syllabi.

Oxymorons I've Seen Recently.

Here are some oxymorons I've seen in print lately: plastic glasses, definite maybe, twelve-ounce pound cake, diet ice cream, rap music, temporary tax increase.

Burriss Authors Lead Article.

Larry Burriss has the lead article in the current (Winter, 1997) issue of *Focus on Elementary,* a publication of the Association for Childhood Education

International. The title of the article is "Safety in the Cybervillage: Some Internet Guidelines for Teachers."

Jimison Undergoes Heart Surgery.

Tom Jimison underwent quadruple bypass heart surgery last Friday and is currently recovering at Centennial Hospital in Nashville. He told me this morning he feels well.

Chris Blanz to Speak in Graphics Classes.

Chris Blanz, creative director for EdgeNet, one of the major ISPs in Nashville, will be speaking to several graphics classes tomorrow. In the morning sessions—9:25 and 10:50—he will discuss the design and technology of Web pages in the Introduction to Graphic Communication classes. He also will be speaking to the Publication Design class at 1:25. He will be joined by Jeff Felertag, EdgeNet's director of Internet training. There will be room for faculty to attend these sessions, especially the afternoon one, according to Ray Wong.

Carlos Cortez Lectures Today, Tomorrow.

Carlos Cortez will lecture today and tomorrow on multiculturalism and civility and gender relations. He will speak this evening at 7:00 p.m. in the Tennessee Room of the James Union Building and tomorrow at 9:30 a.m. and 1:00 p.m. in the KUC theater.

Have a good week.

Monday Morning Memo / Print

October 28, 1997

TO: All Faculty

FR: XXXXX

RE: Monday Morning Memo

Fall Alumni Banquet.

The Journalism Alumni Association's fall banquet will be November 2 at the Radisson (social hour at 6 p.m. and banquet at 7 p.m.). As you already know, George Arnold and James Casto will be honored. Tom Miller has given me tickets to sell. They are $20 per person. Yes, they plan to make some money on the event. And as you know, they always give whatever is left after expenses to the School of Journalism. Bev McCoy also has tickets.

Televised Courses.

Keith Spears sends word that the Higher Education Instructional Television Consortium is interested in faculty proposals for courses to be taught by public television in 1998-99. NEW: The deadline on this is no later than November 13 because the state selection committee meets on November 14. To propose a course the department must complete a simple form. Let me know if you're interested in teaching by television.

Curriculum Committee.

The Curriculum Committee will meet at 3:00 p.m. Wednesday in the conference room.

Journalism Faculty Meeting.

Our next faculty meeting will be on Thursday, November 14 at 4:15 p.m. in the conference room. Please mark your calendars.

Graduate Faculty.

On the back of this memo is a memo from the Graduate Committee that was sent by memo to all deans who sent a memo to all chairpersons who were instructed to share the information by memo with all faculty. I'm not sure why the Graduate Committee didn't send a notice to all faculty directly, but then where would the bureaucracy and the paper industry be?

Guest Speakers.

Jeff Seglin of *Inc.* magazine has committed to a date for his visit next semester. He'll be on campus from Sunday evening, February 16, until late afternoon or early evening on Tuesday, February 18. A public presentation will probably be scheduled for Monday evening, and he is available for classroom visits at other times. First come, first served.

Wil Haygood of the *Boston Globe* will be visiting in the early part of second semester, too, but the days of his visit aren't yet determined. Do you think Boston is far enough away to keep us from being considered insular and provincial?

Resource Materials. The Placement Services Center has agreed to purchase *Current Jobs in Writing, Editing, & Communications.* It should be available for our students' use in about one month. While visiting campus last week, Brent Archer of Columbia Gas Transmission left copies of *Bacon's Publicity Checker* for magazines and newspapers. They're available in the journalism library.

Follow up to Last Faculty Meeting. At Thursday's faculty meeting, a number of issues were left unresolved. First, I asked for volunteers for two ad hoc committees, one to decide what equipment to include in our request to the Clay Foundation and another to help with a five-year plan as related to Dr. Gilley's desire to have journalism as one of the centers of excellence. Janet, Ralph, and Corley have volunteered for the equipment committee. Other committee members are welcome, but I don't think we need anyone else. The second committee now has Wayne and Chuck as volunteers and needs at least one, probably two, additional members. The discussion of the proposed School of Journalism plan regarding female/minority representation led to an agreement that the faculty will provide additional ideas for the committee about specific tactical approaches; the committee will write objectives for the plan (keeping in mind the university's multicultural plan); and the committee will attempt to include more about issues of gender.

Peer Evaluation Form

The thrust of peer evaluations is to assess the scholarship and organization that goes into the class. Thus, the most important phase of evaluation are the discussions between evaluator and teacher before and after the observation. Before visiting the class, the evaluator collects data such as instructional materials, reading assignments, tests, texts, instructor philosophy, scholarly quality, etc.

The evaluator should also find out about what has been covered in previous classes and receive an overview of the concepts to be covered during the evaluator's classroom visit. The evaluator should then visit the class on the scheduled date. Upon request of either the evaluator or the teacher, a second visit may be scheduled. After the visit, the evaluator should again meet with the teacher to provide feedback. When the evaluator has filled out the rating forms, a copy should be given to the teacher for inclusion in his or her files.

	excellent	good	marginal	poor	unacceptable
Instructor Knowledge					
How good is the scholarship that goes into the course?	1	2	3	4	5
Methods of Instruction					
Scholarship gets incorporated into the class	1	2	3	4	5
Tests and assignments are fair	1	2	3	4	5
Stresses important material	1	2	3	4	5
Vocational and Personal Advising					
Keeps regular office hours and is accessible to students	1	2	3	4	5

	excellent	good	marginal	poor	unacceptable
Is involved in students' activities outside of the classroom	1	2	3	4	5
Overall evaluation of teaching	1	2	3	4	5

Narrative Comments:

Recommendation to Hire, Faculty Position

COLLEGE OF MASS COMMUNICATION
Position description:

Position number:

1. Were there any exemptions to the college's recruitment procedures and the university's Affirmative Action Guidelines? [ ] Yes [ ] No
   If so, attach appropriate authorization.

2. Recommended rank: ________________
   Does candidate have terminal degree in field? [ ] Yes [ ] No
   Justification:

3. Number of years of full-time teaching:________________
   List below the institution(s) and number of years the candidate has taught.

4. Candidate is recommended for tenure at this time: [ ] Yes [ ] No
   If yes, provide justification, including number of years as a tenured professor at other institution(s).

5. Number of years recommended that the candidate be allowed to count toward tenure: ________ Candidate's tenure year would be: ________
   Justification:

6. If you are not recommending tenure at initial hiring, did you provide the candidate with the university promotion and tenure guidelines, and does he or she understand them? [ ] Yes [ ] No
   Comments:

7. Salary recommended: ____________________ Does this salary create any inequities in the department? [ ] Yes [ ] No
   Justification:

8. Describe the procedures used in checking the candidate's qualifications. Be specific—list the names of individuals who submitted letters, as well as names of persons contacted by telephone.

9. List below any additional comments relative to this recommendation.

____________________________________ ____________
(Search Committee Chair) (Date)

____________________________________ ____________
(Department Chair) (Date)

Dean's Recommendation for approval: [ ] Yes [ ] No
Comments:

____________________________________ ____________
(College Dean) (Date)

Review of Accomplishments, Dean or Department Chair

Memorandum

To: Liberal Arts Faculty and Staff

Fr: John McDaniel, Dean

Re: 1996–97 Year-in-Review

Date: June 6, 1997

It is time again for a brief review of academic-year highlights, along with some comments on major directions and developments for AY 1996-97 and beyond. In fall 1996 university enrollments rose to 17,924 (+2.87% over fall 1995). Liberal Arts enrollments increased 6%, giving us a 13th consecutive year of record enrollment. Cliff Gillespie is predicting 18,299 (+2%) for AY 1997–98. Cliff also reports that 141 new Presidential Scholars have declared their intent to enroll in the fall; of these, 25 are liberal arts majors and 37 are undeclared. Our freshman class for AY 1997–98 is averaging 22 on the ACT (which is above state and national averages), African-American enrollment is up 15% in the freshman class, and 31 Floyd Scholars are coming on board. For us, staffing will be a major concern once again, with numerous full-time temporary faculty holding down tenure-track lines as a result of the budget crunch. Our space problems should be ameliorated to some degree by the limited opening (on a "phase-in" basis) of the new Business/Aerospace Building this fall. The provost is intent on doing away with the portables and finding new office space for faculty housed therein, a project now headed by Bob Jones. And now to the year in review.

Tenure and Promotion

The president has made the following recommendations to the Tennessee Board of Regents:

Promotion to Full Professor: Raphael Bundage, Jackie Eller, Ron Zawislak, Elizabeth Nuell, and Ron Bombardi

Promotion to Associate Professor: William Brantley, Madeline Bridges, Richard Moser, Elyce Helford, Doug Heffington, Timothy Rouse, Sharon Shaw, Steve Jones, Warner Cribb, Robert Holtzclaw, Karen Lee, and Dewayne Pigg

Tenure: William Brantley, Robert Bray, Madeline Bridges, Warner Cribb, Doug Heffington, Elyce Helford, Michael Hinz, Mary Hoffschwelle, Robert Holtzclaw, Steve Jones, Michael Linton, Richard Moser, Tim Rouse, Sharon Shaw, and Anne Sloan

Staffing

This year we have made and continue to make excellent additions to our Liberal Arts staff. We are in the process of adding 16 full-time faculty as replacements or add-ons for AY 1997-98. Because of the proposed budget cuts, we were required to do some creative hiring, with some full-time temporaries filling tenure-track lines. The total number of full-time faculty for AY 1997-98 will be 209, with an additional 130 part-time faculty, including 54 GTAs. Retiring this year are Norman Ferris (1962), Dan McMurry (1968), Larry Lowe (1963), and Wilma Barrett (1975), with a combined total of 154 years at MTSU. Ron Zawislak has been appointed chair of the geography/geology department as a replacement for Ralph Fullerton; Bill Connelly has been appointed chair of English as a replacement for David Lavery; and Jim Brooks will serve a second year as interim chair in music while we continue that search in AY 1997–98.

Budgets

FY 1996–97 was a "tight" budget year, as will be the upcoming FY 1997-98 budget year. The 4.28% budget cut proposed by Governor Sundquist has had a "chilling" effect on all of our operations, of course, but the provost is committed to preserving our academic programs and to underwriting expenses occasioned by growth. This past year the VPAA Office contributed

$93,000 for additional adjuncts; Technology Access dollars in the amount of $55,300 were allocated for computer-lab upgrades in English, geography/geology, and art; and the college was able to distribute $210,666 to Liberal Arts departments for faculty development and general operational support. The legislature, with the leadership of Senator Womack, is considering some ways of modifying the governor's proposed $40 million budget cut to minimize the impact on growing universities like MTSU. Still, it appears that budgets on campus will once again be lean—especially in light of an additional impoundment of reserves in the amount of $1,380,500 (our share of a $20 million reversion for higher education in 1996-97 budgets). Just hold on: We will ride out the storm.

Salaries

Although the state has provided no new monies for salary increases, you are all aware that the provost's market equity study with strong presidential backing is being readied for implementation this fall. The plan initially targets for salary improvement those faculty who fall below 92% of predicted salary based on salaries at 78 peer institutions. When this plan is implemented in August 1997, 71 Liberal Arts faculty will receive a salary increase, with a total of $157,909 for the college (27% of the $586,286 to be allocated to the University faculty). The goal, to be achieved in a phase-in plan for the next few years, is to reach 100% of market equity for everyone (a moving target, to be sure). There will be continued discussion and debate as the president and provost move forward with the market equity plan, but we are undertaking a good first step.

Faculty Internships

As a new feature this year, the college is preparing a Liberal Arts Newsletter, one that will detail faculty activities more fully than I have been able to do in the past in this year-in-review memo. This project is being undertaken by Karen Lee (social work), on a Liberal Arts internship. The newsletter should be out within the next few weeks. I would like to have your reactions to this new approach to publicizing faculty activities. Larry Mapp (English), also working on a Liberal Arts internship, is preparing what we hope will be an expansive and extensive Web site for the College of Liberal Arts. This too should improve our dissemination of faculty activities and college information—not only locally but throughout the world. Another Liberal Arts intern, Laura Jarmon (English), has done a valuable study on retention and persistence to graduation for African-American students in Liberal Arts. This study is in my office, available for your perusal.

Final Thoughts

The recent reports of the General Studies Task Force and the Academic Master Plan Committee have placed Liberal Arts departments at the center of the academic enterprise at MTSU—now and for years to come. Both reports stress the importance of strengthening "academic core" courses by providing interdisciplinary approaches and threshold and capstone courses. The Academic Master Plan calls for us to capitalize on areas of "competitive advantage," including communications, arts, law and government, and health and human services. And the recommendations for an Honors College, for improvements in library holdings and in arts and sciences facilities, and for the development of high quality graduate programs (including Ph.D.'s in such areas as English and history) provide opportunities that Liberal Arts faculty will welcome. This year we have seen the development of interdisciplinary minors in film and writing, along with a new major in anthropology; the Leonardo Project, an interdisciplinary approach to teacher preparation cosponsored by Liberal Arts and Education, has witnessed a dramatic increase in student and faculty participation; and a School of Fine Arts within the College of Liberal Arts is already on my drawing board as an arrangement with much interdisciplinary potential. Community outreach has been a strength of a number of our programs—not only in the obvious areas of speech and theater, arts, and music, but also in social work programs, public history and political science internships, the activities of the Gore Center and The Center for Historic Preservation, and the University Writing Center. Having had the opportunity to serve on both the General Studies Task Force and the Academic Master Plan Committee, I was pleasantly reminded once again of what I have known all along: the Liberal Arts are alive and well at MTSU—always have been, always will be. In the upcoming year we will be invited to rethink traditional methods of teaching and to move toward a "student learning-centered" environment. This could make for an interesting year indeed.

Student Exit Interview

DEPARTMENT OF MASS COMMUNICATION
SOUTHEAST MISSOURI STATE UNIVERSITY

1. As you conclude your course work at Southeast, there may be courses that you remember as being especially good.

   (a) Identify two courses you have taken during your college experience that have been especially memorable. (Include a course in the major/minor and a University Studies course.)

   (b) Similarly, there must be courses that you found to be less satisfactory. Take a few moments to identify two courses you have taken during your college experience that have been less than memorable. (Include a course in the major/minor and in University Studies.)

   (c) What is the basis that you used to classify the courses as either good or bad?

2. Think about the faculty you have had in your major courses. Can you assess their quality as compared to other faculty on campus?

   (a) Choose two words that you think best describe the department's faculty. Why?

   (b) If you asked other faculty outside the department to assess the quality of the mass communication faculty, what two words do you think they would use to describe our faculty? Why?

3. Think about the students that have been in your major courses. Can you assess their quality as compared to other students on campus?

   (a) Choose two words that you think best describe your classmates. Why?

   (b) If you asked other students outside the department to assess the quality of mass communication majors, what two words do you think they would use to describe your classmates? Why?

(c) If you asked faculty outside the department to assess the quality of mass communication majors, what two words do you think they would use to describe your classmates? Why?

4. The department stresses the value of your working with our student media and participating in the student organizations. Did you take advantage of these opportunities?

   (a) If you participated, did you find the experience rewarding?

   (b) What could be done to improve the experiences for others?

   (c) What could be done to help students understand the value of participating?

5. The department offers internship opportunities to students having a 2.5 GPA to a 2.75 GPA in course work in the department. Did you complete an internship?

   (a) If you completed an internship, what was the value of the experience?

   (b) Did the department satisfactorily assist you in securing an internship?

   (c) Do you think your supervisor at the cooperating agency also found the experience valuable? If yes, how do you think your performance compared with that of previous interns/or interns from other schools?

6. If the department could make any two changes, what would you suggest those changes be?

   (a) The department is considering changing ______________________. Would you support that change to the curriculum?

7. Having completed the requirements to apply for graduation and looking back at your experiences in the department, would you choose to be a mass communication major again if you were just now declaring a major? Why/why not?

8. While you might be willing to be a mass communication major, it is a very different matter to advise your friends to consider majoring in mass communication.

   (a) Would you recommend this major?

   (b) Why/Why not?

Tenure and Promotion Guidelines

COLLEGE OF MASS COMMUNICATION

The following guidelines, effective in the 1997–98 academic year, supplement the general university policies and procedures on tenure and promotion and are specific to the College of Mass Communication.

Degrees and Professional Experience

At the time of employment, an initial determination is made of the suitability of the candidate's professional experience and academic background for purposes of tenure and promotion. The chair (in consultation with the departmental tenure and promotion review committee), dean, and vice president for academic affairs are responsible for this evaluation. Because of the diversity of backgrounds and qualifications required for faculty membership in the college, this evaluation assumes great importance, and the candidate's letter of offer should make explicit its outcome.

Creative Activity

The college values both traditional research and creative activity. University guidelines offer explicit direction in the area of traditional research. The following guidelines offer general direction for those who will present creative activity as part of their record for tenure and promotion.

"Creative activity" consists of the creation, production, exhibition, performance, or publication of original work. Such activity should demonstrate originality in design or execution, and reflect, comment on, or otherwise contribute to the forms and practices of any endeavor represented by the disciplines in the College of Mass Communication. The product of creative activity may be communicated through print media, photographs, film, video recordings, audio recordings, graphic designs, digital imaging, live performances, or other technologies.

Examples. Creative activity may include, but is not limited to: (1) published books (professional, trade, or consumer), and articles, reviews, and commentaries in professional and popular publications; (2) graphics, visual materials, photographs, video productions, multimedia productions, or other visually-oriented media for professional or general audiences; (3) audio and/or audio-related productions, sound design for theater, film, video, or other media for professional or general audiences; (4) performances or exhibitions of creative works before professional or general audiences; (5) original musical works or original arrangements of preexisting works, including, but not limited to, scores (traditional, electronic, or other fixed media) engineered, produced, or performed for professional or general audiences; (6) software development, multimedia authoring, and/or unique and innovative applications thereof for professional or general audiences.

Review. Review of creative activities may be satisfied in one or more of the following ways: (1) acceptance for exhibition, publication, or performance in popular or professional media where submissions are judged by independent referees who are respected practitioners of the creative activity; (2) acceptance by an editorial staff or someone who is charged with a selective review process; (3) published review of performances or productions by recognized critics, scholars, or industry professionals. In fields where published reviews or their equivalents are difficult to obtain, independent reviews of the individual works, projects, or performances may be solicited. Such reviews are separate from the evaluation of the faculty member's research and/or creative record as a whole, which occurs as part of promotion and tenure review.

Responsibilities. As indicated in the university policy, documentation of creative activity should represent the cornerstone of the evaluation process. It is the responsibility of the faculty member to provide detailed documentation of creative activity in materials accompanying the application for tenure or promotion, or where the creative activities are being judged as part of the annual evaluation for retention in a tenure track position. This documentation must accompany the initial submission of materials to the department chair and departmental promotion and tenure review committee. The faculty member may also include supporting materials that would assist colleagues in assessing qualitative aspects of the work. Faculty are encouraged to submit whatever is significant to document "their direct participation in the creation or creative performance of the work" (MTSU Policy No. II:O1:05B, Policies and Procedures for Promotion and Appointment, August 1, 1996; Paragraph 1(B) (2) (b) 1).

Documentation

In documenting the record for tenure and/or promotion review, candidates, and departments when appropriate, should marshal evidence in the following ways:

Teaching. Candidates are expected to present the following: (1) an orderly summary of teaching evaluations that uses tables to chart responses to important questions about teaching over time in relation to departmental averages (supplied by the department); (2) copies of class visitation reports as prepared by the senior faculty of the department; and (3) other evidence of quality teaching, including records of teaching innovations, course improvements, honors received, teaching portfolios, and participation in national, regional, and state symposia.

Research and Creative Activity. Departments are expected to solicit three outside evaluations of the research and/or creative record as a whole. For research, the evaluations should be written by an appropriate panel of scholars; for creative activity, the evaluations should be written by an appropriate panel of professionals and/or scholars. The evaluators should be chosen by the chair in consultation with the candidate and with the advice of the departmental tenure and promotion review committee. In order to fulfill university deadlines in the decision year, the candidates should discuss evaluators with the chair during the spring semester in the year prior to being reviewed. The chair, in turn, should consult with the departmental tenure and promotion review committee to finalize the evaluators. The candidate should provide the chair with a package of materials for the evaluators by the first week of classes in the decision year. The outside evaluations should address the quality of the scholarly or creative activity as a whole, delineate the unique contribution to the field, comment on future prospects, and, if appropriate, evaluate the quality of the candidate's work in relation to those evaluated for tenure at the evaluator's institution.

Public Service. Candidates may solicit letters that document substantial accomplishments, whether they are service to the university, profession, or society. University guidelines offer ample direction for documenting excellence in public service.

Tenure

The probationary period in the College of Mass Communication is ordinarily six years. Candidates who began employment at MTSU prior to August 1, 1997 may choose to undergo tenure and promotion review in their fifth probationary year.

Candidates for tenure must demonstrate excellence in two of the following areas and average performance or above in the third: (1) instruction; (2) research and/or creative activity; (3) public service. Candidates must distinguish the two areas in which they claim excellence and marshal evidence to document the claim.

People hired as assistant professors under the master's degree plus 30-hour provision in the university guidelines must complete the doctorate to be eligible for tenure.

Promotion

Candidates for promotion to associate professor will normally be reviewed in the same year as for tenure.

Candidates for promotion to professor must demonstrate a national reputation in one of the following three areas: (1) instruction; (2) research and/or creative activity; (3) public service. It is expected that candidates will name their areas of excellence and offer appropriate documentation to support the claim.

Committees in the College

Departmental tenure and promotion review committees should be organized early in the year and should meet within the first month of the semester to select a chair. Meetings to evaluate candidates for tenure and promotion should be announced as early in the semester as possible and, at the latest, 10 days prior to the meeting. The chair leads the deliberations of the committee and coordinates the committee's work with the departmental chair and with the candidates. The chair functions as a participating member of the committee and may vote on all issues facing the committee. All voting on issues of tenure and promotion is done in person at meetings; no absentee or proxy votes are accepted. In the case of multiple votes, including votes taken after consultation with departmental chairs to resolve splits, only the final vote is reported.

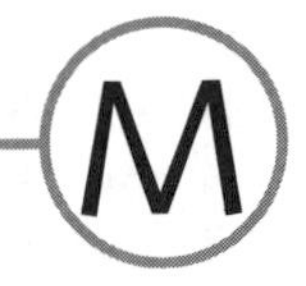

Tenure and Promotion Procedures

DEPARTMENT OF PSYCHOLOGY

Criteria for Tenure and Promotion

To be tenured and/or promoted, one must score at least "good" in each of the categories listed. Furthermore, a ranking of "excellent" in teaching or research must be made for each promotion decision. Only those holding a PhD degree will be eligible for tenure or promotion to the rank of associate or full professor in the department of psychology. The above standards apply to all promotion and tenure decisions.

Times for Evaluations

New tenure track faculty will be evaluated according to the procedures outlined as follows in their second, fourth, and sixth year at Marshall. Faculty are eligible for promotion to the next rank if they have been in their present rank for at least four years. Experience at the same rank at another institution can count for tenure and promotion. A candidate will submit the promotion and tenure credentials on or before Oct. 31 of the year of evaluation. Tenure and promotion are to be based on identical criteria. Each promotion is to be based on the same criteria, with the restriction that materials submitted in a prior evaluation cannot be counted again.

Composition and Voting Procedures

The tenure and promotion committee will consist entirely of tenured faculty. They will elect their chair. The evaluation scores from the attached forms will be the basis of all tenure and promotion decisions. These evaluations will then be summarized by the chair of the tenure and promotion committee. The chair's responsibilities are to organize the score sheets and provide a summary sheet. The committee will vote to determine if this final document reflects the views of the committee. If there is no consensus on this document, then a "minority" document may be written by members if they wish. All documents will be turned into the chair of the department by Dec. 10. The chair will use the same evaluation procedures and forms as the department members of the tenure and promotion committee. The chair of the department will use the enclosed forms and procedures in his/her evaluations.

The following weightings will be used as the basis for the overall score of an individual being evaluated.

A.	Teaching score	50 %
B.	Research score	35 %
C.	Committee score	10 %
D.	Community score	5 %
	Total score	100 %

The following formula will be used in calculating the overall performance score:

A.	Teaching score	_____	× .50	=	_____
B.	Research score	_____	× .35	=	_____
C.	Committee score	_____	× .10	=	_____
D.	Community score	_____	× .05	=	_____
	Total score		= 1.00	=	_____

These will be analyzed by the following scale:

outstanding	good	marginal	poor	unacceptable
1–1.75	1.76–2.5	2.6–3.0	3.1–3.9	4–5

It should be noted that each score must be of the accepted levels listed as follows for a person to be promoted or tenured. If it is not, then even if the applicant's overall score is in the good or excellent range, the applicant will not be promoted or tenured.

Committee's Cover Sheet

Name of candidate: ______________________________

Present rank: ______________________________

Rank being applied for: ______________________________

Committee members: ______________________________

Summary of evaluation:

A.	Teaching score	____	× .50	=	_____
B.	Research score	____	× .35	=	_____
C.	Committee score	____	× .10	=	_____
D.	Community score	____	× .05	=	_____
	Total score		– 1.00	–	_____

Recommendation:

Evaluator's Cover Sheet

Name of candidate: ______________________________

Present rank: ______________________________

Rank being applied for: ______________________________

Committee members: ______________________________

Summary of evaluation:

A.	Teaching score	____	× .50	=	_____
B.	Research score	____	× .35	=	_____
C.	Committee score	____	× .10	=	_____
D.	Community score	____	× .05	=	_____
	Total score		= 1.00	=	_____

Recommendation:

A. THE EVALUATION OF TEACHING

Teaching is the most important feature in retention, tenure, and promotion decisions. It will count for 50% of the weight in all tenure and promotion decisions. There will be three different measures of teaching effectiveness: Student evaluations will count 40%, peer evaluations will count 40%, and the promotion and tenure group's evaluation of course development and teaching related factors outside the classroom will count 20% as applied to retention, promotion, or tenure decisions. A final score will be calculated such that questions 1–15 on the student evaluations will be averaged over all evaluations conducted for the review period, and then the scores on the peer evaluations and evaluations of teaching activities outside of the classroom will be averaged in a similar manner. These will then be averaged to produce a "Teaching Score" calculated by the formula:

A. Teaching Score:

1. Student evaluation score	_____	× .40	=	_____
2. Peer evaluation score	_____	× .40	=	_____
3. Outside classroom teaching score	_____	× .20	=	_____
Total score		= 1.00	=	_____

If the total Teaching Score falls at "marginal" or below (i.e., an average score of 2.6 or worse), then the person applying for promotion or tenure will be turned down. Thus, one must demonstrate good teaching to be retained, tenured, or promoted in the department of psychology. If the average score is 1.75 or better, then this person is considered to be "outstanding."

1. Student evaluations of teaching: _____

Every year, student evaluations of teaching must be performed on four sections taught for all faculty in the department. More evaluations may be done if the individual faculty member desires. The chairperson or his/her designee will be responsible for data tabulation. A minimum of four evaluations per year must be entered into one's calculations including each course topic that is taught or all sections if fewer sections are taught in a particular year. One does not have to calculate a course into one's evaluations the first time the course is taught by that person. To calculate student evaluations, the computer center will generate the means for all students on all questions for each section taught. The means for each question will be added together and divided by the number of questions on the form such that an overall mean is calculated for each course. These individual course means will be summed and this sum will be divided by the number of evaluations creating the student evaluation score. This will be the number entered into the "Teaching Score" on the cover sheets for the tenure and promotion committee's evaluation. The chair will use the same student evaluations but use her/his own peer score for determination of the Teaching Score on the chair's Evaluator's Cover Sheet.

2. Procedures for peer evaluation of teaching: ______

The peer evaluation procedure (Appendix H) is the only one that will be recognized by the department tenure and promotion committee and by the chair of the department. It is to be used in all cases of promotion and tenure, and in the second, fourth, and sixth year of a nontenured faculty member's employment. This should be initiated by the applying faculty member at the beginning of the semester, and completed before the deadline for application. The peer evaluations will be conducted by the chair and a faculty member appointed by the tenure and promotion committee. Each evaluator should evaluate a different section.

If someone has released time to conduct other activities in the university, e.g., chair of the department, clinic director, etc., that person's performance must be evaluated and weighted into the teaching score proportionally to the percentage of released time they hold. Because these activities can vary, the applicant will provide the chair of the department and tenure and promotion committee careful documentation of their duties and accomplishments in the position. Each evaluator will use the following scale to calculate into the teaching dimension.

outstanding	good	marginal	poor	unacceptable
1	2	3	4	5

3. Teaching activities outside of the classroom: ______

The third component of the teaching score involves the evaluation of course organization, development, and other nonclassroom-related aspects of teaching. Because opportunities differ for various faculty to teach a large number of different preparations, supervise research, etc., this area must be analyzed subjectively by the committee. The candidate will present evidence of the committees served on, students supported in research, number of courses taught, number of preparations offered, participation in student activities, participation in honors courses, team teaching, special topics, advising loads, etc. Each member of the committee will use the following scale to calculate this dimension.

outstanding	good	marginal	poor	unacceptable
1	2	3	4	5

B. EVALUATION OF SCHOLARLY ACTIVITY

As with the other areas, the following scale will be used to evaluate each research criterion.

	outstanding	good	marginal	poor	unacceptable
	1	2	3	4	5
Points	250+	200–249	150–199	100–149	0–90

To be tenured or promoted, one must score a minimum of 200 points. Points can be generated from all areas, but the department expects that there be evidence of published works from one of the first three categories. The values for each type of scholarly activity is listed below. Use APA style to list all accomplishments as appropriate.

1. Books: _______

(0–250 points per submission) Describe the publisher of the published or in-press work, and then list the contributions of the coauthors if appropriate. Include a copy of the book in the appendix. Factors to be considered include magnitude of the work, relative contribution to the work, etc.

Evaluator's justification:

2. Refereed journal articles: _______

Weighting the value of the published or in-press article will include how significant the research is and the applicant's role in generating the ideas, methods, analysis, data gathering, write-up, etc. For example, if it is in a refereed journal and involves a substantial amount of work and/or creativity, then one would probably get maximum credit. Evaluators will use the following scale for each submission under this category. They will add the scores from each publication according to the areas of "primary contribution" and "quality of research/journal."

	low	med	high
Primary contribution to work:	25	50	75
Quality of research/journal:	25	50	75

Evaluator's justification:

3. Chapters in edited books: _______

Describe the published or in-press book and how it is refereed. Weighting the value of the chapter will include how significant the research is, and the applicant's role in generating the ideas, methods, analysis, data gathering, write-up, etc. For example, if it is in a refereed text and is done by a sole author and involves a substantial amount of work and or creativity, then one would probably get maximum credit. Evaluators will use the following scale for each submission under this category.

	low	med	high
Primary contribution to work:	25	50	75
Quality of research/book:	25	50	75

Evaluator's justification:

4. Conference presentations: _______

	low	med	high
Primary contribution to work:	5	10	20
Quality of research/conference:	5	10	20

Evaluator's justification:

5. Invited addresses: ______

	low	med	high
Primary contribution to work:	5	15	30
Quality of research/audience:	5	15	30

Evaluator's justification:

6. Consultations: ______

This refers to any application of professional skills. Describe the nature of the project and its scope. List the contributions of the coauthors if appropriate. If possible, include a copy of a paper in the appendix. This can also include clinical work, reviews of texts, consultations on research designs, consultations with businesses, etc. Evaluators will use the following scale for each submission under this category. This area can count as no more than 100 points toward the final score.

	low	med	high
Primary contribution to work:	0–5	10	20
Quality of research:	0–5	10	20

Evaluator's justification:

7. Editorial boards for journals: ______

(50-200 per submission) Factors to be considered include the nature of the journal, its readership, status, level in hierarchy of editors, number of papers edited per year, years of service, and other pertinent information.

Evaluator's justification:

8. Review work for journals: ______

List journals, reviews performed.

Evaluator's justification:

9. Articles and consultations in preparation: ______

(Up to 20 points per submission) The applicant should explain why this material should be rated prior to its completion.

Evaluator's justification:

10. Professional development: ______

Mention conferences attended, trips completed with the topics covered, and professional development that occurred. Up to 5 points per activity.

Evaluator's justification:

11. Other scholarly activity: ______

This could include grants from NSF, NIMH, etc., contracts on books, etc. Begin with APA-style bibliographic reference, then describe the nature of the project and its scope. List the contributions of the coauthors if appropriate. If possible, include a copy of the paper in the appendix. Up to 150 points depending on the scale of the project.

Evaluator's justification:

B. Overall research score: _____ (Add points from items 1–11 and determine score from scale on p. 306)

C. PROCEDURES FOR THE EVALUATION OF SERVICE TO THE UNIVERSITY

The following scale will be used to evaluate each service criterion. There must be service beyond the department level.

	outstanding	good	marginal	poor	unacceptable
	1	2	3	4	5
Points	20+	15–19	10–14	5–9	0–4

1. University committees: ______

(0–7 points) Personal characteristics may affect the rating in this area. However, they will enter into the numerical ratings only if the behavior inter-

feres with teaching, research, or committee accomplishments. A negative score up to −5 may be given in any of the below mentioned categories.
List committees, responsibilities, and accomplishments:

(a) Committee (b) Responsibilities (c) Accomplishments

Evaluator's justification:

2. College committees: ______

(0–7 points) List committees, responsibilities, and accomplishments:

(a) Committee (b) Responsibilities (c) Accomplishments

Evaluator's justification:

3. Department committees: ______

(0–7 points) List committees, responsibilities, and accomplishments:

(a) Committee (b) Responsibilities (c) Accomplishments

Evaluator's justification:

4. Contributions to official student organizations: ______

(0–7 points) List service and responsibilities

(a) Student group (b) Responsibilities (c) Accomplishments

Evaluator's justification:

5. Other: ______

(0–7 points)

(a) Activities (b) Responsibilities (c) Accomplishments

Evaluator's justification:

C. Overall university service score: _____ (Add points from items 1–5 and determine score from scale on p. 309.)

D. SERVICE TO THE COMMUNITY

As with the other areas, the following scale will be used to evaluate each service criterion

	outstanding	good	marginal	poor	unacceptable
	1	2	3	4	5
Points	20+	15–19	10–14	5–9	0–4

(10 points per activity) List committees, responsibilities, and accomplishments:

(a) Committee (b) Responsibilities (c) Accomplishments

Numerical rating: _______

Evaluator's justification:

D. Overall community service score: _____

Workshops for Department Chairs

Some organizations that offer workshops and seminars for department chairs include:

Academic Chairpersons Conference
Division of Continuing Studies
Kansas State University
247 College Court
Manhattan, KS 66506-6006

American Council on Education
One Dupont Circle, NW (#800)
Washington, DC 20036

Cornell University School of Continuing Education
Education and Summer Sessions
Box 530, B20 Day Hall
Ithaca, NY 14853-2801

Council of Colleges of Arts & Sciences
College of Liberal Arts & Sciences
Arizona State University
PO Box 873901
Tempe, AZ 85287-3901

Harvard Institutes for Higher Education
339C Gutman Library
Harvard Graduate School of Education
Cambridge, MA 02138

National Community College Chair Academy
Mesa Community College
145 N. Centennial Way
Mesa, AZ 85201

NCHEMS Management Services, Inc.
P.O. Drawer P
Boulder, CO 80301-9752

University of Alabama
College of Continuing Studies
Box 870388
Tuscaloosa, AL 35487-0388

Index